634 WAYS TO KILL FIDEL

634 WAYS TO KILL FIDEL

Fabián Escalante

Seven Stories Press
New York • Oakland • London

Published by Seven Stories Press on behalf of Ocean Press, Melbourne, Australia.
Direct all rights inquiries and permissions questions to rights@sevenstories.com.

Library of Congress Cataloging-in-Publication Data

Names: Escalante Font, Fabián, 1940- author.
Title: 634 ways to kill Fidel / Fabián Escalante.
Other titles: 634 maneras de matar a Fidel. English | Six hundred thirty
    four ways to kill Fidel
Description: Second edition. | New York : Seven Stories Press, [2021] |
    "Published in Spanish by Ocean Sur as 634 Maneras de matar a Fidel,
    ISBN 978-1-92575-634-0 (paper); ISBN 978-1-64421-124-3 (e-book)"
Identifiers: LCCN 2022007425 | ISBN 9781644210987 (trade paperback) | ISBN
    9781644210994 (ebook)
Subjects: LCSH: Castro, Fidel, 1926-2016--Assassination attempts. | United
    States. Central Intelligence Agency. | Intelligence service--Cuba. |
    Subversive activities--Cuba--History--20th century. |
    Mafia--Cuba--History--20th century.
Classification: LCC F1788.22.C3 E83313 2021 | DDC
    327.7307291--dc23/eng/20211008
LC record available at https://lccn.loc.gov/2022007425

Printed in the USA

Published in Spanish by Ocean Sur/Seven Stories as
634 Maneras de matar a Fidel, ISBN 978-1-92575-634-0 (paper);
ISBN 978-1-64421-124-3 (e-book)

9 8 7 6 5 4 3 2 1

Contents

To Fidel.

To my comrades in struggle, past and present.

To my children, grandchildren and siblings.

To Teresita, beloved compañera for life and partner in this literary adventure.

"Recently someone was arguing with one of our people in the United States, and he vehemently disagreed with her, saying, "You say there were 30 planned attempts. There weren't 30. There were no more than six…"

"In fact, there were neither 30, nor six. There were over 300! Because you don't only count the plans the CIA organized using bombs, a gun powerful enough to kill an elephant, a pen that shoots a little poisonous dart, a mask that has some sort of fungus, and who knows what else… No!"

Fidel Castro, 1993

Preface to the Second Edition

This is a new, updated edition of a previously published book *Executive Action: 634 Ways to Kill Fidel Castro* (Ocean Press, 2006) that documented the plans to assassinate Fidel Castro through 1993. This new edition now covers some of the main homicidal plots to kill the Cuban leader through 2000.

We hope this work, written by a key player in this story who has been intimately involved in investigating these criminal conspiracies, will reveal to the reader the extent to which the irrational obsession of generations of US leaders has damaged relations between both countries, simply because Cubans overthrew a US-backed dictator and initiated a social, political and cultural revolution that has become an example for the Americas.

Introduction

On July 20, 1961, I was assigned to the special bureau of the Cuban State Security Department (DSE) unit responsible for investigating plots and conspiracies against revolutionary leaders.[1] It was a memorable day, not only because it marked my debut as an operative officer, but also because I had the pleasure and honor of meeting the people who, from that moment, would be my compañeros.

The first was Mario Morales Mesa, known as Miguel — our chief, who had been an internationalist combatant in the Spanish Civil War (1936-39) and was a staunch communist and a born investigator. A small, slim man with a fine mustache, like those worn in the 1940s, he possessed an ironclad will and courage in the face of every test. Dozens of anecdotes were told about him, some from his time fighting in the International Brigades in Spain. In one story, he was responsible for a light submachine gun of Soviet manufacture known as a Maxim, and was thereafter known by that nickname, as he had a particular way of firing the gun so that, his compañeros claimed, it imitated the sounds of a Cuban rumba.

Later, as some of his compañeros related, he was taken prisoner and placed in a concentration camp in Nazi-occupied France, where he managed, together with the Senegalese guards who looked after the prisoners, to open a little store which sold milk

---

[1] DSE: Department of State Security or G-2, which, after the establishment of the Ministry of the Interior in June 1961, replaced the Rebel Army Investigations Department (DIER).

to the bosses of the place and gave it away free to the most needy. Mario was a real character who lived for 80-plus years. When I met him, I had just returned to Cuba after training in the Soviet Union, with lots of theory but little practical knowledge. Mario taught me skills in daily combat and investigation that cannot be acquired in any school, however good it might be.

He was an unpredictable person. On one occasion, tired and hungry, we went to eat hot dogs from a van parked behind the famous Hotel Nacional in Havana. He recognized one of the owners of the place as a former officer in Batista's army.[2] After identifying him as a sympathizer of General Batista, he set about playing along with him, while indicating to me that I should eat as quickly as possible. Once we had finished eating, the subject took us to a corner of the van and, with some pride, showed us a crate of incendiary devices: explosives made with "live phosphorus," at that time one of the CIA's most sophisticated inventions for acts of sabotage. As quick as a flash, giving me no time to react, Mario pulled out his revolver and arrested the whole gang.

Perhaps because of that speed with which he always acted, he would constantly pepper his speech with "You understand?"

Carlos Enrique Díaz Camacho, whose nickname was Trillo, was one of the compañeros who has left a lasting impression on me and with whom I was friends until his death at enemy hands in 1964. He was a man in his 30s, an old man to those of us who had just turned 20. One day I found him in Mario's house, where our office was located, with a cache of valuable jewels in his hands, wrapped in a woman's handkerchief. The jewels had been given to him from wealthy Cubans who were frantically trying to get them out of the country. Trillo was an agent who, himself, had belonged to the small world of the Havana bourgeoisie. He hung out with

---

[2]   General Fulgencio Batista was the Cuban dictator who came to power through a coup d'état in March 1952 and ruled until December 31, 1958.

people of his own social milieu who knew he had close ties with various European ambassadors, whom they hoped would assist them get documents, valuable jewelry and assets — which had not always been legitimately obtained — out of the country. On many occasions, those riches were rightfully returned to the Cuban people at a time when they were most needed.

We were with Trillo another time in the anteroom of the office of Captain Eliseo Reyes (known as San Luis), who was then chief of the revolutionary police.[3] Another police officer was also waiting there. In a low voice, Trillo exchanged words with the policeman, making him believe I had brought him in as a prisoner; within a few minutes, Trillo succeeded in exposing the policeman as an active conspirator within the police ranks.

Trillo always wore a light-colored suit and had a mischievous look in his eyes as he'd say "Tell you later," which of course he never did.

Another of my compañeros was José Veiga, better known as Morán, who had worked undercover in the United States, spoke English perfectly, enjoyed opera and had an inexhaustible imagination.[4] He always had an idea at the ready, even if it was a crazy one.

Carlos Valdés, Pedro Piñeiro, "Mayiyo" and many others were part of the group of no more than a dozen men who played an outstanding role in the fight against the assassination plots of the CIA and its Cuban accomplices against the revolutionary leadership, particularly compañero Fidel.

---

[3]   Eliseo Reyes was a captain of the Rebel Army who fought with Che Guevara in his Bolivian campaign where was killed in the struggle for Latin American independence.

[4]   José Veiga was lieutenant colonel in Cuban State Security who managed agent Fausto (Luis Tacornal) and dismantled the Rolando Masferrer conspiracy.

I have so many recollections of those years, when sometimes we had no working budget or a cent to buy something to eat, while in the desk drawers there were thousands of pesos, dollars or valuable jewelry. It never occurred to us to use of this, including to meet expenses related to our work.

All my compañeros are acknowledged in this story, not just those who are mentioned by name, but also so many more who gave the best of themselves in this silent war against terrorism. In addition to performing these heroic deeds, in many cases they have been witness to the incidents related. This story is a sincere tribute to that group of anonymous combatants, to whom I dedicate these pages with all the love and affection that emerged in the heat of those years and the adventures we experienced.

Perhaps readers will find it strange that I have used the word "love" in introducing the following chapters. This is because it is the love of our homeland and our people that has been, is, and always will be the motivation for our undertakings and struggles, as well as the basis for this great adventure that is the Cuban revolution. To the revolution and to my compañeros, present and fallen, my eternal gratitude and homage.

Preamble to an Obsession

He consulted his watch again. For several minutes he had been concealed in the dark doorway of an empty house facing the little airport of Fort Lauderdale in Florida. His gaze was fixed on some lights in the airport administration area. At his feet was a can of gasoline, waiting to be put to use. Suddenly, the lights went out and the guard left in the direction of a nearby café.

The silent observer picked up the can of fuel, crossed the street and entered the airport with swift and sure steps. Once there, he headed for an area where three P-51 Mustang aircraft were parked. He opened the can and meticulously spilled its contents around the planes until it was empty. He then retreated to a prudent distance and threw a lit match in the direction of the three aircraft, which were rapidly engulfed in flames. A voracious fire illuminated the night, while the man made his getaway in a waiting car. As the car pulled away, the sirens of a firefighting unit began to wail nearby.

Alan Robert Nye had been recruited a few months earlier by the Federal Bureau of Investigation (FBI) to penetrate groups of revolutionary Cuban émigrés who were conspiring against the dictatorship of General Fulgencio Batista. Nye was a pilot and had apparently been expelled from the air force after his base chief received an anonymous note accusing him of conspiring with the Cubans to launch air attacks on military targets in Cuba.

In fact, Nye's "expulsion" was a plan carefully laid by the FBI to give him a convincing introduction to the Cuban émigrés fighting the Batista dictatorship. The plan spiraled out of control when the

Cubans, overly enthusiastic about the project to bomb military targets on the island, acquired an aircraft to undertake the mission. Nye found himself in a blind alley, because if he did not attack the proposed targets, the revolutionary émigrés would become suspicious. As a way out, the FBI ordered him to destroy the planes and to blame supposed Batista agents for the sabotage.

After that action, the FBI introduced Nye to Efraín Hernández, the Cuban consul in Miami and an agent of the Batista dictatorship responsible for keeping the émigré community in Florida under observation. Hernández briefly explained that the FBI had entrusted him with an important mission in Cuba. The details would be provided later but he assured Nye that a large sum of money would be paid for his services, and that top members of the US administration were aware of the plans.

Nye did not know much about Cuba, only that it was seen as a paradise for tourism, gambling and prostitution. So he regarded the mission as a Caribbean vacation. On November 12, 1958, he arrived at Havana airport, where a black car waited for him at the foot of the aircraft steps. The vehicle drove him at speed to the Hotel Comodoro, located near the beach in a tranquil Havana neighborhood.

Waiting impatiently for him there were colonels Carlos Tabernilla and Orlando Piedra — the former, chief of the air force, and the latter, head of the secret police. After the usual introductions they moved to the hotel bar, where they began to talk at a table set at a distance from the others. Tabernilla explained to Nye the details of the plan in which he was to be involved: to assassinate Fidel Castro, the rebel leader who was challenging the Batista dictatorship from the country's eastern mountains, the Sierra Maestra.

The idea seemed simple enough. Nye was to infiltrate the rebel ranks in the area where Castro was operating. Once with him, he would present his "revolutionary" credentials and the project to bomb military airports in Cuba from Florida. The colonels were convinced that Castro would be seduced by Nye's personality. They had two reasons for this belief: one, Nye was a US citizen, a Yankee representing the most powerful nation on Earth; and two, the rebels needed planes to respond to Batista's air force, which was constantly bombing the civilian population in the rebel zones and causing serious destruction. Nye was a pilot and had an impressive letter of introduction from the Cuban émigrés in Florida, and thus would be an ideal pilot for any small aircraft the rebels could get their hands on, which could also be used to strike Batista's military positions.

Tabernilla and Piedra explained to Nye that he would be protected by an army command and, most importantly, that $50,000 would be deposited in his bank account once Castro was eliminated.

That same afternoon, the three men headed for Camp Columbia, the headquarters of Batista's army to coordinate the project with Colonel Manuel García Cáceres, chief of the fortress in Holguín, capital of the northern region of Oriente province. Nye and García quickly agreed that the former would travel to the colonel's command post within a few days and initiate the operation from there.

Despite the brevity of his stay in Havana, Nye found the time to visit the capital's main nightclubs and was able to understand why his fellow countrymen were interested in supporting the government of General Batista, who guaranteed to maintain Cuba as a haven for safe US investments as well as gambling and entertainment.

On December 20, 1958, Nye was in Holguín going over the main aspects of the homicidal plot with Colonel García. Four days later, in the company of a squadron of Batista's soldiers in the vicinity of the town of Santa Rita, he was infiltrated into the operational zone of Fidel Castro's rebels. That night, they stashed a .38-caliber revolver and a Remington .30-06 rifle with a telescopic sight in a previously selected site, and Nye bade farewell to the troops.

The following day he went on alone. Within a few hours he was captured by a rebel patrol and he informed them of his desire to join the revolutionary combatants and to meet Fidel Castro. Initially, things did not go according to plan. The young officer commanding the patrol did not appear very interested in him and confined him to a camp where wounded soldiers were recovering, explaining that in due course his case would be considered.

This did not overly bother Nye. On the contrary, it provided a way for him to familiarize himself with the territory. He imagined that as soon as Castro, who was in that area, knew of his presence, he would send for him and the opportunity would come. He would just have to wait until nightfall to get to his cache, retrieve the weapons and ambush Fidel in a convenient location.

On January 1, 1959, he heard the stunning news: Batista had fled, and the rebels were preparing to deal the final blow to the battered and demoralized government forces. He was in total shock, because nobody had given him any reason to consider this possibility. In his conversations with Batista's officers, he had not detected any hint of weakness in their government, let alone that the troop of "bearded ones" were on the verge of defeating it. Nevertheless, he thought to himself, there was no evidence against him, and as soon as the situation normalized, the rebels would set him free. If they did not, he would turn to his embassy for help. At the end of the day, he concluded, he was a US citizen and his rights were guaranteed.

On January 16, 1959, he was transferred to Havana for a routine investigation, or so he was told. An amiable rebel captain took a statement from him and then explained that he would have to wait a few hours while his story was verified. Nye committed a major error by mentioning the Hotel Comodoro as the place he had stayed on arriving in Cuba. In a matter of hours, the investigators had discovered two elements that convicted him beyond any doubt: first, the name he gave in the hotel, G. Collins, was not his real name; and second, his expenses there had been covered by Colonel Tabernilla.

The rebel officer interviewed him again and asked him to clarify the situation. Nye was unable to conceal the truth for very long. He confessed to the plot and named its instigators. In April of that year, Nye was convicted by the courts and expelled from the country through the US embassy. That was the end of the first criminal attempt on Fidel Castro's life undertaken with the participation of a US government agency — the FBI — and the complicity of Batista's police force.

Other assassination plans devised against Fidel Castro over many years involved weapons such as lethal poisons, powerful plastic explosives, cigars containing dangerous substances, grenades to be launched in public areas, guns with sophisticated telescopic sights, poison-filled syringes so fine that contact with the skin would be unnoticed, rocket launchers and bazookas, and explosive charges concealed in underground drains with a timer ticking down the minutes and seconds.

Only a few months after the triumph of the revolution, the United States proposed the elimination of the Cuban leader as the most expeditious way to overthrow the revolutionary government. This was hardly something new in US politics, as various presidents, politicians and human rights activists have been assassinated to prevent their ideas affecting public opinion. Leaders from other parts of the world have also been eliminated on the advice or encouragement of US ambassadors and consuls when they have been regarded as potential enemies of Washington's political and economic strategies, to the point where this method became an instrument of policy — the end justifying the means, but always allowing the US government the cover of "plausible denial."

The assassination of President Kennedy in 1963 was undoubtedly one of the most dramatic episodes in US political history. Over the years, various commissions were created to determine who instigated the crime and who carried it out. Nevertheless, those investigations, supported by million-dollar budgets, have only produced various hypotheses and lists of groups possibly interested in the president's demise.

Prompted by the Watergate scandal, which confirmed that CIA agents actively participated in clandestine activities against foreign politicians and US citizens, and under public pressure, in 1975 the US Senate created a commission headed by Senator Frank Church to investigate intelligence activity related to the assassination of foreign political leaders hostile to Washington's policies.[1] Senator Church's commission report exposed, for the first time, the existence of an institutional mechanism for political killings that deployed all kinds of special weapons, poisons and other sophisticated means that were created in CIA laboratories.

The Church Commission, however, only uncovered a minor part of the CIA's criminal plans. A complicitous silence sealed the lips of the organization's agents and chiefs who, headed by CIA director at the time, Richard Helms, refuted and withheld information that would have unmasked the shady assassination mechanism. In the case of Cuba, the commission concluded that there were merely eight conspiracies hatched against Fidel Castro, some of which, according to the investigators, never materialized. But this is far from the truth.

---

[1]   See US Senate Select Committee Report, *Alleged Assassination Plots Involving Foreign Leaders*, (Washington: US Government Printing Office, 1975), [referred to here as the Church Commission report].

From 1959, the youthful revolutionary government had to confront countless acts of terrorism from supporters of the ousted Batista dictatorship, such as war criminals who had fled from justice, and organized crime syndicates, who saw the new regime as detrimental to their economic interests. Later, with the official approval of President Dwight D. Eisenhower's administration, the CIA instigated a program to eliminate Fidel Castro and defeat the Cuban revolution.[2]

The most powerful CIA base within US territory was established in Florida with more than 400 case officers and 4,000 Cuban agents who, backed up by maritime and aerial fleets, launched an unprecedented secret war against Cuba. Some 300 clandestine organizations were formed, armed and directed by the United States for this purpose. An army — Brigade 2506 — was organized, trained and landed at the Bay of Pigs in Cuba in April 1961, with the aim of defeating the revolutionary government. This US aggression against Cuba even extended to bacteriological warfare.

Understanding how hundreds of conspiracies against Fidel Castro's life have been intercepted and neutralized is not easy without comprehending the extraordinary work of the people involved — the men and women who succeeded in exposing enemy plots, not only in Cuba but in the United States itself. The hundreds of these men and women who infiltrated the ranks of the CIA and the counterrevolutionary groups, often without the most basic training for the work involved, have been the real heroes of this effort.

In recent years, the CIA's responsibility for the conspiracies against Fidel Castro has been questioned in the United States.

---

[2]   See #481 A Program of Covert Action Against the Castro Regime, 16 March 1960, in *Foreign Relations of the United States, 1958-1960, VI: Cuba* (Washington: U.S. Government Printing Office, 1991), 850-851. This program was approved by President Eisenhower on 17 March 1960.

Certain journalists and scholars have been convinced that only a few bad apples within the Agency were responsible for such actions, operating behind the backs of their unwitting chiefs. The actions of William Harvey, Ted Shackley, Howard Hunt, David Phillips, David Sánchez Morales and others are presented as aberrations. This is completely untrue. The Church Commission report, based on an extensive examination by members of Congress of declassified documents, showed that in early 1961 it was the two principal CIA chiefs, Richard Bissell and Allen Dulles, who ordered the creation of Operation ZR/Rifle with the explicit mission of eliminating of foreign political leaders.

That operation was directly or indirectly responsible for the hundreds of homicidal plots against Fidel Castro. In some cases, these were both directed and funded by the CIA, which was also aware of others that it encouraged through the control it had over a multitude of counterrevolutionary organizations. Furthermore, the CIA utilized the extremely powerful weapon of psychological warfare, with thousands of radio broadcast hours transmitted from the United States inciting and exhorting the revolutionary leader's assassination.

The "Cuban-American Mechanism" of the CIA and the Agency's use of Mafia hit-men described in this book were activated by President Kennedy's government in 1962 after the Bay of Pigs defeat in order to unleash a civil war within Cuba. This cost US taxpayers millions of dollars and resulted in the emergence of the Cuban-American lobby as a powerful independent force in the US politics. Some investigators — including the author of this work — have argued that this "Cuban-American Mechanism" grew out of control and played a significant part in the assassination of President Kennedy.

The incidents narrated in this book are based on multiple investigations in Cuba and the experiences of the author, who participated in several them; dozens of interviews with participants; extensive documentary evidence; and the generous collaboration of compañeros, officials and undercover agents who dismantled these plots. Only some the most significant cases — some of them previously unknown and whose connections with the CIA and the US Mafia are irrefutable — have been selected for this book.

While based on factual events, certain fictional devices have been deployed to make for easier reading, and to present the events and characters involved in sharper relief, without affecting historical accuracy. This book records the history of how successive US governments tried 634 times to assassinate one man, Fidel Castro, who, like the mythological David, defied Goliath by committing himself to the defense of his people's sovereignty and independence.[3]

---

[3]   See the chronology at the end of this book for details of the main homicidal plots aimed at Fidel Castro.

1

With the Tigers

The alarm clock awoke Colonel J.C. King, who mechanically switched it off, throwing it a glance to confirm the time. Still half asleep, he gazed up at the ceiling and tried to put his thoughts in order.[1]

With the exception of Sundays, King got up at 4:00 in the morning. At that early hour, he devoted himself to studying the most important news of the day before considering his tasks in his current projects. Then he read a passage from the Bible, as, contrary to comments made by his detractors, he was a deeply religious man. He liked to compare certain passages of the Bible to actions he had taken, which gave him profound satisfaction.

This day marked an important moment in his career. He had been invited by his bosses, Allen Dulles and Richard Bissell, to give a special report on the situation in Latin America. For the first time during his years as CIA chief for the Western Hemisphere he felt intensely concerned. More and more organized political movements opposed to the policies of the United States were appearing on the continent, disturbing the peace and threatening the prospects of US investors. There had been earlier conflicts in what the United States considered its backyard, but the victory of Fidel Castro's revolution in Cuba had convulsed the usually passive Latin Americans like never before.

---

[1] Colonel Joseph Caldwell King (alias Oliver G. Galbond) was chief of the Western Hemisphere Division of the CIA in the 1950s and 1960s.

Cuba was once again the issue for discussion, as it had been in recent months since the United States had become aware of the need to remove Fulgencio Batista. It had become evident that political maneuvers to replace him "democratically" could not prevent the triumph of Fidel Castro and his rebels in the Sierra Maestra.

The political situation on the island had been worrying King for some years. The growing anti-US demonstrations, the strong communist movement built during the 1930s and 1940s, and finally, the assault on the Moncada Garrison in July 1953, indicated that communist subversion had reached the US border.[2] They could no longer sit back with their arms folded.

At the end of 1958, one of his closest friends, William D. Pawley, President Eisenhower's former ambassador and the owner of various businesses in Havana, had warned of the danger presented to the United States if Castro succeeded in Cuba, but his words went unheeded. It was assumed that Castro's rebels were just another group seeking power, but events had unfolded rapidly, clearly threatening US interests.

King recalled that Robert Weicha, the CIA agent who operated as US consul in Santiago de Cuba, was convinced Castro's group was not communist. Another informant who had reported on the group was Frank Sturgis, a mercenary who had joined an expedition led by Pedro Luis Díaz Lanz, then chief of the rebel air force.[3]

---

[2]   On July 26, 1953, Fidel Castro led an assault on the Moncada Garrison in Santiago de Cuba, the second largest military fortress in Cuba, with the aim of arming the people and defeating the Batista dictatorship. Many of the combatants were killed and while others were captured and imprisoned.

[3]   Frank Sturgis (Frank Angelo Fiorini) was a US armed forces veteran and member of the Rebel Army's air force under Pedro Luis Díaz Lanz. Under CIA orders, Sturgis participated in attempts on the life of Fidel Castro and the training of the Cuban exile brigades to attack Cuba. He was linked to the conspiracy to assassinate President Kennedy and was involved in the Watergate incident.

Nevertheless, King still believed they could control the Havana government's future actions. Not only did they have Díaz Lanz in the Rebel Army, there were other "sympathizers" like Huber Matos and various government ministers, all of whom discussed everything with the embassy. But Castro was unpredictable. His speeches on agrarian and urban reform in which he announced his intentions to lower rents and redistribute the land among the *campesinos*; the trials of notorious Batista followers were a particular cause for concern. Independent action had to be prepared so that events did not take them by surprise.

King rose from his bed, and, as was his custom, shaved and dressed with care. A final glance in the mirror revealed the image of a man in his 50s of military bearing, white-haired and with a penetrating gaze. He felt satisfied at confirming once more that, although the years were passing, he retained his distinguished appearance.

He descended the stairs of his house with an agile step, headed for the kitchen and prepared a cup of coffee. His long years of military service had taught him that it was better not to have a full stomach before battles or important meetings. With his cup in hand, he moved to a comfortable armchair in the large sitting room of his mansion. At that early hour the servants had not arrived, and he could allow himself the luxury of working there, where sunlight was beginning to filter through the large windows. He picked up his files, extracted various documents, and started reading attentively. One of them caught his attention; he reread it several times and then underlined two paragraphs in red pencil:

> Castro had contacts with Communist-front groups during his university days and there have been continuing reports of possible Communist affiliations on the part of some of his top leaders. However, there is no present firm indication that Castro

is a Communist sympathizer. . . Castro seems to be nationalistic
and somewhat socialistic; and although he has criticized alleged
US support for Batista, he cannot be said to be personally hostile
to the US.[4]

He took the pencil and distractedly placed it between his lips.
It was a personal habit he adopted when he was absorbed in
thought. He had before him the evaluation of the CIA station in
Havana and had to consider it as the most authoritative. But those
opinions did not concur with Washington's current view of what
was happening in Cuba.

The diplomats were confused in their analysis of events.
They thought that what was happening was merely the result of
premature optimism after the revolutionary triumph and that
things would subsequently follow the usual pattern. Was there
anyone who had defied the United States and lived to boast about
it? Fidel Castro was not, as they saw it, an exception to the rule.

The clock marked 8:30 a.m. His closest colleagues were expecting
him in an hour to discuss the issue. There was an established
procedure: everyone who worked under his command had to be
heard before making any decision on a specific subject.

When he was ready to leave, the telephone rang. It was the
operations officer who, as always, was responsible for ascertaining
whether the colonel was ready to start his program for the day.

He went out into the garden and made himself comfortable in
his car, a black, four-door Oldsmobile that gleamed immaculately.
Willy, his driver, an elderly sergeant who had been in his service
for years, switched on the ignition and moved off in the direction
of the Agency's central offices, located in an old navy building
known as Quarters Eye while its future headquarters in the

---

[4]   #224 White House Special Staff Note, Washington, January 13, 1959, in
    Foreign Relations of the United States, 1958–60, Vol. VI, Cuba, (Washington:
    US Government Printing Office, 1991), 356.

discreet district of Langley, on the outskirts of Washington, was under construction.

He walked to his office with a confident step, and to his satisfaction, found the people he wanted there ready for the briefing: Tracy Barnes, Richard Bissell's aide; Frank Bender [Gerry Droller], a veteran agent of German origin who had fought behind Nazi lines during World War II; Robert Amory, deputy director of intelligence; and various other officers. After the customary greetings, King asked Bender to relate the content of his talks with Augusto Ferrando, the Dominican consul in Miami, believing them vital for a full evaluation of the situation in Cuba. In his particular Germanic style, Bender explained:

"Ferrando represents Colonel John Abbes García, head of Trujillo's intelligence, and they want to know our official position on Cuba.[5] They believe that Castro is a dangerous communist, who will take revolution to all the countries of the continent. He confirmed that President Trujillo is planning to form an army with exiles from General Batista's forces located in his country in order to block Castro's plans, but needs Washington's blessing. He proposed we should send someone there to gather additional details."

When the report was over, King observed the rest of the officials and fixed his gaze on Amory. King did not like him. He was a dapper, Harvard-educated liberal with a penchant for adopting a contrary position, particularly when it came to analyzing proposals from his division. King motioned him to give his opinion.

At one point in his career, Amory, a slim man with a long face, refined manners, and a solid background in matters of hemispheric politics, had aspired to a State Department post, but he had lacked

---

[5]   Rafael Leónidas Trujillo Molina was the ruthless Dominican dictator also known as the Sultan of America. He earned himself the nickname of "Chapitas" due to his fondness for braid and medals. He died in May 1961, the victim of a CIA conspiracy.

the necessary sponsors to secure one. He knew King did not like him and took any opportunity to irritate the colonel with his sharp political reflections.

"To me it seems premature to draw conclusions on Fidel Castro's intentions. Trujillo sees phantoms everywhere and fears his dictatorship could be attacked by thousands of Dominican exiles in Cuba and other parts of Latin America. As you know, Colonel, I have expressed reserve over the support we are still lending that government, as in my understanding it is compromising us with other nations on the continent. What we are doing in this case is very similar to the experience with Batista, and look what has happened there."

Amory's words were followed by a silence. King's face was slowly changing color. He was aware that the "analyst" was attacking him for his public sympathies for Batista. Barnes, who knew what the colonel was thinking, intervened to avoid a sudden explosion from King, and explained that the Agency heads had not defined their position in relation to Castro and that all options should be kept open, including that suggested by Trujillo. Everyone in the meeting knew that Barnes spoke for Richard Bissell and as long as the "great strategist" (as the deputy director of plans was called behind his back) kept an open mind, CIA Director Allen Dulles would be receptive to any proposal.

The meeting concluded, King collected his reports and meticulously put them away as he always did due to habits acquired in the army. On returning to his office he recalled, for a few seconds, his years as an officer, his ascent through the ranks and his service as a military attaché in various Latin American countries. That was his great school, where he had learned that one had to treat Latin Americans with a heavy hand so that their fragile democracies did not collapse. That was why he had sympathized with Batista when he led the coup in Cuba in the early 1950s. But Batista could no longer be kept in power because weak Washington politicians refused to commit themselves to overt US involvement in the Cuban conflict. Bureaucrats like Richard Amory thought that communism could be contained with liberal theories, not realizing that, in fact, they were aiding it. King consulted his watch once more and left his office to head for the meeting with his chiefs.

Allen Dulles, the much-admired director, received him with his customary pipe between his lips and the pleasant manner of a venerable, elderly man. He was the undisputed chief of the CIA. Founder of the Office of Strategic Services (OSS), the CIA's predecessor, he played a dominant role in US covert actions in Europe during the war. There he undertook operations that were still legendary among younger officers. His brother, John Foster Dulles, was secretary of state, and both had an established legal practice in New York that, among other clients, represented the powerful United Fruit Company.

Richard Bissell, a brilliant Harvard graduate in economics, was seated in a comfortable armchair, his long legs crossed. He saluted King with his characteristic professorial gesture. After a brief exchange, King slowly read out the report and then gave a brief account of the conversation between Bender and the Dominican consul, deliberately omitting Amory's views. When he concluded his report, King waited expectantly. He knew Dulles perfectly well. He had the habit of asking his subordinates to express their opinions so as to attack them with sharp questions in order to discover the weak aspects of their proposals. On this occasion, however, he remained silent, a strange experience for the others in the room. After a few seconds that seemed interminable to King, he made a movement with his head in Bissell's direction. The latter, as if on cue, stepped in, interpreting the thoughts of the "great chief."

"We have nothing to lose in finding out what Trujillo has up his sleeve. I propose sending Bender himself so that he can report back, avoiding any commitment. Then we can make the pertinent decisions. In addition, it would be interesting to seek out one of the men we have in Havana for firsthand information on what is going on there. I fear," he concluded, "that our people are very polarized in one way or another and are not being objective."

Dulles, comfortable in his armchair, had his eyes half closed. He looked at King in a questioning manner.

"What is your opinion?" he asked.

King straightened in his chair, and with a rapid movement of his head indicated his agreement.

"Clearly, as Mr. Bissell says, we have nothing to lose by sending Bender."

The Tigers
Santo Domingo, Dominican Republic, January 1959

The day had been too hot for a Caribbean "winter." In the presidential palace two men were engaged in animated conversation. They were Trujillo, president for life and "Supreme Father of the Homeland," and Batista, who, up until a few weeks earlier, had been the "strongman of Cuba." Gone were the days when they contested for the title of bloodiest and most reviled dictator on the continent, and for the crumbs thrown them now and again by Uncle Sam. In his still-recent period of "democratic" urges, Batista had adopted a threatening attitude toward the Trujillo regime on more than one occasion. But now Batista's time was over, and apparently all disagreements had been overcome.

Both were impeccably dressed: Trujillo, spruced up for an imminent press interview, was decked out in a military suit covered in medals and braid. For his part, Batista was wearing an elegant white drill suit. Each of them held a glass of whiskey in their hand, from which they sipped from time to time.

The former Cuban dictator was starring in his new role as deposed president exiled in the Dominican Republic after a hazardous journey in the small hours of January 1, 1959, when he was forced to flee Cuba, besieged by the triumphant revolution.

He could not complain of the treatment he had received. He was accommodated in one of the capital's finest hotels and even given a bodyguard. It was true that he had to pay for everything in hard cash, but between old foxes like these two men, such trivialities did not cause offense. As the old saying goes: "You today and me tomorrow."

Trujillo was satisfied, as he had demonstrated to the illiterate general that his regime was the stronger. He took the floor, and after a "historical-political" preamble, explained his fears of the repercussions that Fidel Castro's victory might have elsewhere in Latin America and particularly for his country. In the final months of the previous year he had anticipated − in a meeting with his closest allies − the probable political outcome in neighboring Cuba and had devised a strategy in response. He would form a new army of anticommunist soldiers that would attack the neighboring island without delay, before the new Cuban government could fortify itself and before the thousands of exiled Dominicans resident in Cuba could organize themselves to counter the invading army.

Thus, during the initial weeks of January 1959, hundreds of men arriving from Cuba − many of them from the ranks of the dissolved regular army − joined the army that was being trained in Trujillo's camps, which were further swelled by mercenaries recruited from throughout the Americas.

In pursuit of that strategy, Trujillo had directed Colonel Ferrando, his consul in Miami, to evaluate the attitude of the CIA and the US State Department toward the new regime in power in Havana. The response could not have been more encouraging. In essence, it consisted of US approval for his plans, to be made concrete with the visit of a top-ranking Agency official. He could move ahead with the project and invade Cuba within six months, he figured.

Nevertheless, something was bothering him. Much of the daily news arriving from Cuba acknowledged Fidel Castro's enormous popularity and charismatic appeal. He would have to find a way to eliminate him. Without a leader, the people would be defenseless against external aggression and everything would be easier. That was precisely the subject of his conversation with Batista.

"Fidel has found a way to deceive my people," the former Cuban dictator explained. "His speeches, full of promises to improve the standard of living of the poorest sectors, are pure demagogy. That's been his biggest mistake because it affects US interests. He is standing up to the Americans and they won't forgive him for that. Perhaps the easiest thing would be to wait until they defeat him."

"I don't think things will be that simple," responded Trujillo. "Moreover, why wait? We have the necessary men and US backing in the OAS [Organization of American States] and the UN [United Nations] if necessary. I believe that now is the right time to resolve this conflict, and that the Americans would be appreciative…" Trujillo thought to himself, "this tight-fisted guy obviously doesn't want to invest and only wants to take refuge on the beaches of Miami. But he's not going anywhere with his wealth. He'll have to get his money out, and if he tries, I'll take it off him."

Batista appraised the situation and grasped Trujillo's strategy. The Dominican was not only after his collaboration but also his money. He got up and took a few paces around the office, a room decorated with antique furniture and heavy drapes. He reasoned: "He thinks I'm going to return to Cuba if Castro is overthrown, and in that he's totally wrong. I've been through many dangers in recent years and what I most want to do is rest. I'll have to find a way so that this little general doesn't suspect my intentions, and escape at the first opportunity to enjoy my fortune."

Batista halted in the middle of the room and, forcing a smile, nodded: "General, I'm in agreement with your plan. I understand you're suggesting we find a way to eliminate our young enemy before your Caribbean Legion reaches Havana.[6] With him dead everything would be much easier. I have attempted it before, and things didn't work out as I had hoped, but I think I can take care of the matter. Obviously, the costs will be down to me."

Trujillo assented. Here was the cooperation he was looking for. Now he could fully dedicate himself to the invasion plans, while his colleague busied himself with eliminating the man who was giving them so many headaches.

After a cordial handshake, the two dictators separated. Batista hurried back to his hotel.

Once there, he got rid of his wife Marta and some of the hangers-on awaiting him and asked for a phone link to Miami. A few minutes later he was talking to one of his henchmen, Rolando Masferrer Rojas, known as the Tiger.[7]

Masferrer was living comfortably in Miami, where the authorities had confined him not so much for his political record, but for his illicit activities and businesses. He was a personal friend of Mafia chief Santo Trafficante and was in ready contact with Colonel King.[8]

---

[6] Caribbean Legion was a mercenary army organised by Dominican dictator, Rafael Trujillo, and inspired by the French Foreign Legion.

[7] Rolando Masferrer Rojas was a politician in the period before the 1959 revolution who ran the so-called Tiger death squads under Fulgencio Batista and was responsible for killing hundreds of civilians.

[8] Santo Trafficante was the head of the Florida Mafia and its representative in Havana prior to 1959.

Batista confided in his man, saying, "Rolando, I need you to send me someone you trust completely for a matter requiring an urgent solution. It has to do with our own future..." He left the rest unsaid.

Realizing that something big was cooking, from the other end of the line, Rolando responded: "I don't think there will be any difficulties, General. You remember El Morito? Yes... the one who was chief of the Tigers in the Manzanillo area. Well, I'll give him instructions to travel there immediately."

CIA Headquarters
Washington, DC, March 1959

Colonel King was standing in front of the large window of his office at Quarters Eye, meditating on political events in Cuba. Despite his recommendations, the administration was going in the wrong direction. With every passing day the communists were taking a greater quota of power in the Havana regime. Castro already had several of his loyal men in key government positions: Raúl, his younger brother, was virtual chief of the army; Camilo Cienfuegos was chief of his general staff; and the dangerous Argentine Ernesto Guevara was behind all the populist and ommunist initiatives being announced in Havana. According to King's agents in the embassy, with every passing day the communists were gaining control over key positions, even though these agents were constantly meeting with sympathetic people in the new government to give them fresh instructions. Events were proceeding in the most disagreeable direction for the United States.

King was so absorbed in his thoughts that he failed to notice the presence of his secretary, who was patiently waiting with a cup of steaming coffee.

"Here's your coffee, Colonel. If you have no other orders, I'll be going as it's already past 9:00."

King took the cup. With a gesture he indicated that she could go and he once more buried himself in his thoughts. He had to convince his chiefs to do something to reverse the course of events in Cuba. He knew of Trujillo's plans, but mistrusted the old dictator, whose alliance with Batista was very fragile. Besides, Trujillo was placing a lot of confidence in the internal forces that he claimed could be mobilized within Cuba to support his invasion. Moreover, King was concerned at Trujillo's lack of standing among other Latin American governments. If the invasion materialized, that factor could trigger significant political and moral support for Cuba.

King sat down at his desk and flipped through various reports until he found what he wanted. It was an interview by CIA case officer Bill Alexander with Rolando Masferrer, an exile who was forming an organization with branches in Cuba to fight against the revolutionary government.

Masferrer had proposed to the CIA agent his anti-Castro plan, explaining that it included the assassination of Castro and that he could count on many men prepared for every contingency. His only condition was that he be given a post of government minister in the cabinet to be formed after the collapse of the revolutionary government.

The report concluded by affirming that Masferrer had become one of the most influential figures within the exile community in Miami, controlling the group of ex-Batista soldiers there, and that he was privately opposed to the Trujillo plan, given his understanding that the Dominican dictator wanted to sideline them from his project.

King tapped the intercom and asked for Bill Alexander. He wanted to know the operative's opinions firsthand. "Colonel," said Alexander, "I believe that Masferrer is our man. He has very powerful allies within the exile movement, including Eladio del Valle, a former member of Congress in the Batista government who is closely linked to Santo Trafficante.[9] It would seem that these people are offering him solid economic backing and want Castro out of power as quickly as possible."

"And how are they thinking of executing the plan?" asked King.

"The idea is to infiltrate a group of men to prepare an ambush for Castro near the presidential palace. They have people ready and trained for this task and it will not be difficult to shoot him. Without their leader, the revolutionaries will descend into power struggles and that will create an opportunity for the United States to bring order to the country."

Miami, Florida, March 1959

Hundreds of kilometers from Washington in his Miami residence, Rolando Masferrer was giving his plan its final touches. He deeply loathed Fidel Castro and anything that sniffed of communism, perhaps because of his past. In the 1930s, he had fought in the International Brigades on the side of the Spanish Republic during the Spanish Civil War. In that period, he was a passionate defender of anarchist ideas. After the conflict ended in the victory of the

---

[9]   Eladio del Valle Gutiérrez (Yito) was a captain in the merchant marines who devoted himself to trade in contraband merchandise from 1941 onwards in complicity with the Cuban government of the time. He was given a position in Batista's government and in 1952 held the post of deputy inspector of the National Secret Police. One year later he entered the Military Intelligence Service (SIM). In 1959 he left Cuba for the United States and became linked to the Junta of the Cuban Government in Exile (JGCE), headed by former President Carlos Prío Socarrás. He was an active participant in the CIA's covert war against the Cuban revolution and was suspected of participating in the assassination of President Kennedy. He was brutally murdered in 1967.

fascists, he felt he had been profoundly mistaken and speedily changed his allegiances.

Initially, Masferrer made contact with various gangster groups acting in Cuba under the protection of President Ramón Grau San Martín.[10] Later, he realized that he did not have to depend on anyone else and that he could be a "capo" himself. So he created his own gang. After Batista's coup d'état in 1952, he joined that gravy train and soon obtained control of a newspaper, a position in Congress, and a paramilitary troop called the Tigers that acted as an executive arm of the dictator. The mere mention of his name terrified people; his gangs acted with particular remorselessness in the eastern part of the island. There they delivered their "justice," executing and torturing the local people.

On January 1, 1959, he was forced to flee in haste to avoid being tried for the crimes he had committed, and his new lair was Miami. There he had influential friends, particularly in organized gambling circles. Being an enterprising man, he set to work immediately, and soon his friend Santo Trafficante made him responsible for extracting the money from the Havana casinos, which remained concealed in the homes of loyal friends.

In the depths of his dark consciousness he wanted "to do something for his country," and when Batista asked him to "eliminate" the revolutionary leader, he dedicated himself to the task with renewed energy. He could count on certain safe houses in Havana that belonged to former associates where he could hide his point men. There were no problems with clandestine entry into Havana: some of the residences of his collaborators adjoined the banks of the Almendares River, a few meters from its estuary, where he could land in a small vessel on a dark night.

The two men selected for the assassination were Obdulio Piedra, nephew of Orlando Piedra, the infamous former chief of

---

[10]   Ramón Grau San Martín was president of Cuba from 1944 to 1948.

Batista's police Bureau for the Repression of Communist Activities (BRAC), and Navi Ferrás, alias El Morito, a notorious Tiger from the death squads. Both had reputations as tough and unscrupulous men. They both had thick mustaches, perhaps to disguise them for their flight from Cuba. The conversation was brief. Everything had already been said.

"I have confidence in you," affirmed Masferrer. "You are well prepared, and I can also inform you that the Americans are supporting us; it's just that they don't want to appear to be involved. This support will be very useful when the time comes because the FBI will take the pressure off us and it will be easier for us to operate our businesses. Plus, Trafficante's people are prepared to pay good money, so we win on both sides."

He continued: "Over there you have to move carefully. You are known and I have news that Castro is developing an efficient police force. You should get in contact with the group that Ernesto de la Fe directs from prison and complete the task as quickly as possible."[11]

The two assassins asked for certain details. They were particularly interested in the pay and how they would return to Miami. After their doubts were allayed, they headed off to plan the journey.

Colonel King received a call at the precise moment the two killers left for Cuba. His officer, ensconced in Miami, kept him abreast of all events. He replaced the receiver and informed Bissell that the operation had begun. "Everything is going according to plan. With luck, we'll have finished with Castro in a few days," affirmed the CIA division chief.

---

[11] Ernesto de la Fe was minister of propaganda during the Batista regime who was detained in 1959 and sentenced by the revolutionary courts for his activities in support of the Batista dictatorship.

Report of the Rebel Army Investigations
Department (DIER)
DIER Headquarters, Havana, March 1959

After illegally entering the country at the end of March, Obdulio Piedra and Navi Ferrás — two notorious Masferrer henchmen — were discovered with several collaborators of Ernesto de la Fe, a former Batista minister currently serving time in prison for his past crimes. The two were hiding in one of the safe houses owned by the group in the Vedado district of Havana. In initial meetings between the new arrivals and various counterrevolutionaries, our agent was unable to discover the objective of their infiltration, and so did not detain them at that point.

A few days later, the two men asked for a car and began to reconnoiter the vicinity of the presidential palace. Alerted by our agent, we directed a National Revolutionary Police patrol to stake out the location and, as soon as they appeared, apprehend them and take them to the closest police station.

On the third day after the orders were dispatched, the patrol located the suspect vehicle, and when the agents moved in to identify the two men, Navi Ferrás opened fire with a submachine gun. The police returned fire, leading to an exchange of shots. Nobody on our side was wounded.

The counterrevolutionaries managed to evade the police pursuit and left the country that night in a vessel awaiting them at a wharf in the Almendares River estuary.

The house serving as a hideout for Masferrer's men was searched, resulting in the seizure of valuable information on counterrevolutionary plots and the planned assassination of Fidel Castro.

A few days later, on March 27, *Revolución*, the newspaper of the July 26 Movement, reported the abortive attempt: "The police authorities discovered a plot to assassinate Commander Fidel Castro led by Rolando Masferrer and Ernesto de la Fe, two notorious Batista henchmen linked to elements of the US Mafia located in Cuba prior to the revolutionary triumph..."

2

A Tough Guy in Havana

US Embassy
Havana, April 1959

David Sánchez Morales was a Chicano. With dark hair, almond eyes and round face he could not conceal his Mexican origin, and this had presented him with numerous barriers in his career within the CIA. He had a strong, brutal character and an uncontrollable taste for liquor. He was accepted into the CIA for his willingness to take on the dirty jobs. Nevertheless, when it came to giving him better-paid and more comfortable positions, everyone wavered, preferring to give him a pat on the back and wishing him better luck next time.

He was part of the task force in the US intervention in Guatemala to liquidate Jacobo Árbenz's "communists," responsible for training the forces of rebel colonel, Carlos Castillo Armas, a former collaborator of the US embassy in that country. The Guatemalans he trained in the "arts of subversion" mockingly called him "El Indio Grande" (the Big Indian), and the nickname stuck. Everyone in the Agency called him that behind his back.

When he was appointed as a "diplomat" in Havana in 1958, he thought his big opportunity had finally arrived. Cuba was a sought-after placement for young officers, not only on account of the agreeable climate and high salary, but for the contacts that could be made with US entrepreneurs based there, particularly those involved in organized gambling and drug trafficking, who could guarantee any young diplomat a promising future in return for their cooperation.

The triumph of the revolution and the subsequent economic measures taken by Fidel Castro cast shadows on Morales's horizon. Several of his agents had warned him that the democratic discourse of the new regime concealed a skillful international communist maneuver to seize Cuba, and he had expressed this belief in various reports sent to the CIA headquarters at Quarters Eye. There was nobody better qualified than him for such analyses. He had agents infiltrated into the Rebel Army, the National Revolutionary Police and other government agencies.

In April, Morales received an urgent call from one of his principal agents, Frank Sturgis, who occupied an important position within the Rebel Army air force.

After talking for several hours with his agent, Morales was left feeling totally convinced that the United States could not allow the Cuban regime to advance in its political project. Through Commander Díaz Lanz, chief of the air force, Sturgis had discovered that in a month Castro was to decree a radical agrarian reform act that would adversely affect big landowners and proprietors of US sugar mills.

Sturgis insisted that the only way to solve the Cuban situation was through Castro's elimination. Díaz Lanz had confided to him that various reformists in the cabinet headed by Manuel Urrutia could channel the process in another direction and eliminate the communists led by Raúl Castro and Ernesto Che Guevara who, in his assessment, were promoting the revolution's radicalization.

With another US collaborator, Gerry Patrick Hemming, a parachute instructor and explosives expert, Sturgis had a plan to assassinate Castro.[1]

That same afternoon, Morales met with Jim Noel, head of the CIA's Havana station and put to him the plan suggested by Sturgis.[2] The plan, he explained, consisted of attracting Castro to the air force headquarters for a meeting and then detonating a powerful explosive previously concealed in the meeting room.

Noel, following his custom of not taking responsibility for any operative who did not provide 100 percent security, posed some of the dangers he could foresee, and finally decided that he did not have the power to approve the proposal. To Morales's total dissatisfaction, Noel decided to consult with the new ambassador to Cuba, Philip Bonsal, a pragmatic diplomat and a specialist on Latin America who was opposed to CIA incursions into foreign policy.[3] Observing Morales's face, Noel ended the interview saying: "In any case, I authorize you to travel to Washington to go over the plan with Colonel King. He will know which way the wind is blowing there."

Morales met once again with Sturgis and Hemming to go over the details of the planned operation. Afterwards, through Marjorie

---

[1]   Gerry Patrick Hemming was a US citizen who was in Cuba in 1959 with a group allegedly training to fight in Nicaragua, which was part of CIA plan to provoke and discredit the new revolutionary government. He was later a Green Beret instructor in the Panama Canal Zone and was linked to Cuban exile groups operating against Cuba from US territory and mentioned in the investigation into the assassination of President Kennedy.

[2]   James A. Noel was head of the CIA station in the US embassy in Havana from 1958 to 1960, and the head of the Madrid CIA station 1961-64.

[3]   Philip W. Bonsal was a US career diplomat, a liberal with knowledge of Latin American affairs; he was appointed ambassador to Cuba in 1959 after previously serving there as a junior diplomat. He was recalled to Washington in late 1960, prior to the rupture of US-Cuba diplomatic relations on January 3, 1961.

Lennox, one of the secretaries at the station, he reserved a seat on the first available Pan American flight from Havana to Miami.[4] Once in Miami, he phoned Washington to inform them he would be there in a few hours and requested an interview with King.

CIA Headquarters
Washington, DC, April 1959

As soon as Colonel King knew of David Morales's presence, he called him to an urgent meeting. He was not accustomed to receiving colleagues at night but the wire from Havana intrigued him. Noel informed him of the need to discuss an emerging plan that could change the course of events in Cuba. This was what King had been waiting for. He knew the men in the Cuban capital very well and their numerous contacts within the government and opposition ranks. Through certain reports that had reached headquarters, he had picked up that a bloc against Castro within the regime was beginning to emerge and organize itself. Maybe the moment to act had arrived.

It was the first time that Morales had met with such a high-ranking chief. Walking through the corridors of CIA headquarters he could sense a growing emotion. He had in his hand a vital plan, and if it met with success, his future would be assured.

Once in King's office, he explained in detail the plot to assassinate Castro and the collaborators who would accompany him in setting the trap, concluding by stating confidently:

"Sturgis is a proven man. He fought in the Pacific during World War II and was wounded on three occasions. Later he worked with the army security agency. In the mid-1950s, he joined Carlos Prío's

---

4   Marjorie Lennox was secretary at the CIA station in the US embassy in Havana. She was detained in 1963 along with several CIA officials while attempting to place concealed microphones in the Chinese Xinhua press agency.

group of exiles in Florida and established good contacts with the Cuban revolutionary movement. He traveled to Cuba with arms for Castro's rebels and recruited several officers, including Díaz Lanz, chief of the armed forces. He enjoyed much respect within that group and Gerry Hemming, a contract agent and demolitions expert, worked with him."

Morales continued expounding on the conspirators' credentials and the project's chances of success.

King reflected while he was listening. He would lose nothing by authorizing the plan because its principal executors were from the Cuban regime itself. Although two US citizens were to be involved, the United States apparently had nothing to do with them. He was aware that the Agrarian Reform Act would divide the Cuban government and that he ran elements who could neutralize the communists and who, in the absence of Fidel Castro, would take control.

"Very well," said King. "I approve the plan with two conditions: one, that our embassy is not seen to be involved in the action; and two, that this project stays between us: you, Noel and me."

David Morales knew precisely how to interpret what the colonel was saying. Accordingly, he asked his chief for justification for an irregular visit, and once the details were agreed, took the first plane to Miami to continue his journey to Havana from there.

Interview with Frank Sturgis[5]
Miami, Florida, July 1977

In April 1959, as captain of the air force in Castro's army, I proposed to David, my case officer and an embassy official, that the solution to the problem in Cuba was the elimination of

---

[5]   Interview with Frank Sturgis by a collaborator with Cuban intelligence, conducted in July 1977 using the cover of preparing an article for the national press.

Castro. By that date it was clear to all of us that the communists controlled the main government positions and that after the drafting of the Agrarian Reform Act, land and sugar refineries owned by US citizens would be confiscated. There was also the issue of tourism. We already knew, through Díaz Lanz, that the casinos would be closed definitively, which would ruin many friends in the gambling industry.

Many people were looking to us, US citizens in the Rebel Army, hoping that we would give them a signal to act, and we could not lose any more time. Raúl Castro and Che Guevara were placing their cadres everywhere and would soon control the main posts within the armed forces.

This was what we proposed to case officer David Sánchez Morales for Castro's execution.

A few days later, Morales returned from a trip to Washington and gave us the green light. I remember that at the beginning of May we met in Díaz Lanz's office and made the decision. Hemming would plant the device we had prepared, and we would then wait for Fidel to visit the chosen location.

One afternoon, in the middle of that month, we placed the explosive device in the meeting room of the air force command. We used two large marble ashtrays there and placed the charge inside them. Then, with some fine cables concealed under the carpet, we took the connection out to the park. There, conveniently hidden among some bushes, we left everything ready to install the electrical connection that would detonate the device at the desired moment.

We waited for Castro's visit with much tension. Díaz Lanz had invited him to a meeting with the central command, but as always, he (Castro) never said when he would come, in order to appear unexpectedly, as was his habit.

In the meantime, we established contact with other army commands, including Commander Huber Matos, head of the Camagüey military fort, whom we knew was against Castro's socialist direction. The idea was that after Castro was eliminated, they would join with us to form a provisional government which would choose a civilian to head the country.

Sergio Sanjenís, chief of the Aviation Military Police, came to see me one day highly concerned. He had received information that G-2 was investigating Díaz Lanz and myself, saying:

"Frank, these people have you under observation. I think Fidel wants to send out a warning by detaining some of his detractors, and many people know that you're considered part of the opposition. I'm leaving the country at the earliest opportunity and I would advise you to do the same."

When I spoke to Díaz Lanz he got very nervous. He told me: "Frank, it's over. Castro suspects us and that's why he hasn't come to the air force command."

Hemming retrieved the explosive device at the request of Díaz Lanz, who, without saying anything to us, took a launch and headed for Florida. When I consulted with David, he ordered me to leave Cuba as quickly as possible, to avoid G-2 discovering the embassy connection. I was left with no alternative but to steal a plane and leave with Gerry.

A Faustian Opera
CIA Headquarters, Washington, DC, December 1959

Colonel King found himself extremely busy that afternoon in the final days of the year. He was examining various cables from the CIA station in Havana, and one of them had caught his attention. It noted the contacts made by Major Robert Van Horne, military attaché at the embassy and a CIA official, with various counterrevolutionary groups active in the Cuban capital.

The month had been decisive in terms of the creation and organization of the counterrevolutionary movement in Cuba. The dismantling of the conspiracy organized by Huber Matos and his associates had forced many people to choose sides. Manuel Artime founded the Movement for the Recovery of the Revolution (MRR), and the Christian Socialists went underground, renaming their party — which had previously played an active role in national politics — the Christian Democrat Movement (MDC).[6] After leaving the government, Manuel Ray founded the Revolutionary Movement of the People (MRP), and thus commenced a lengthy list of counterrevolutionary groups, almost all of which, at that point, originated in the lay structures of the Catholic church.

Nevertheless, King's attention was focused on another organization that had already been operating for a few months. It was the Anticommunist Workers Movement (MOA), composed of bourgeois elements, landowners and businesspeople who, fearful of the measures taken by the revolutionary government, had decided to participate in a counterrevolutionary coup.

One of the principal leaders was US citizen Geraldine Shamma, who was married to a Cuban businessman with a large personal fortune.[7] Shamma — a covert CIA agent — was the MOA's link with the US embassy and affirmed that the group had organized units in every province of the island.

Colonel King saw that events were moving quickly. The cable listed some of the group's proposed activities and one proposition

---

[6]   Manuel Artime Buesa joined the armed struggle against Batista in the last days of his dictatorship (December 28, 1958). As minister of agriculture he embezzled 100,000 pesos from the Agrarian Reform budget and left Cuba on December 8, 1959. He was prominent in the Brigade 2506 that invaded Cuba in April 1959 and founded the anti-Castro group Movement for the Recovery of the Revolution (MRR), carrying out numerous attacks against Cuba under the direction of the CIA. He was later suspected of participating in the assassination of the Panamanian president, General Omar Torrijos.

[7]   Geraldine Shamma acted under the orders of the US embassy in Havana and was detained in 1960 by Cuban authorities for conspiring against the revolutionary government. Before she completed her sentence, she was released and went to the United States, where she maintained links with exiled Cuban counterrevolutionaries.

had caught his attention: an attempt on the life of Castro during one of his visits to the residence of Commander Ramiro Valdés, head of G-2.[8]

"Perhaps," mused King, "this is the opportunity I was waiting for. Only in this case," he concluded, "they will have to do it themselves, directly, so as to not leave any traces. We mustn't repeat the same mistakes."

Nevertheless, they needed to cover their backs; to find a way to eliminate the leader without appearing to be involved. King knew that Dulles and Bissell would support him, but the Harvard liberals and academics in the government would protest or even oppose such an extreme measure.

With those thoughts running through his mind he took up his pen and began to write a long memo to Allen Dulles, highlighting his view that "a 'far left' dictatorship now existed in Cuba, which, 'if' permitted to stand, will encourage similar actions against US holdings in other Latin American countries." Among other actions, King recommended:

> Thorough consideration be given to the elimination of Fidel Castro. None of those close to Fidel, such as his brother Raúl or his companion Che Guevara, have the same mesmeric appeal to the masses. Many informed people believe that the disappearance of Fidel Castro would greatly accelerate the fall of the present government.[9]

A few hours later Allen Dulles received the report and, after consulting with Richard Bissell, who had already been consulted,

---

[8]   Ramiro Valdés Menéndez participated in the Moncada attack and was an expeditionary on the *Granma* cabin cruiser. He was one of the combatants closest to Fidel Castro. He became chief of G-2 (Cuban State Security) and subsequently minister of the interior.

[9]   J.C. King Memorandum, December 11, 1959, cited in *Alleged Assassination Plots...*, 92.

noted his approval in a corner of the document and recommended that the matter should be handled with the greatest delicacy. Ambassador Bonsal should not be informed and all necessary measures taken to avoid the United States being seen to be officially involved in the operation.

Testimony of Luis Tacornal, "Fausto"[10]
Miami, Florida, January 1960

I was sitting in the lobby of the America Hotel in downtown Miami when I overheard a conversation on the situation in our country. I immediately caught on that the people in the meeting were against us, so, perceiving the opportunity to establish a friendship with them, I followed the current.

Two days later, Masferrer himself appeared at 9:30 a.m. accompanied by four friends: one called Antonio, who is lame; El Morito [Navi Ferrás]; and two others, one of them a relative of Orlando Piedra. In that first meeting they told me they had planned a joint action with the people of Huber Matos and Tony Varona in Camagüey, that the plot had failed because events had moved faster than expected, and that he wanted me to get in contact with his man in Havana.[11] A second meeting was agreed for 3:00 p.m. that same day.

At the agreed time Masferrer reappeared, accompanied by the lame one, Antonio. El Morito didn't leave me alone for a second. I think they may have checked me out in Havana, or

---

[10]   Luis Tacornal Saíz (Fausto) was a Cuban security agent who infiltrated into Rolando Masferrer's counterrevolutionary group.

[11]   Manuel Antonio (Tony) de Varona Loredo was prime minister during the Carlos Prío Socarrás government (1948–52). He was president of Congress and headed the Cuban Revolutionary Party (*Autenticos*) during the 1948 presidential campaign. He led the Revolutionary Democratic Front (FRD), a group organized by the CIA that initially united Cuban exile counterrevolutionary organizations in the United States. Later, he joined the Cuban Revolutionary Council (CRC), which had the objective was to form a provisional government in Cuba after the 1961 Bay of Pigs invasion.

something like that, because they arrived more ready to talk. On that occasion they asked me to learn by heart a note with the addresses of certain people in Havana, and they explained what code to use with each one of them in order to make contact.

Some weeks later, Masferrer phoned me again at my house in Miami to explain the plans they were preparing related to an invasion of Cuba.

They believe that with State Department support they can obtain the moral and material aid necessary for their invasion plan. At the point when they land and initiate the battle, the State Department will ask the OAS to intervene in Cuba, backed by six to eight Latin American countries. If the OAS decides to intervene in the Cuba issue, President Eisenhower will designate Admiral Burke to command troop landing operations.[12]

Colonel King from the CIA, head of the Latin American division, is in charge of reviewing and presenting the plans from the different groups, which in their turn are called to Washington to discuss them. The day before I left Miami, Colonel King called Rolando Masferrer and told him he was thinking of approving his plan and, as it was impossible for him to go to Washington, some CIA agents would visit him in his house in Miami to discuss the plans more thoroughly.

Masferrer thinks that at "Zero Hour" the men can leave Miami for the intermediate base in the direction of Guatemala, as if they were going on a work contract with another group leaving from Tampa supposedly en route for Panama that they would meet up on a little island they had in the Bahamas and subsequently land in Cuba. Once they had seized power, they would convene elections as soon as possible and impose a "democratic regime."

---

12   Arleigh Burke was chief of the US Army and a friend of President Eisenhower. He had amicable relations with the government of General Batista, from whom he received various commendations. He was one of the Pentagon officers proposing the defeat of the Cuban revolution by means of direct US military action.

During this meeting in Masferrer's house, Yito [Eladio] del
Valle came to visit him. Masferrer explained that he was going to
Washington to meet with Carlos Márquez Sterling and also with
CIA agents. He asked me to accompany him to Washington. [13]

As soon as I have fresh information, I will send it via the
same channel.

Luis Tacornal Saíz (Fausto), was educated in New Orleans. The
triumph of the revolution surprised him there while he was
involved in establishing the July 26 Movement in that city. He
soon realized that his duty was elsewhere, within the ranks of the
enemy, which was already organizing to attack the revolution.

He became an infiltration agent for Cuban State Security,
which selected Lieutenant Colonel José Veiga Peña, a young officer whom he had known when they were both students in New
Orleans, to work with him. Fausto and Veiga were an inseparable
pair. They moved to Havana and from Geraldine Shamma's
residence infiltrated the conspiratorial network, whose Cuban
State Security code name was *Caso Ópera* (the Opera Case), until it
was dismantled in November 1960 with the arrest of most of the
conspirators. Both of them were exposed to countless risks but as
Veiga recalled the most difficult time was when the counterrevolutionaries received a CIA directive to assassinate Fidel Castro.

Testimony of José Veiga Peña
Havana, November 1994

At the end of 1959 and the beginning of 1960, I made contact
with Geraldine Shamma, who lived on 1st Street in Miramar
and operated as the link with the CIA station in Havana, and
who was also Manuel Artime's representative in Cuba. Up until

that point Shamma had dedicated herself to hiding war criminals and Batista regime fugitives.

We were aware from the first meeting that she reported directly to Major Robert Van Horne, military attaché at the embassy and one of the CIA chiefs on the fifth floor of the building. His secretary was called Deborah and his typist Mildred Perkins.

Van Horne was almost always accompanied by Lieutenant Colonel Nichols, who, according to Shamma, was in charge of military intelligence.

We met both of them in the Methodist church on 110th Street, Miramar. One Sunday, Fausto and I received instructions to organize Masferrer groups nationwide and have them ready to initiate an uprising in the Escambray, to engage in sabotage and to make an attempt on the life of Fidel Castro, for which Geraldine would act as our support.

On several occasions, we observed Geraldine filming and taking photos of the house adjacent to hers, the home of Commander Ramiro Valdés. She said the material was for Van Horne and that was correct, as I accompanied her to his office on various occasions to hand over the film. In fact, they were studying the possibilities of assassinating Fidel on a visit to Ramiro's house.

On inquiring what ideas they had to execute the attempt, she explained that three groups would take part in the action: two would seal off the streets and the third would fire on the commander from the attic opposite. I discovered that she already had M3 submachine guns and grenades and only needed telescopic rifles that the Agency was going to provide.

Bearing in mind the threat posed by the group, we decided to focus on delaying the operation. This tactic resulted in the visit to Havana in January 1960 of a high-level CIA figure to put pressure on Fausto to speed up the assassination attempt.

Given the CIA pressure, we proposed to simulate an attack on Commander Abelardo Colomé Ibarra, another enemy objective, and when that failed, to go underground and divert the main project.[14] The supposed attack on Commander Colomé was organized on the corner of 20th and 3rd Street in Miramar, with a shoot-out that allowed Fausto and me to flee with the weapons, which, as we explained afterwards, we threw into the sea, thus neutralizing the operation.

Geraldine hid Fausto in her house for a few weeks, having advised the US embassy, which confirmed the attack on Commander Colomé, but added that the US government was not planning to give it publicity. I was hidden on 21st Street in Vedado in the house of counterrevolutionary Isabel del Busto, until headquarters decided to activate the case.

On December 28, 1960, the Havana newspaper *El Mundo* published the following article on its front page: "27 Detainees Sentenced in La Cabaña."[15]

The public prosecutor's report noted that the individuals tried some months ago were conspiring against the stability of the state, in conjunction with the enemies of the revolution who are attacking the Cuban government from abroad... Those sentenced had conspired to assassinate senior government figures and to plant bombs... according to the testimony of investigating agents of the armed forces, José Veiga Peña, Manuel Franco, Antonio Cervantes, and Luis Tacornal Saíz.

---

[14]   Abelardo Colomé Ibarra was operations chief of Cuba's security services 1959–61. An outstanding combatant in the revolutionary war who rose to the rank of commander, he was later a founding member of the Cuban State Security Department.

[15]   La Cabaña is an 18th century fortress complex located on the eastern side of Havana Bay.

3

La Cosa Nostra

A cold front had swept over Washington, obliging its residents to swathe themselves in heavy overcoats and walk rapidly along the almost deserted streets. An important meeting was underway at CIA headquarters, which had brought together several chiefs and officials of the Western Hemisphere Division. Under discussion, and not for the first time, were contingency plans to combat and defeat the regime of Fidel Castro in Havana.

In one of the airconditioned rooms set aside for special meetings, with white walls and no windows, soundproofed and with rigorous protection measures against bugs, a group of men who had recently arrived in Washington from various countries were talking animatedly around a large oak table.

They were all high-profile specialists in espionage and veterans of PBSUCCESS, the secret war plan that had defeated the "communist" government of Jacobo Árbenz in Guatemala in 1954. From left to right, first was Jake Esterline, who had been chief of the CIA station in Venezuela until news arrived that "something important" was being prepared against Cuba. He had been in Caracas when Fidel Castro visited there in early 1959 and had realized then that the man was a very dangerous leader for the United States. As soon as Esterline heard that a task force against the Cuban revolution was being organized, he offered his services. Bissell immediately accepted him and assigned him to head the task force.

Then came Howard Hunt, back from Uruguay after an incident with the US ambassador there, who accused him of refusing to accept orders in front of President Eisenhower during the president's visit.[1] The ambassador was inflexible with his staff and immediately demanded that Hunt be replaced as head of station.

Next was veteran Office of Strategic Services (OSS) spy Frank Bender, who had been personally recruited by Dulles during World War II; he was the CIA's link to the Domincan dictator Trujillo. He was handling the mercenary action through which the Dominican dictator was unsuccessfully trying to defeat the Havana regime. He already had solid experience and knowledge of the Cuban exile groups, with which he had established close connections.

David Atlee Phillips, a specialist in psychological warfare who had recently operated underground in Cuba and had an excellent base of agents, came next.[2] His credentials also included participation in the conspiracy that brought down the Árbenz government in 1954.

The cowboy of the group was William "Rip" Robertson, who belonged to the legendary paramilitaries, always ready for action. It was true that he had blundered on certain occasions and was still recovering from the huge error committed in Guatemala when CIA

---

[1]   Everette Howard Hunt (Bill Williams), better known as E. Howard Hunt, was a US intelligence officer who published 73 books. From 1949 to 1970, Hunt served as an officer in the CIA. Along with G. Gordon Liddy, Frank Sturgis, and others, Hunt was one of the Nixon administration's Watergate "plumbers," a team of operatives charged with identifying the source of leaked national security information, such as the Pentagon Papers, to the media.

[2]   David Atlee Phillips (alias Harold Bishop): recruited by the CIA in the early 1950s in Chile, where he published a national newspaper. In 1954, as a specialist in psychological warfare operations, he was part of a CIA task force to overthrow Jacobo Árbenz's government in Guatemala. At the end of the 1950s he established himself in Havana under the cover of a publicity agency. He later became chief of the CIA's Western Hemisphere Division.

aircraft, acting on his instructions, mistakenly sank a British cargo boat in the belief it was a Czechoslovakian vessel. The United States had to pay substantial compensation to Britain and, since then, he had been somewhat left out in the cold.

Finally came Tracy Barnes, with his slicked-down hair, dark tailored suit, the Agency's rising star, an adviser to Bissell and his logical successor in the event of the latter's promotion to CIA chief.

The conversation became quite animated as Barnes read out President Eisenhower's recent instructions to proceed with a covert operation to overthrow the Cuban government. The language was rambling but clear enough for everyone to get a clear grasp of the strategy they were to execute: to set up a responsible and unified opposition to the Castro regime outside of Cuba; to develop mass media aimed at the Cuban people as part of a propaganda offensive; to create a secret intelligence and action organization in Cuba to follow the instructions of the opposition-in-exile; and to build a paramilitary force outside of Cuba for future guerrilla actions.

Once Barnes had finished, Colonel King, who suspected the decision to establish an independent task force would once again keep his team sidelined from any action, asked to speak:

"In general, I think Barnes's notes summarize the mission to be carried out. However, I insist that if Castro is not removed from the field, our plans could fail."

A silence followed the colonel's words. The rivalry and differences between the head of the Western Hemisphere Division and Bissell's principal adviser were no secret to anyone. The same thing had occurred with the intervention in Guatemala. Everyone thought that King was too slow for such complicated tasks. Without any doubt, this was why Dulles had assigned Esterline and his group to the leadership. Bissell, sitting in the corner of the room, looked at him intently and his myopic eyes, hidden behind heavy-lens glasses, reflected an explosion of anger. "Colonel, as you will understand, such recommendations cannot be written in an official memorandum that has to be signed by the US president. You have the approval of Dulles and myself for that task, which, I repeat, is highly classified. What more do you want?"

With a brusque gesture, King moved on, setting March 1 as the date for each person to submit plans in their area of expertise for Dulles's consideration. These plans would then go to the president for his signature and inclusion in a National Security Action Memorandum.

At the end of the task force meeting, Colonel King, still annoyed at the treatment he had received, headed for his office. He was approached in the passage by David Phillips, who asked him for an urgent meeting.

Once seated inside the office, Phillips began:

"Colonel, as you know, I participated in the recruitment of Cuban exile Manuel Artime. He is a very useful man who heads the MRR with the support of the Catholic church and influential sectors within the national business community. We are training some of his men and he thinks he'll be ready to liquidate Castro within a couple of months."

King settled himself in his chair. His bad mood had begun to lift. This was an attractive proposal he could not ignore. If everything worked out well, his position within the CIA would be strengthened and maybe he could even get the chief off his back.

"Very good," he said, softening his expression. "Explain the matter to me in detail."

Phillips embarked on a long explanation. The project was essentially based on the access of certain members of Manuel Artime's group to the University of Havana, a location frequently visited by Castro. It would be easy to shoot him there and then melt back into the crowd.

After listening to Phillips, King felt more relaxed. He shook Phillips' hand as he was leaving and said:

"I have confidence in you. Keep me up to date with the plan. I would only ask that, for now, this stays between us."

He accompanied Phillips to the door and patted him on the back with an affectionate gesture, unusual for him.

"Who do you suggest should coordinate the plan?" asked King.

"I think Howard Hunt is our man. He has been in Havana and is an experienced agent."

"Very well, take care of the details. Of course, if everything goes according to plan, I would like to have you on my team and who knows what in post-Castro Havana!"

In his memoir, Howard Hunt recalls he went to Havana in early 1960.

Havana, Early March 1960?????? MAY – he went to Madrid in April to manage the defection of Col Barquin. Soviets had just shot down a U2 plane and captured pilot.

> Our cover staff provided me with documentation that would support the operational alias I was to live with for the duration of the project. I drew a travel advance and flew to Tampa where I boarded a National Airlines flight to Havana.
>
> Checking in at the Vedado Hotel, I exchanged my dollars for Cuban pesos, surveyed my small and cheerless room and began a walking survey of the Cuban capital.
>
> The atmosphere of repression struck me almost at once. Uniformed *barbudos* [bearded rebels] with carelessly slung Czech burp guns guarded the hotels and other confiscated property. Women and girls of the *Milicia* paraded through the main streets to the cadence of "Uno, dos, tres, cuatro. Viva Fidel Castro Ruz!" Obviously, the cult of personality had taken hold in Cuba.
>
> Newsstands that once held *Life, Look, Time and Vision,* offered little more than gaudy imports from Peking, the USSR and the Agrarian Reform Institute's INRA. I walked to the Malecón

[esplanade along the sea front in Havana] and saw long lines of Cubans waiting at our consulate for visas to the US. From there I turned back to Sloppy Joe's, where I lunched on draft beer and a poor boy sandwich, alone in the great bar where once you had to fight for service. . . .

I dozed off and woke near midnight to the scream of brakes in the street below. Looking down I saw the flasher of a police car escorted by two jeeps. Uniformed *barbudos* swarmed out and into the neighboring apartment building where lights were going on. In a few minutes two men and a woman were dragged out, forced into the Black Maria. Machine guns menaced the crowd. The three cars drove off and quiet fell over the sultry Havana night. . . .

[On returning to Washington flight to Washington] I prepared a report of my impressions. When it came to recommendations related to the project, I listed four:

1. Assassinate Castro before or coincident with the invasion (a task of Cuban patriots);

2. Destroy the Cuban radio station and television transmitters before or coincident with the invasion;

3. Destroy the island's microwave relay systems just before the invasion begins;

4. Discard any thought of a popular against Castro until the issue has already been militarily decided.[36]

Report of the Rebel Army Investigations Department (DIER)
Havana, April 1960

According to our sources, on April 9 this year, elements infiltrated from the United States under the orders of Manuel Artime Buesa and the CIA planned to unleash a series of terrorist attacks, including the dynamiting of power stations and oil refineries in the country. At the same time, armed gangs would attempt to assassinate national leaders and army and militia officers.

A commando force comprising counterrevolutionaries Rogelio González Corzo, Juan Manuel Guillot Castellanos and Roberto Quintairos Santiso, previously trained in Miami, were to attend a tribute for those who died on April 9, 1958, held at the University of Havana. There, dispersed among the public, they would attack Commander Fidel Castro and assassinate him.

Our man, responsible for facilitating the two cars to be used in the action, was detained by the police who, under instructions, held him all day with the explanation that the vehicles had incurred outstanding traffic fines, which was a fact.

Meanwhile counterrevolutionaries José Quintana García, Joaquín Benítez Pérez and Martina Otero Salabarría, coordinators of the attempt, were arrested. This led to the dispersal of the group and allowed us to continue its penetration for further objectives.

Eduardo[3]

A Present for Castro
CIA Headquarters, Washington, DC, July 1960

Sheffield Edwards was a career officer who served for many years in the Defense Intelligence Department, where he rose to the rank of colonel. There he won acclaim not in combat trenches, but within the institution's bureaucracy. He was an astute person who knew how to perform in the presence of senior officials. Some time back, his friend J.C. King had proposed him to head the CIA Office of Security, a unit set up to oversee the protection of secrets within the Agency, and he had accepted. The CIA would certainly offer new horizons very different from military life, he thought.

---

[3]   Carlos Arocha Pérez (alias Eduardo) subsequently achieved the rank of brigadier general in Cuba's Department of State Security.

Six feet tall, with whitish hair, blue eyes and a military bearing, Edwards enjoyed a reputation among his colleagues as a reserved, loyal and disciplined man.

One day in mid-July 1960, Bissell and King called him to an important meeting. After formal greetings, they discussed events in Cuba and the state of the project to defeat the revolutionary regime. While Bissell was explaining details, Edwards wondered why he was being informed of such classified plans, which had nothing to do with his usual work. He did not have to wonder for long. When the Harvard professor had finished, King took the floor to give him a mission, just as he had done previously when both of them were in the army.

"We think you could play an important role in helping us get rid of Castro. Some of your personnel have relations with the Las Vegas gambling syndicate. They are as interested as we are in solving this problem. Using a credible front, perhaps posing as the representative of businessmen who have lost a lot of money in Cuba, select the most suitable individuals and offer them a contract on Castro's life."

The request did not take Edwards by surprise. Under the cover of protecting CIA secrets, he was developing a secret program, one of whose objectives was to maintain relations with individuals involved in organized crime who would occasionally take on dirty operations in which the Agency did not want to, or could not, be involved. They were the experts in assassination and extortion, which were supposed to be off limits to the elegant, pristine and delicate men of the CIA.

The conversation continued for several hours, with the participants all proposing different solutions, from a shoot-out in the streets of Havana to the use of poison. It was not the first time that US intelligence had used the services of the Mafia to promote US foreign policy interests. At the end of World War II, the OSS proposed and achieved the release from prison of Lucky Luciano, one of the principal Mafia capos, to serve as ambassador to La Cosa Nostra in Sicily.

At the end of the meeting, Bissell suggested that Edwards meet with Joseph Scheider, head of the Agency's laboratory, the Technical Services Division (TSD), who had been successfully experimenting with synthetic botulinum toxin — a powerful poison more effective than cyanide that left no trace — to determine the state of his research and assess its usefulness in the plot.

Some hours later, alone in his office, Edwards analyzed the various proposals discussed for effecting the crime and decided not to reject any of them: poisoning, a surprise shoot-out, or the use of a lone assassin.

He picked up the phone and dialed the number of one of his men, Jim O'Connell, operational Support Chief, under whose mantle the Mafia contacts were concealed. That night, O'Connell and Edwards met in a dark Washington parking lot, since matters of that nature were not discussed in offices.

O'Connell was very pale, blond, over six feet tall, and with the look of a killer. He always carried a revolver hidden under his arm. He was notorious for his crude habits and was the best person for the task at hand. After Edwards' explanation, the agent understood what was required and assured his chief that he had the means and the right people for the job.

The following day, O'Connell met with Joseph Scheider who, like a traveling salesman, offered him a range of products: a lethal poison and chemical agents capable of inflicting temporary disorientation, uncontrollable hysteria and hair or beard loss.

O'Connell left the meeting elated. He had not imagined the Agency would have such a variety of means for undertaking that type of task. The era of waiting with submachine guns at the exit of some public place was ending. Now, one could not only kill, but also leave the victim crazy, beardless or subject to constant and uncontrollable fits of laughter. Marvelous, he thought.

As soon as he got back to his apartment, he took a hot shower and made some coffee. He dialed a New York phone number and waited a moment until someone picked up.

"Mr. Maheu, please."

He waited a moment while the servant advised her boss. Seconds later, a familiar voice answered.

O'Connell said: "How are you, my friend? I imagine you must be surprised by this unexpected call, but I need to see you urgently."

With a positive response from his colleague, O'Connell continued: "OK. I'll be on the first plane and I'll call you."

Robert Maheu was a veteran CIA agent who had started his career in the FBI. Later, he became a private investigator and lent the Agency valuable services. At that time, he was working as head of public relations for Texan multimillionaire Howard Hughes. Short, brown-eyed with a doglike face, he could rub shoulders — without calling attention to himself — with the regents of the gambling city of Las Vegas, where Hughes had key businesses.

As soon as he arrived in New York, O'Connell took a taxi to the luxury apartment of his old collaborator. There, sipping a glass of bourbon, he brought Maheu up to speed with the reason for his visit: a contract on Fidel Castro.

It was not the first time that Maheu had received a task of that nature. He had close ties with the right people for such jobs. The small man moved about the room. "Perhaps," he thought, "Johnny Rosselli, one of the right-hand men of Giancana, the capo of La Cosa Nostra in Chicago, could be the man." He knew Rosselli had friends in Florida, the home of the largest number of Cuban exiles. Santo Trafficante, the czar of gaming in Havana before Castro took power, was also there in Florida. "Yes, Rosselli's the man," he concluded.

Rosselli and Trafficante would be the men given the task. They would surely find good people for the job among their contacts in Havana. For his part, O'Connell would seek out other ways of executing the plan. He knew that in the near future — in September — Fidel Castro would be attending a UN meeting in New York and maybe the opportunity they sought would present itself there. "Perhaps an explosive device at a public event," he mused.

During the last year of the Eisenhower administration, the CIA considered plans to undermine Castro's charismatic appeal by sabotaging his speeches. According to the 1967 report of the CIA's Inspector General, J.S. Earman, an officer in the Technical Services Division (TSD) recalled discussing a scheme to spray Castro's broadcasting studio with a chemical, but the scheme was rejected because the chemical was not reliable.[4] During this period, the TSD impregnated a box of cigars with a chemical which produced temporary disorientation, hoping to induce Castro to smoke one of the cigars before delivering a speech. The Inspector General also reported on a plan to destroy Castro's image as "The Beard" by dusting his shoes with thallium salts, a strong depilatory that would cause his beard to fall out.[5]

Edwards and Maheu agreed that Maheu would approach Rosselli as the representative of businessmen with interests in Cuba who saw the elimination of Castro as the first essential step to the recovery of their investments.[6] According to Rosselli, he and Maheu met at the Brown Derby restaurant in Beverly Hills in early September 1960. Rosselli testified that Maheu told him that

---

4   J.S. Earman, CIA Inspector General, *Report on Plots to Assassinate Fidel Castro*, 1967, published as *CIA Targets Fidel* (Melbourne & New York: Ocean Press, 1996), 29.

5   *CIA Targets Fidel*, 30.

6   *CIA Targets Fidel*, 33.

"high government officials" needed his cooperation in getting rid of Castro, and that Maheu asked him to help recruit Cubans to do the job.[7]

A meeting was arranged for Maheu and Rosselli with Support Chief Jim O'Connell at the Savoy Plaza Hotel in New York. The 1967 CIA Inspector General's report placed the meeting on September 14, 1960.[8] A note in this report indicates that on August 16, 1960, an official was given a box of Castro's favorite cigars with instructions to treat them with lethal poison. The cigars were contaminated with a botulinum toxin so potent that a person would die after putting one in his mouth. The official reported that the cigars were ready on October 7, 1960.[9]

Michael Murphy, chief inspector of the New York police, entered the suite of the Waldorf Astoria, a luxury hotel that served as headquarters for his men in charge of protecting Castro, and met there with a CIA agent waiting for him with a hair-raising story. The Agency had a plan to place a box of cigars in a location where they could be smoked by Castro. If and when he lit one, the agent said, the cigar would explode and blow his head off. Murphy, who could hardly believe his ears, was dismayed, as it was his responsibility to protect Castro rather than to bury him. So he took no part in the plot.

Meanwhile, the Mafia continued moving its criminal tentacles in accordance with the orders received. John Martino was one of the top Mafia strongmen in the casino of Havana's Hotel Nacional. Mike McLaney afforded him privileges over and above those enjoyed by the rest of the gangsters operating in organized

---

7   *Alleged Assassination Plots...*, 75-76.

8   *CIA Targets Fidel*, 34.

9   *CIA Targets Fidel*, 37.

10   Michael Julius "Mickey" McLaney was a Mafia-linked US golf and tennis player, who made a fortune in the casino business.

gambling.[10] Within a few years Martino had bought a house in the Cuban capital, while also occupying a suite at the neighboring Hotel Capri, where he was constantly visited by the most beautiful chorus girls from Havana's cabarets. The revolution complicated his life. He soon realized that the Cuban government would eradicate gambling and prostitution and do away with the lucrative businesses they had set up.

One afternoon, at the beginning of August 1959, McLaney instructed Martino to begin to smuggle the Mafia's money out of Cuba via the maritime link between Havana and Key West in Florida. A tip-off to the Cuban police led to his detention on October 5 with a suitcase full of dollars. At that time Cuban police were waging a full-scale battle against organized crime figures, who, through the use of couriers, were attempting to save their fortunes. One such "courier" was Jack Ruby, who some years later would be Lee Harvey Oswald's assassin.

Martino was detained in the Havana jail in the lower part of El Castillo del Príncipe, an old fortress dating back to the colonial era. Only the payment of a large bond made his release possible, whereupon he fled the country aboard a cabin cruiser bound for Miami. But he never forgot that "insult."

Fidel Castro's trip to New York in September 1960 to address the UN General Assembly provided the opportunity Martino was hoping for. Through the New York press, which gave front-page coverage to the activities of Castro on his second visit to the United States, Martino learned of a public event organized by Cuban émigrés in Central Park in honor of their leader. A call from the "godfather," Sam Giancana, was the catalyst for his decision that the park was an ideal place to assassinate the revolutionary leader.

He called his brother Walter, a gunman, and told him to place a powerful dynamite charge under the speakers' platform to be used by Castro and his followers. He could not have known that US police agents would surprise Walter in that operation, arrest him, and inform the press, thus thwarting the homicidal plot.

That same month, *Bohemia* magazine in Havana published an article based on information collected from the US news agencies:

> During the visit by Prime Minister Fidel Castro to New York, police agents in that city surprised US citizen Walter Martino attempting to place a powerful 200-pound TNT explosive device in Central Park, where the Cuban leader was to attend a public meeting.

A Contract to Kill
New York and Havana, October 1960

At the end of the 1950s, Sam Giancana (Momo) was chief of one of the most important Mafia "families" in Chicago and possibly the entire country. His relations with various labor unions ensured his control of legitimate businesses in ports and road transportation, which were highly lucrative. He was a descendant of Italian émigrés who had fought hard to give him his position. More than one of his colleagues had to pay very dearly for trying to muscle in on one or another of his businesses. His "family" had commercial interests in many countries, including in Cuba and its leisure industry.

Informed by Rosselli of the CIA's proposal to take out Fidel Castro, Giancana understood that in providing his services, not only would he be doing the Agency a favor, which he could call in when needed, but he would also be solving a problem affecting him and his associates. Since the revolutionaries had taken power, everything was going backwards, and businesses were collapsing. So he decided to accept the contract and assign one of his most outstanding captains for the operation.

Giancana's choice was Richard Cain. He had a background in the police force, as did many members of the "family," through which he had acquired experience and useful contacts for his current work as a private detective, a role that provided a cover for his activities as a link between CIA agents and the Mafia.

Two telephone calls to Santo Trafficante produced what Giancana needed: a backup in Havana who could help Cain set up and execute the mission. The choice of the thug was ideal: he was a former associate of Trafficante's from his time as director of the casino in the Sans Souci cabaret, Eufemio Fernández.[11]

It was early October 1960 when Cain arrived at Havana airport. From there he went to the Hotel Riviera, and after changing into lighter clothes, phoned Fernández to arrange a meeting in L'Elegant, the hotel's discreet bar.

Tortoiseshell spectacles framed the cold eyes of the US killer while he assessed his new Cuban acquaintance. Both sat down at the bar and ordered rums, one in an expectant pose and the other mentally weighing up his words. Finally, Cain spoke:

"Mr. Trafficante told me you were a man he could trust, prepared to do anything to serve him. Is that still true?"

"My friend," Fernández replied, "All I can say is that I have only one word and that is pledged to *Señor* Trafficante. Tell me how I can help you."

Considering each word, Cain explained what was required of them. At the end, as if in passing, he assured Fernández that he himself was a good shot and would have no objection to directly participating in the action.

"These people are crazy," thought the Cuban gangster. "They don't realize how much Havana has changed." He had to find some way of making the Cain understand so he would not think he was scared of undertaking the mission. Trafficante might

---

11   Eufemio Fernández Ortega was a notorious gangster in the 1940s. He was arrested in 1961 when he was coordinator of the Triple A terrorist organization.

still return to Cuba one day, which would give him a chance of recouping his job as front man in the capo's casino.

Choosing his words carefully, Fernández explained why Cain's proposal would not be easy. Fidel Castro moved about at high speed and had no fixed habits. Moreover, he had loyal men who could not be bribed. "Nevertheless," he said, "I would like to consult with some friends." Noting the look of displeasure reflected on Cain's face, Fernández went on:

"Don't worry. They are proven people whom Trafficante knows very well. I'll vouch for them."

After a courteous farewell, he left the hotel with a smile on his thin lips.

The next day they met up again. This time Fernández came with a tall, light-skinned Afro-Cuban with gleaming white teeth, whom he introduced as Herminio Díaz.[12]

"This is Santo's latest bodyguard in Havana."

The three of them made themselves comfortable at the bar of the 21 Club — an elegant establishment opposite the Hotel Capri — and began to talk. The Cubans tried to explain to Cain that the proposed operation would not be easy. It could take months, given that it involved stalking the victim. There was also another factor that could not be overcome: Castro's personal guard was very effective and well trained.

---

[12] Sandalio Herminio Díaz García had been a gangster and extortionist since the 1940s, who served prison terms for various crimes. At the end of the 1950s, he was closely linked to Santo Trafficante and was named chief of police at the Hotel Riviera, owned by the Mafia. In 1962, he left Cuba for the United States, where he was linked to Santo Trafficante and former President Carlos Prío Socarrás,. A member of the Commandos L terrorist organization, he took part in numerous actions against Cuba. He is suspected of having participated in the conspiracy to assassinate President Kennedy. He died on March 26, 1966, while attempting to infiltrate Cuban territory via the northern coast of Havana province with other counterrevolutionaries.

Cain knew his collaborators were right. He thanked his new friends and told them he would let them know when he left the island, which, naturally, he did not do.

Report of the Church Commission
Washington, DC, November 1975

It was arranged for Rosselli to go to Florida and recruit Cubans for the operation. Edwards informed Bissell that contact had been made with the gambling syndicate.

During the week of September 24, 1960, the Support Chief [O'Connell], Maheu and Rosselli met in Miami to work out the details of the operation. [. . .] After they had been in Miami for a short time, and certainly prior to October 18, Rosselli introduced Maheu to two individuals on whom Rosselli intended to rely: "Sam Gold" [Sam Giancana] who would serve as a "back-up man" or "key" man, and "Joe" [Santo Trafficante], whom "Gold" said would serve as a courier to Cuba and make arrangements there.

The Support Chief testified that he learned the true identities of his associates one morning when Maheu called and asked him to examine the "Parade" supplement to the Miami Times. An article on the Attorney General's ten-most-wanted criminals list revealed that "Sam Gold" was Momo Salvatore Giancana, a Chicago-based gangster, and "Joe" was Santo Trafficante, the Cosa Nostra chieftain in Cuba.[13]

O'Connell said "the Agency had first thought in terms of a typical, gangland-style killing in which Castro would be gunned down. Giancana was flatly opposed to the use of firearms. He said that no one could be recruited to do the job because the chance of survival and escape would be negligible. Giancana stated a preference for a lethal pill that could be put into Castro's food or drink."[14]

---

[13]   *Alleged Assassination Plots...*, 76-77.

[14]   *CIA Targets Fidel*, 39.

4

The Sacred Monsters

Wherever the Agency needed experienced men, William Harvey was to be found in the front line. He was one of the CIA's "sacred cows," belonging to the group of officers trained in the heat of the Cold War. Six feet tall, 200 pounds in weight, fair-skinned and with a habit of making crude gestures that had earned him the reputation of a man of action and few scruples, he enjoyed wandering around the Agency, toying with the .45-caliber pistol that he always carried.

For some years, he led the task force spying on the Soviets in West Berlin. He was responsible for the construction of the much-publicized tunnel that crossed the border to the eastern part of the city, through which communications from Soviet troops stationed there were intercepted. Nevertheless, he was unlucky. Soviet counterintelligence had discovered the tunnel project from the outset and initiated a disinformation campaign that confused US spies for quite some time.

Of course, that fact was not widely publicized. Supported by his Langley protector, Richard Helms, then second to Richard Bissell, Harvey made out that the Soviets had discovered the tunnel after it had been functional for some time, and that the information acquired in the first few months was reliable. Thus, an aura of success surrounded Harvey, granting him inclusion in the highest-level CIA operations.

Nonetheless, Richard Helms had pulled him out of Berlin to prevent Harvey's constant bragging from revealing the truth about the tunnel and damaging the CIA's reputation, assigning him to a bureaucratic post, albeit an important one: Chief of CIA foreign intelligence, with responsibility for agents and collaborators involved in Agency operations all over the world.

Harvey was working in that role when, one January afternoon in 1961, he received an invitation to meet with Deputy Director Bissell.

"I've sent for you because we have an urgent and delicate mission for you. Given certain failures and unfortunate events, we have decided to organize a secret operation within our organization to create the capacity to overthrow and eliminate political leaders hostile to the United States in any part of the world. As you will understand, this is a very delicate matter, above all because our country cannot be seen to be openly committed to this program. Moreover, the incoming Kennedy administration doesn't know anything about it, and we think the less they know the better. Your job is to select the right people, train them and, when the need arises, we will give you the relevant orders."

Harvey swallowed. He was no novice and he knew this kind of thing went on, but he never imagined it would be elevated to the point that it became so structured. Regardless, he was not a man to wilt in the face of difficult tasks. So he agreed, asking about the modus operandi and the objectives to be prioritized.

Bissell explained: "We want to give you a cover for the operation, so we'll appoint you chief of Division D, in charge of deciphering the codes utilized by our allies. Under that cover, you will organize the ZR/Rifle program. Your job is to find people with the capacity for this kind of work from among our agents, and to contact the lab chief and also Colonel Edwards, who is working along similar lines. Our priorities are Fidel Castro and Dominican

President Rafael Trujillo. As you know, Trujillo was our ally but is becoming a nuisance. Castro is a dangerous communist. A plot against Castro is already underway and you need to check it out and give it the OK. We need to eliminate him before the exile brigade training in Guatemala lands in Cuba. That's our top priority."

Harvey experienced a feeling of satisfaction. Once again, he was in the field of action and with a project in his hands worthy of a significant rise through the ranks. With a "Thank you very much, sir" and a smile on his lips, he took his leave of Bissell and hastily immersed himself in Agency files, searching for his criminal candidates.

Bissell testified to the 1975 Church Commission that sometime in early 1961, Harvey, who was then chief of CIA foreign intelligence personnel, "was assigned the responsibility for establishing a general capability within the CIA for disabling foreign leaders, including assassination as a 'last resort.'" This capability was called "Executive Action" and later included under the cryptogram "ZR/Rifle."[1]

William Harvey confirmed:

> [H]e was "almost certain" that on January 25 and 26, Services Division (TSD), and a CIA recruiting officer, to discuss the feasibility of creating a capability within the Agency for "Executive Action." After reviewing his notes, Harvey testified that the meetings occurred after his initial discussion of Executive Action with Bissell, which, he said, might have occurred in "early January."
>
> Harvey testified that the Executive Action capability was intended to include assassination. His cryptic handwritten notes of the January 25/26 meetings, preserved at the CIA, contain phrases which suggest a discussion of assassination: "last resort beyond last resort and a confession of weakness,"

---

[1]   *Alleged Assassination Plots…*, 83.

"the magic button," and "never mention word assassination."
Harvey confirmed this interpretation.[2]

Bissell ultimately explained that "the development of an Executive
Action capability was 'undoubtedly,' or 'very much more likely'
initiated within the Agency, acknowledging that "this would not
have been unusual," stating:

> It was the normal practice in the Agency and an important part
> of its mission to create various kinds of capability long before
> there was any reason to be certain whether those would be used
> or where or how or for what purpose. The whole ongoing job of
> [REDACTED] a secret intelligence service of recruiting agents is
> of that character [...] So, it would not be particularly surprising
> to me if the decision to create [REDACTED] this capability had
> been taken without an outside request.[3]

CIA Headquarters
Washington, DC, January 1961

Harvey picked up the intercom linking the Agency's principal
chiefs and dialed Colonel Edwards' number. After greeting each
other briefly, they agreed to meet the next day in a well-known but
discreet Washington restaurant.

At the appointed hour, Harvey and Edwards installed
themselves at a secluded table and, while savoring spaghetti à
la Milanese accompanied by an excellent rosé wine, discussed
pending issues. The colonel explained that the failure of attempts to
eliminate Fidel Castro up to then was the result of poor professional
planning on the part of the executors.

---

2   *Alleged Assassination Plots...*, 183.
3   *Alleged Assassination Plots...*, 186.

"It is essential to liquidate Castro before the invasion takes place," Edwards insisted. "We have various plans underway. The first consists of infiltrating a team of Cuban agents trained in Panama who, in collaboration with the internal resistance, will gun Fidel down outside his secretary Celia Sánchez's house, which he frequents regularly. The second, consisting of two alternatives, is to give poison capsules filled with botulinum toxin, an invention of our laboratories, to two groups associated with Santo Trafficante operating in Cuba. We plan to execute the third option through a young agent who is one of the leaders of the Cuban underground movement and should be infiltrating Cuba in the next few weeks to lead the internal front. This option consists of blowing up the meeting room of a minister whom Castro regularly visits. What's your opinion?" he asked.

"It sounds foolproof," Harvey replied. "Thanks for the information, and if there's no problem, I'll meet with O'Connell and Scheider to go over some of the details."

The Undercover Agent

Félix Rodríguez Mendigutía was a CIA man. He came from a wealthy family in the Sancti Spíritus region of central Cuba. Like many of his friends, after the triumph of the revolution he escaped to the United States and there immediately placed himself at the command of anyone who talked of attacking Castro. This naturally led him to the CIA. In January 1961 he was in an Agency safe house in Miami. Some months previously he had been recruited by the special missions group, organized in Panama to develop subversive action within Cuba to pave the way militarily and psychologically for the brigade of mercenaries which was to invade Cuba at the Bay of Pigs.

He had proposed Castro's elimination to his bosses as the most expeditious means of overthrowing the Cuban government. His plan had the backing of an underground group, which would give them the necessary support. He dwelt on the plan a lot before disclosing it, but everything seemed relatively easy to him. It was true that he did not have up-to-date information on the internal political situation, but he knew the locations selected for the action, and his training was excellent.

Years later, Félix Rodríguez would go on to participate in the murder of Che Guevara in Bolivia, the US adventure in Vietnam, and finally, the war against the Sandinista government in Nicaragua.

In his memoir Rodríguez recalls:

> One day [in Miami, in January 1961] I was talking to a friend of mine with whom I had served in the [Pedro Luis] Díaz Lanz group. . . . We were talking about the probability of success our infiltration teams would have, and I suggested that by assassinating Castro I might be able to save lives. He agreed, and I took the plan to the acting camp commander, an American we knew as Larry, and volunteered our services.
>
> Soon thereafter Larry told me my idea had been accepted by the people in charge. Early in January we were all flown to Miami where we were assigned a third Cuban to be our radio operator, and where I was given a weapon. And what a weapon it was: a beautiful German hold-action rifle with a powerful telescopic sight. . . .
>
> Apparently the resistance had obtained a building in Havana facing a location that Castro frequented at the time, and they'd managed to presight the rifle.
>
> The Americans moved the entire infiltration unit to a place in the Homestead area [in Miami] while we waited for our boat. It looked like an old motel, although it was out in the boondocks, right near a bunch of tomato fields. The place had a pool, where we practiced paddling the rubber rafts we'd use to go from our

boat to the shore. From our "headquarters," we drove by car down into the Keys, where at a predetermined spot we'd blink the headlights and a small boat would come to shore, retrieve us, and carry us to the yacht that would take us to Cuba.

Three times my friends and I tried to infiltrate Cuba with that damn rifle, and three times we failed. The boat we used was a power cruiser, maybe 40 feet long, with air conditioning, luxurious appointments and fancy cabins. The captain was an American, but our crew were all Ukrainians. They spoke no Spanish — at least not to us — and they were tough-looking s.o.b.s who carried Soviet bloc automatic weapons.

Our problem was, we never managed to get ashore. We were supposed to [disembark] onto a Cuban boat near Varadero Beach, an area I knew well from my childhood. From there we would be taken to rendezvous with members of the anti-Castro resistance and be driven to Havana. We would be provided a safe house, then move to a room where we'd be able to shoot Fidel, do it, and then try to escape somehow. . . .

We were already well on our way to Cuba for the third time when the American captain canceled the mission. The reason he gave us was a hydraulic failure [in one of the boat's engines]. When we got back to Florida, they took away the rifle and ammunition, and said that they'd changed their minds about the mission.[4]

Poison Capsules
Miami, January–March 1961

Santo Trafficante was 41 when he arrived in Cuba on December 26, 1955, describing himself as a successful US businessman "interested in developing tourism." He had been in Havana on several previous occasions and had decided to base himself there

---

[4]   Félix I. Rodríguez and John Weisman, *Shadow Warrior: The CIA Hero of a Hundred Unknown Battles*, (New York: Simon & Schuster, 1989), 65-66.

permanently. He promptly opened the Sans Souci night club and casino. A few months later he bought shares in the Comodoro and Deauville hotels and extended his activities to other commercial spheres, particularly trade in contraband items from the United States.

A Cuban police report of that same year noted:

> Having expanded the investigation ordered with the purpose of identifying "the high-level government official," it has been discovered that it is *Señor* Amleto Barletta, the owner of the hotel where the subject Santo Trafficante is staying... He is currently representing of one of the parties supporting the government. In relation to the paragraph: "with the gaming business in Havana," in my assessment, it lacks specific importance, bearing in mind that the informants used a generic term to refer to those who live off and exploit gambling in any country, using the word "business" because — licit or illicit — it is without doubt a business, just like the word "traffic" is used to mean "trade"... Attached is a press cutting from the March 26 edition of the *Miami Herald*, which reveals that the subject and his brother Henry violated the gambling laws, were detained and charged on those grounds, and also that they have a record of being imprisoned for the crime of bribery and for infringing the Lottery Law, sentenced to five years on each count...

Slowly but surely, Trafficante became the owner of, or principal shareholder in, Havana's most important casinos. According to the ruling ordering his expulsion from the country, drawn up by the Cuban government's director of public order:

> Trafficante was arrested in November 16, 1953, in Tampa, Florida, and again in Tampa on May 29, 1954. Cuban police arrested him on June 15, 1956. He made more than 30 telephone calls to racketeers in the United States during the final months of 1957, according to Lieutenant Pena of the Cuban police. The

accused attended a grand Mafia council at the house of Joseph Barbara in Apalachin, New York, in November 1957, in which gambling and other illicit operations in Havana were considered an important agenda item, and geographical divisions were designated to each gambling syndicate. The territory of the Republic of Cuba was included in the eastern zone of the United States.

Trafficante was detained on those grounds by the Cuban police on June 11, 1959, and he was interned in a camp for undesirable foreigners until August 18 of that year, when he had to be released given the absence of any extradition claim on the part of the US authorities.

A DIER report dated November 11, 1959, lists Trafficante's main associates as Eufemio Fernández, Néstor Barbolla, John Rivera, Sam Mondell, Joseph Bedami, Ciro Beluccia, Joe Cacciatore, John Martino and Mike McLaney.

In January 1960, Trafficante was arrested again by Cuban authorities in the Hotel Riviera along with his bodyguard Herminio Díaz García on account of their criminal and counterrevolutionary activities; he was then finally expelled from the country. Once back in Miami, profoundly resentful of the revolutionary process, he called together various Cuban émigrés he knew from his dealings in Cuba, including Manuel Antonio (Tony) de Varona, a veteran politician and former collaborator in major illegal operations. Varona was then head of Rescate, one of the largest underground groups acting against the Cuban government, composed mainly of members of the Cuban Revolutionary (*Authentico*) Party from the late 1940s.

Trafficante's strategy was clear: By backing one of the most important exile groups, which was sponsored by the CIA and the State Department, once Castro was defeated the members of that group would be part of the new Cuban government, with all their property and privileges restored. This would give Trafficante significant influence. Toward the end of 1960, the news he received of the US government's plan to overthrow Castro convinced him he had made a sound medium-term investment.

As soon as Rosselli was contracted by the CIA to kill Fidel Castro with poison, Trafficante knew about it. After all, it was he who facilitated the contact with his friend Eufemio Fernández in Havana when Richard Cain traveled to that city to fine-tune the details of the crime. But Trafficante kept his distance. He wanted government officials to come to him, asking for "favors." Finally, Rosselli called him, informing him that "somebody" from the CIA wanted to meet with him, to which he agreed with pleasure. The opportunity to offer a important service to the US national security interests had arrived.

Trafficante had various additional options for the contract. One of them was his old friend, Juan Orta Córdova, an individual linked to gambling interests and who, at that time, was acting as chief of staff for Prime Minister Fidel Castro. Orta owed him favors and could not refuse a request from him. The other alternative was Tony Varona's group in Havana. He decided to dispatch poison capsules to both of them, so at least one of them would take out Castro. "It can't go wrong," mused the gangster. Orta could mix the poison into one of the many coffees Fidel consumed in his office; and if that failed, Tony's people could use one of their men who worked in the Pekín Chinese restaurant the Cuban leader patronized regularly.

Report of the Church Commission, *Alleged*
Assassination Plots...
Washington, DC, November 1975

[Colonel] Edwards rejected the first batch of pills prepared by TSD because they would not dissolve in water. A second batch, containing botulinum toxin, "did the job expected of them" when tested on monkeys. The Support Chief [O'Connell] received the pills from TSD, probably in February 1961, with assurances that they were lethal, and then gave them to Rosselli.[5]

The record clearly establishes that the pills were given to a Cuban for delivery to Cuba some time prior to the Bay of Pigs invasion in mid-April 1961. . . .[6]

The Inspector General's Report states that in late February or March 1961, Rosselli reported to the Support Chief that the pills had been delivered to an official [Juan Orta] close to Castro who may have received kickbacks from gambling interests. The Report states that the official returned the pills after a few weeks, perhaps because he had lost his position in the Cuban government, and thus access to Castro, before he received the pills.[7]

In any event, Rosselli told the Support Chief that Trafficante believed a certain leading figure in the Cuban exile movement might be able to accomplish the assassination. The Inspector General's Report suggests that this Cuban may have been receiving funds from Trafficante and other racketeers interested in securing "gambling, prostitution and dope monopolies" in Cuba after the overthrow of Castro. . . .[8]

The Cuban claimed to have contact inside a restaurant frequented by Castro. As a prerequisite to the deal, he demanded cash and $1,000 worth of communications equipment. The Support Chief recalled that Colonel J.C. King, head of the Western Hemisphere Division, gave him $50,000 in Bissell's office to pay the Cuban if he successfully assassinated Castro. . . .

The money and pills were delivered at a meeting between Maheu, Rosselli, Trafficante and the Cuban at the Fontainebleau Hotel in Miami. As Rosselli recalled, Maheu "opened his briefcase and dumped a whole lot of money on his lap . . . and

---

5   *Alleged Assassination Plots...*, 80.

6   Ibid, 80.

7   Ibid, 80.

8   Ibid, 80.

also came up with the capsules and explained how they should be used." […]

The attempt met with failure. According to the Inspector General's Report, Edwards believed the scheme failed because Castro stopped visiting the restaurant where the "asset" was employed. Maheu suggested another reason. He recalled being informed that after the pills had been delivered to Cuba, "the go signal still had to be received before in fact they were administered."[9]

What really happened was that Orta took fright at measures being adopted against people conspiring in one way or another against the revolution and sought asylum in the Venezuelan embassy. When the Pekín restaurant employee realized the enormous risk he was running if something should go wrong, he took refuge in another embassy to wait for the mercenary invasion that everyone thought was imminent.

Operation Generosa
JM/WAVE Base, Miami, February 1961

Miami was a hotbed of Cuban exiles. They all knew of the brigade that was receiving military training in Guatemala and the special missions group training in Panama whose objective was to spearhead the internal counterrevolution when the mercenaries invaded. Of course, what they were trying to do was not at all easy; to organize an army while developing leaders for an internal resistance movement that, like the exiles, was profoundly fractured by competing ambitions, each faction demanding a specific quota of power once the revolutionary government was overturned.

Well aware of these problems, the CIA had assigned one of its most outstanding negotiators to unite these groups into one

---

[9] Ibid, 80.

internal front. This was Howard Hunt, who rose to fame some years later as one of the Watergate "plumbers." Hunt clearly favored one particular group, the Movement for the Recovery of the Revolution (MRR), having reached a certain agreement with its leader, Manuel Artime, on his prospects in the new government once the revolution was defeated. The Cuban Revolutionary Council (CRC) was created to unite the exile movement prior to the April 1961 invasion. Dr. José Miró Cardona, a former dean at the University of Havana, who was prime minister in the initial revolutionary government, was selected to lead it. Other appointees were Manuel Artime (the political delegate of Brigade 2506), Tony Varona, Manuel Ray and other leaders from the Cuban émigré community in Miami.

The most delicate issue, however, was the question of who should take charge of directing the underground groups. Various meetings were needed to reach agreement among the exile leaders, who each proposed their own delegates, realizing that positions in a post-Castro provisional government would be filled by those on the ground in Cuba.

It was finally agreed that Rafael Díaz Hanscom, an engineer who had left Cuba illegally and who was allied to Varona's group (Rescate), would be general coordinator; the military chief would be Humberto Sorí Marín, an ex-commander of the Rebel Army, who had also been minister of agriculture in the first revolutionary cabinet; and Rogelio González Corzo, Artime's delegate within Cuba, would act as the link with the CIA and thus be in charge of supplies. The choice of Díaz Hanscom was not accidental. He had recently arrived from Cuba, where he worked in the National Savings and Housing Institute, bringing a proposal for a new plot to assassinate Castro in the days leading up to the planned invasion.

Testimony of Mario Morales Mesa[10]
Havana, November 1994

Around the time of Girón [the Bay of Pigs], I was designated to organize a counterintelligence unit in charge of investigating plots and conspiracies to assassinate revolutionary leaders, particularly Fidel, who was the focus of all the hatred of the counterrevolution and the CIA.

We had received various reports on planned assassination attempts on Fidel in the run-up to the Bay of Pigs attack. These were clearly intended to decapitate the revolution — which those responsible believed would make the invaders' task easier.

At that time, we had coordinated with Federico Mora, the captain of G-2 who, on Fidel's instructions, was handling the case of Humberto Sorí Marín, who had fled to the United States early in 1961 after being involved with the US embassy in Havana in various conspiracies.

Mora had infiltrated an agent into the group: Alcibiades Bermúdez, also a captain in the Rebel Army, who had been instructed by Sorí to create an uprising in the Pinar del Río mountains and to prepare the ground for a landing in support of the Bay of Pigs invasion.

Thus, we knew about the landing of Sorí, Díaz Hanscom and a group of CIA agents on March 13, 1961, who entered the country at a point on the border of Havana and Matanzas provinces.

In their initial conversation, Sorí informed Alcibiades of their plans, including the unification and arming of all the counterrevolutionary groups, the unleashing of an internal war in support of the invaders, and the assassination of the commander in chief [Fidel]. The codename the Americans used for the assassination plot was Operation Generosa.

---

[10]   Mario Morales Mesa was the chief of Cuban counterintelligence responsible for averting attempts to assassinate members of the revolutionary leadership. He was a veteran of the international brigades in the Spanish Civil War.

Informed of the plans and their imminent execution, Captain Mora passed on the details to our chief, Commander Ramiro Valdés, who authorized an operation against the infiltrators.

Through our intensive investigation we discovered that the meeting to establish a united internal front of the counterrevolution was scheduled for March 18 in a house in Reparto Flores, Marianao. Headquarters assigned compañero José Luis Domínguez as head of the operation, and at 18:00 on the day indicated, our compañeros surrounded the house and raided it before the counterrevolutionaries had time to react.

There we seized a large number of weapons, plans and sketches, and, most important of all, details of a plan to assassinate Fidel on March 26 during a meeting to discuss a construction project to house poor families that was scheduled to take place in the Housing Institute. That particular assassination project involved Rafael Díaz Hanscom, who had absented himself for a few days in order to travel clandestinely to Miami, and he was one of the people invited to the meeting. The plan consisted of placing an explosive device in the meeting room to be detonated by remote control.

That day dealt the first blow to the invasion plans, given that the counterrevolutionary general staff and various CIA agents who were specifically trained to sabotage the country's industries were captured. But above all, one of the most dangerous conspiracies to assassinate Commander Fidel Castro prior to the attack at the Bay of Pigs was dismantled.

Report of the Rebel Army Investigations Department (DIER)
Havana, March 28, 1961

In accordance with instructions received, the house at 110 106th Street, Reparto Flores, Marianao, was searched and its occupants arrested. They were:

• Rafael Díaz Hanscom, in charge of the internal front, who, according to documents seized, was to assassinate Dr. Fidel Castro at the Savings and Housing Institute.

- Rogelio González Corzo, with false documents from the CIA in the name of Harold Boves Castillo. González was the MRR representative, a CIA agent and the coordinator of a plan to create a provocation at the US Guantánamo naval base to coincide with the invasion of our country currently being prepared by the United States.

- Humberto Sorí Marín, a former commander of the Rebel Army, a traitor to the revolution, involved in conspiratorial efforts with individuals from the US embassy in Havana dating back to the previous year, and associated with notorious counterrevolutionaries Manuel Artime and Huber Matos. In early 1961 he fled the country for Florida. There he received instructions from the CIA to join an internal front in Cuba, intended to unite all the counterrevolutionary groups, which would act as a fifth column as soon as the Yankees attacked us. One of his basic tasks was to try to recruit as many officers as possible from our armed forces for this purpose.

- Manuel Lorenzo Puig Miyar, CIA agent.

- Nemesio Rodríguez Navarrete, CIA agent, former leader of the Martí Democratic Movement (MDM), who traveled to Miami in January 1961 to receive instructions.

- Gaspar Domingo Trueba Varona, CIA agent, responsible for training military chiefs of the counterrevolutionary movements affiliated to the new united internal front.

- Eufemio Fernández Ortega, ex-collaborator of *mafioso* Santo Trafficante when he managed Trafficante's gambling room in the Sans Souci casino in Havana. He was chief of the Triple A counterrevolutionary group and a convenor of the united internal front. A large quantity of arms and military equipment were found in his residence.

Also detained were counterrevolutionaries Dionisio Acosta Hernández, Pedro Céspedes Compay, Felipe Dopaso Abreu, Orestes Frías Roque, Eduardo Lemus Pérez, Narciso Peralta Soto,

Gabriel Riaño Zequeira, Yolanda Álvarez Balzaga and Berta Echegaray Garriga.

In various searches undertaken and in the Reparto Flores house itself the following weapons were seized: 11 Colt .45 pistols, six M1 rifles, eight M3 submachine guns, six boxes of ammunition containing more than 5,000 bullets for different weapons, 11 cans of security flares, 16 rolls of time fuses, 13 rolls of detonator fuses, 15 boxes of M2 fuses, 12 boxes of M1 fuses, 10 boxes with 160 hand grenades, three boxes containing 120 incendiaries, a box of 21 fragmentation grenades, 24 packets of nitro-starch (11 in jute sacks and 13 in backpacks); one radio and a transmission plant, maps, minutes, orders, six pages of plans and a document signed by a group of counterrevolutionary organizations constituting a so-called United Revolutionary Front.

5

Alternatives to the Crisis

The heat in Colonel J.C. King's office was intolerable. The air conditioning had broken down and the security measures for Agency establishments meant the windows could not be opened. They were afraid that the Russians, or any other of the enemies of Western "democracy," would overhear the secret assassination and terrorist conspiracies planned there.

King mopped beads of sweat from his forehead from time to time and fanned himself with a file. He had before him fresh information from agents who had radioed messages from Cuba on the situation after Castro's defeat of the brigade of Cuban exiles at the Bay of Pigs. The invasion had ended in failure. To a certain extent, King believed he could not be held responsible, as Bissell — the great strategist — had designated Jake Esterline to head the operation. He had warned on various occasions that things were not as simple as his superiors thought, and that Cuba was no Guatemala. Brigade 2506 had been defeated in less than 72 hours by the Cuban forces. The internal front of the counterrevolution that had cost so much to construct was in pieces, many of the best agents had been captured, and Castro had rubbed the nose of the US government in its own debacle.

King believed Kennedy bore much of the blame for what had happened. The president did not want to commit US armed forces when the brigade called for help from the Cuban beaches.

The president was weak, pusillanimous and too receptive to the ideas of liberal advisers who talked to him of democratic change in Latin America. The Russians were gaining ground; with the defeat at the Bay of Pigs they had consolidated a beachhead in the A mericas.

Following the debacle, Kennedy formed a government commission headed by General Maxwell Taylor to investigate the causes of the defeat.[1] It had been leaked that the commission had orders to find "guilty parties," and blame was sure to fall on the CIA, as everyone was aware of Kennedy's animosity towards the Agency.

With those thoughts in mind, King sent for the officers waiting outside his office: David Phillips, James Noel, Frank Bender and Karl Hetsh. The objective of the meeting was to seek alternatives to the crisis that would be unleashed as a result of the report by General Taylor's Commission. If possible, they might also be able to take revenge for the blow by making Castro pay for his audacity.

"We have to act rapidly," King stated.

"We have an important network in Cuba that has not been discovered by G-2," Bender said. "This is the AM/BLOOD group of trustworthy agents, including Tito, Ernesto, Brand, Javier and 2637 [Juan Manuel Guillot Castellanos]. Also, there are underground groups that were not damaged by Cuban security operations and have decisive and dependable men. I think we still have an opportunity to do something. Unfortunately, Rogelio González was arrested, but it would seem that nobody squealed, as our people have not been picked up by G-2."

"We shouldn't lose our heads," commented King. "We still have some cards to play. We just need a good plan; but this time

---

[1]   Maxwell Taylor was a general in the US armed forces, who would later become chief of staff and finally US ambassador to Vietnam. A military theorist, he designed the scheme of low- and medium-intensity warfare used to combat national and revolutionary movements.

we'll do it alone. Nobody will hear about it in Washington, and when it takes place, they will have no option but to follow our directions."

"I agree," interjected Phillips, "but I think we should decentralize operations, separate them out. We shouldn't put all our efforts into just one undertaking. If the G-2 discovers one group, the others will still be viable. I remind you, colonel, that we have the Grau siblings' Rescate group and other individuals from the [former] FRD [Revolutionary Democratic Front] allied with Tony Varona.[2] All of them are men of action who have the weapons we infiltrated prior to the Bay of Pigs."

"Yes, that's an interesting idea. But how are we going to get in contact with them? I don't think they have their own means of communication and if they did, they would surely have lost them in the communist raids," King replied.

"We have just the person for that," Phillips explained. "Rodolfo León Curbelo, the courier Tony Varona used to send the poison capsules to Cuba in March. He has good contacts with Caldevilla, an attaché at the Spanish embassy in Havana who works for us. We can send instructions through him. They don't have the men for large operations, but they would be excellent for an attempt on Castro."

At that point the telephone rang. King picked up the receiver, and after a brief conversation, explained to those present, "Hunt reports that agent Tito has just arrived in Miami. He says he has talked with him for several hours. He wants to come to Washington to talk with us and find out what future awaits him in Cuba."

"That could be very good or very bad," Hetsh cut in. "If he comes here, we can't keep him away from the Taylor Commission and he could say things that would harm us."

---

2   María Leopoldina Grau Alsina (Polita) and her brother Ramón (Mongo) were niece and nephew of former President Ramón Grau San Martín.

"He's a man we can trust," Phillips put in, "and I think it would be good for him to come and see for himself what the administration is devoting its efforts to while we are sacrificing our best men in this country."

After confirming the impact his words had made, he extracted a bunch of papers from his file, saying he had a message from agent Luis in Santiago de Cuba who reported:

"The failure of the Bay of Pigs invasion has caused confusion and desperation, but now they are beginning to react again. The lack of direction and action is impeding the activities of the civil resistance. Although he is a highly regarded man, Miró Cardona's council will not give people any inspiration whatsoever. In reality, they [the council members] do not identify with the people. They are figureheads rather than leaders. That's the reason for the lack of an open opposition."

"We have to reflect before adopting a line of action," said Frank Bender. "Nevertheless, I think we should act quickly, or that son-of-a-bitch Kennedy is going to have us all by the balls."

King remained silent. He realized that something had to be done and as soon as possible. He paced the room while the others watched him closely. They knew him and understood that something was buzzing in his mind. Suddenly he stopped and sat down again at the table to say:

"Gentlemen, we have to stake everything on this. It's time to launch our men into the final combat. We have lost the battle but not the war. The only solution is to eliminate Castro and his closest supporters, which would plunge the communists into deep confusion and would be the ideal moment for an armed uprising by the groups we still have on the island. The president would have no option but to send in the marines to help the Cubans, because if he didn't, he would lose all authority. Bring Tito to Washington and initiate contact once more with the most capable agents operating in Cuba and send them the necessary instructions. Everything is not lost yet. I think we can kill two birds with one stone."

Operation Patty
Report of the Department of State Security (DSE)
Havana, May 1961

Alfredo Izaguirre de la Riva, alias Tito, was a journalist and descendant of one of the richest families in Cuba; he was recruited in 1959 by the CIA station in Havana and lent it immeasurable services from that time. With his collaboration, microphones were placed in the penthouse of the Hotel Rosita de Hornedo, prior to the Soviet embassy installing its offices there.

On two occasions — September 1960 and February 1961 — Izaguirre de la Riva went to the United States for espionage training. He was instructed to organize a network in Cuba to supply weapons and explosives to counterrevolutionary groups for an operation envisaged as a backup to the Bay of Pigs invasion. The intention was to create internal chaos by disrupting communications, killing revolutionary cadres, damaging electricity and water supplies, and eventually creating such instability that the US-backed invaders would be received as saviors.

In March 1961, the CIA dropped a significant arsenal from a plane onto one of his farms in the vicinity of San José de las Lajas. The materials included a bazooka with shells, 14 Garand rifles, five Thompson submachine guns, two .30-caliber machine guns, four Bar rifles and a large volume of munitions and explosives.

In that same month, agent Jorge García Rubio, alias Tony, was sent to him as a radio operator to maintain communications. García also facilitated contact with other heads of CIA agent networks undertaking similar tasks, including Emilio

Adolfo Rivero Caro ("Brand"), José Pujals Mederos ("Ernesto"), Luis Torroella Martín-Rivero ("Luis"), Javier Souto Álvarez ("Javier") and Juan Manuel Guillot Castellanos (known as 2637).

The mission consisted of supporting counterrevolutionary leaders, including by Rafael Díaz Hanscom and Humberto Sorí Marín, who had infiltrated the country in the first half of March to direct the underground organizations to prepare for a planned invasion. After the Bay of Pigs debacle in April, they found they were on their own with no contact with the internal front. Their US contacts went silent and the agents who escaped detention agreed that Alfredo Izaguirre (Tito) should go to Miami to clarify the situation and the prospects for continuing the struggle. Tito reached Miami in the second half of May 1961.

After talking with various CIA officers, he asked for a meeting with the Washington chiefs and subsequently met with General Maxwell Taylor, one of the hawks in the administration in charge of the Cuba Project. It was not difficult for them to reach agreement. In a matter of days, they had drawn up a new plan, this time bearing in mind the information received from those people in Cuba who were at risk. Tito then returned to Cuba.

As soon as he had ensured that nobody was suspicious of his brief absence, he initiated an intensive series of meetings with the main counterrevolutionary leaders. He had to get their agreement in order to then communicate it to the United States, and if everything were approved, give each of them their new mission.

The idea was to eliminate Fidel and Raúl Castro, taking advantage of their presence at events in Havana and Santiago de Cuba to commemorate the anniversary of July 26. At the same time, a unit of their men, with arms supplied by the CIA, would attack the US military installation at Guantánamo with mortars and light cannon fire to provoke a response from troops stationed there. Believing they were under attack, the US troops would return fire and ask their government for support, providing pretext to intervene militarily in Cuba.

Everything was perfectly planned. Everything, except they had not counted on the G-2 agents in Santiago and Havana, who were informed of their plans. On July 22, four days before the scheduled date of the assault, the Cuban security operation began. The conspirators were all captured, their weapons seized, and their plans, down to the last detail, uncovered. The world would learn of the extent of the conspiracy in August 1961 at the conference of the OAS in Punta del Este, Uruguay, where Commander Che Guevara exposed it in full.

Testimony of Alfredo Izaguirre de la Riva[3]
Havana, July 1961

After the defeat at the Bay of Pigs, with the consequent demo-ralization and detention of contacts and leaders, you can understand the disorganization of the group. We received no word from the United States for two weeks. Finally, they instructed us to go ahead and reorganize the groups, with no further explanation. This was for Ernesto [José Pujals] and myself as we knew nothing at all about Brand. After various meetings between Ernesto and César [Octavio Barroso Gómez, another CIA agent], to whom Ernesto had introduced me as operative chief of the United Front along with Hipólito [Carlos Bandín, MRR coordinator], he brought me to Juanito from Liberation, who in turn introduced me to Justo, head of Liberation and the civil coordinator of the United Front. The Democratic Insurrectional Movement (MID), headed by Víctor [Raúl Alfonso García] came up with the idea that somebody had to go to the United States to find out why the Bay of Pigs operation had failed...

---

[3]   This testimony is part of Izaguirre's account to his captors after he was detained for his terrorist activities.

When I got to Miami, I met with CIA officer Bill Williams [Howard Hunt], who explained the plans they had drawn up and awaiting Washington's approval.

In summary, the plans were: to reorganize the navy and refit all the groups' vessels with artillery; use the vessels to lay mines in Cuba's most important bays in order to blow up supply vessels; to organize attacks on Cuban objectives near the coast to raise counterrevolutionary morale; to obtain maritime and aerial control of the country through a rapid deployment to take Cayo Coco (north of Camagüey province), which was out of range of the Cuban battery; to fill Cayo Coco with artillery to repel attacks; set up a powerful transmission tower; to install a provisional government; to continue supplying arms to the underground groups; to provoke general destabilization in the country; and to eliminate Fidel Castro.

Hunt said they had weapons for 50,000 men for this undertaking.

A few days later I left for Washington to meet with the CIA bosses, as per usual staying at the Mayflower Hotel in the city, and made contact with Karl Hetsh, aide to General Jim Bowdin [Frank Bender], who, as I was informed, was the Agency's politico in the Cuban case.

The next day, Hetsh took me to the Raleigh Hotel where an apartment was reserved for me. Shortly afterwards, Bowdin appeared and explained that everything was on hold for the time being.

When I asked why the Bay of Pigs operation failed, he stated that, as he saw it, everything was well planned from the military point of view and that the failure was due to an executive error [referring to President Kennedy]. He explained that the Cuban government had stopped the invasion with six or seven aircraft that could have been destroyed in a second bombardment, and, were therefore able to hold the beachhead the brigade had taken at Girón [the Bay of Pigs].

We had a lengthy discussion on the situation in Cuba. Bowdin explained the need to unite all the underground groups in one front in order to coordinate future operations.

We reviewed our contacts in the country: the MDC in Santiago de Cuba, directed from the Guantánamo naval base by El Zorro [José Amparo Rosabal], closely linked to Nino Díaz; the MID in Camagüey, headed by Víctor; Javier's group in Las Villas; and Ernesto, Brand and myself in Havana. What he proposed was to create a "resistance unit" of all these groups and others that could be deployed to trigger a plan to deal the final blow to the revolution.

The plan consisted of: organizing a provocation at the US Guantánamo base, through an attack on the installation by counterrevolutionaries disguised as Cuban troops; preparing an uprising of underground groups in all the provinces where we had contingents, for which they would send weapons; and assassinating Fidel and Raúl.

I felt there were no great difficulties with the first two points. They would take care of informing the MDC [Christian Democratic Movement] people in Oriente province and I would send instructions to the Camagüey and Las Villas groups. Good communications already existed and various points on the coast had been selected to land the materiel. Osvaldo Ramírez and Benito Campos, chiefs of the insurgency groups in Las Villas province, had been contacted and unity in terms of action was agreed.

But the planned assassinations would be very difficult because Fidel and Raúl's movements were not easy to pin down.

The MRR had an old plan to assassinate Fidel in Revolution Plaza and eliminate Raúl in his home on 26th Street in Nuevo Vedado, shooting from the Chinese cemetery opposite. I informed Bowdin of those plans and he asked me to study them and confirm things later by radio.

The next day I met with General Maxwell Taylor in his Pentagon office. There I explained the situation in Cuba after the Bay of Pigs and our ideas for moving forward. By then I had absorbed Bowdin's plan and I put it forward as an idea of the "internal front."

One of the people at the meeting told me that we should forget it and that the marines were going to make a "surprise intervention in Cuba" to sort out the Cuban problem. But this would depend on "your people creating a situation allowing for direct intervention."

A few hours later I met again with Bowdin and Hetsh in the hotel. They were very satisfied and brought congratulations from the CIA executive. The ideas discussed had been approved and would be initiated as soon as I returned to Cuba. The operation was codenamed Patty.

Report of the Department of State Security (DSE) Provincial Headquarters
Santiago de Cuba, June 25, 1961

One of the counterrevolutionary leaders, José Amparo Rosabal, alias El Zorro, was head of the ministry of transportation in the early days of the revolution and an old collaborator of Carlos Prío and Tony Varona. He was in contact with the CIA through Nino Díaz, who got him into the intelligence service at the US base.

His plan was to place weapons close to the perimeter of the [Guantánamo] base on the morning of July 17. Antonio Marra Acosta and Emilio Quintana González were in charge of picking them up from a US sergeant named Smith. When arrested, the counterrevolutionaries were found with the following weapons: two 57 mm. cannons, four bazookas, 23 Garand rifles and several hand grenades.

Subsequent operations turned up other weapons from the US base, including 35 Springfield rifles, a 60 mm. mortar, a

.30-caliber submachine gun, 12 M3 submachine guns, munitions, grenades and explosives.

Report of the Department of State Security (DSE) Provincial Headquarters
Santa Clara, August 19, 1961

Investigations uncovered an operation being executed by agents José Ángel González Castro, Segundo Borges Ranzola, Miguel Pentón Alfonso and Javier Souto Álvarez.

These agents' plans involved: uniting the different counterrevolutionary groups; illegally introducing paper money from the United States in order to damage the country's economy; systematic sabotage attacks on production, such as poisoning cattle; and sabotage in the industrial sector, particularly against the Antonio Guiteras power plant.

In addition, military plans were aimed at organizing commando groups in the main cities and aiding insurgent groups, mainly those of Osvaldo Ramírez in the Escambray and Benito Campos in Corralillo.

This was confirmed by the interception of coded radio message 124 requesting an arms shipment to Dutton Cay, north of Isabela de Sagua, consisting of 192 M1 carbines, 12 .30-caliber submachine guns, 24 pistols, 500 pounds of explosives, 200 pounds of incendiary material, three bazookas, three recoilless cannons and large quantities of ammunition. This shipment, which also included special weapons fitted with silencers for personal attacks, was requested for July 22.

Report of the Department of State Security (DSE) Headquarters
Havana, December 22, 1961

Through investigations that led to the arrest of Alfredo Izaguirre de la Riva, we discovered that he commenced his counterrevolutionary activities in the early months of 1959, trying to unite all the counterrevolutionary organizations under his command in response to a CIA directive.

This resulted in numerous meetings with the coordinators of such groups, including Carlos Bandín Cruz (Hipólito) of the MRR; Reynold González of the MRP; Raúl Alfonso of the MID; and Octavio Barroso of the United Front.

He was the main advocate of actions planned for July 26, including those in Oriente province, which involved an attempt on the life of Commander Raúl Castro, an attack on the Santiago refinery and a provocation at the Guantánamo naval base.

Also planned were sabotage operations in Camagüey and Las Villas, and finally, an assassination attempt on Commander Fidel Castro at the commemorative event in Revolution Plaza, using a mortar deployed in a house on Amezaga Street.

Testimony of Carlos Valdés Sánchez[4]
Havana, November 1993

In Havana, a group of men dressed in military uniform would place a 60 mm. mortar within 200 meters of the platform in Revolution Plaza. From there they would open fire on the Cuban leaders with the aim of assassinating Fidel and his compañeros.

There were two alternatives for the attempt on Commander Raúl Castro. One consisted of firing at him with a .30-caliber machine gun while he was speaking at the July 26 event. And if that failed, an ambush was planned on the highway to the airport, where several men armed with submachine guns would attack him. The second option was based on the assumption that as soon as he knew about the attack on Fidel in Havana, Raúl would leave for the local airport, thus providing them with an opportunity.

---

[4]   Carlos Valdés Sánchez was a Cuban officer who was part of the Operation Patty investigation team.

Meanwhile, a group of counterrevolutionaries dressed in Rebel Army uniforms would fire mortars in the direction of the US base in Guantánamo, which would give the signal to underground groups in Santiago and other eastern cities to initiate their subversive action.

In summary, that was the plan of Operation Patty, which Cuban security gave their own codename: *Candela* [Trouble].

A Perfect Target
Havana, May 1961

One day towards the end of the month, Rodolfo León Curbelo received a phone call from Jaime Caldevilla, press attaché at the Spanish embassy. The diplomat wanted an urgent meeting with him at the embassy. León knew Caldevilla well and was aware that when such a request was made it was in connection with a message from the "Americans." So he quickly dressed and took off for the meeting.

Jaime Caldevilla was a veteran CIA agent who used the Spanish embassy for his espionage activities, for which he was expelled from Cuba in 1965. When León was comfortably seated in the diplomat's office, Caldevilla explained that he had received instructions from the Agency to direct the assassination of Fidel Castro using two of the most trustworthy counterrevolutionary groups in the country. They had attempted this task some months earlier, in January, but the operation had failed when Cuban agent Félix Rodríguez could not be infiltrated. Nevertheless, they now believed the conditions were ripe for Mario Chanes's and Higinio Menéndez's men to act.

Mario Chanes de Armas was a resentful, bitter man. He had fought against the Batista dictatorship, but after the revolutionary triumph, felt disillusioned at not being given the position he expected. He became involved in various conspiracies until he finally decided that Fidel was the cause of all his ills, and thus dedicated himself wholeheartedly to his elimination.

Higinio Menéndez Beltrán and his group had different roots. Their political background was linked to the criminal groups that had devastated the country in the 1940s. Menéndez had reached the same conclusion on his own account and was offered the job of assassinating Castro.

One attack was planned at a location in close proximity to a house Castro often visited in the capital. The other plan was for a gangster-style shoot-out on one of Havana's main avenues.

Once he had given his explanation, the Spanish diplomat informed León that after committing the crime he should keep a low profile, or if he had family in the rural part of the country, go stay with them for a reasonable period of time. Within a few days, León had passed on instructions to the chosen assassins and each of them got down to planning.

Carrying a Springfield rifle with a telescopic sight obtained in an earlier adventure, Mario Chanes would fire as soon as the target was in range. He was an accurate shot and had practiced a great deal. The location was ideal: an apartment located above a grocery store on the corner of 11th and 12th Streets in Vedado, a few meters from the home of Celia Sánchez, executive secretary of the Council of Ministers and one of Fidel's close collaborators.

They only had to wait for an opportunity to kill Fidel. After several meetings, the conspirators selected the week July 19–26, 1961, for the operation. They had reached the conclusion that prior to the events for July 26 Fidel would visit Celia's home at some point, to finalize details for the commemoration of an event so important to the revolution.

A few days before, on July 17, G-2 discovered the homicidal plot, captured everybody involved, and thus frustrated this assassination attempt.

Testimony of Florentino Fernández León[5]
Havana, November 1994

I don't remember dates, but I think it would have been mid-1960 when I started to attend meetings of revolutionary combatants organized by Mario Chanes in the Puentes Grandes brewery club. I didn't have much of a friendship with him, but we had been compañeros-in-struggle against the Batista dictatorship.

At those meetings, Chanes expressed his displeasure at the direction being taken by the revolutionary government because he felt he was underestimated and that he was more worthy than other people in key posts in the administration.

At one of those meetings I met a friend of Chanes', called Orlando Ulacia Valdés. He was a type of agitator who explained at the meetings how the real revolutionaries were being relegated, while others without merit, like those from the [Popular] Socialist Party, were occupying important positions.[6]

Ulacia and I soon discovered we agreed politically and, through him, I soon began to gather information about their conspiratorial activities and Mario Chanes's role as a leading figure in them.

Ulacia "recruited" me for these activities and we began to meet regularly. I had the credentials of having been detained for a few days for alleged counterrevolutionary activities. In reality that was a story prepared for me by a compañero from G-2, which had already become suspicious of the Chanes brothers' conspiratorial activities and set me up for my undercover role.

In the early months of 1961, I went to a meeting in the office of the Nela butter factory, where Ulacia worked. Two other individuals whose names I've forgotten were there. Ulacia explained that it was necessary to activate counterrevolutionary

---

[5]   Florentino Fernández León was a Moncada Garrison assailant who uncovered this assassination conspiracy and informed the authorities.

[6]   The Popular Socialist Party (PSP) was the former communist party in Cuba.

activities. He specifically focused on a plot to assassinate Fidel, whom he stated had to be killed.

He sketched the corner of 11th and 12th Streets in Vedado on paper and pointed out the place from which they would shoot with a rifle fitted with a telescopic sight. They planned the attempt on one of Fidel's visits to compañera Celia Sánchez's home. Ulacia stated that he had checked Fidel's movements at her house from the balcony of a house on the corner, where a family he knew lived. He said that when Fidel got out of the car, he usually went around the back of it and that was the moment to shoot. He said there would be several participants in the attack and a car would be parked with its engine running on the corner for a quick getaway.

They held various other meetings elsewhere to fine-tune the plan, at a bar on Puentes Grandes Avenue close to the Pavo Real match factory and also in Ulacia's house.

At the beginning of July everything was ready, and we informed the compañero looking after us, who, after consulting with headquarters, explained that we couldn't wait any longer to move in.

That was how these traitors were caught.

Testimony of Mario Morales Mesa
Havana, July 1961

On July 17, 1961, I was working on the Pinar del Río case involving brothers Mario and Francisco Chanes and others.

We had been investigating these individuals for their counterrevolutionary activities from January of that year, and had discovered that they were in contact with CIA agents from that time and were planning to assassinate Fidel Castro during one of his visits to the house of compañera Celia Sánchez, located on 11th Street, between 10th and 12th in Vedado.

Originally, they were to support a group of agents who were to be infiltrated from the United States to execute the action. When that operation failed, a commando unit consisting of the Chanes brothers and others was organized to attack the apartment from the upper floor of a warehouse on 11th and 12th, barely 50 meters from the target.

The operation included the 30 November Revolutionary Movement, People's Revolutionary Movement and the FRD [CRC] groups. The date selected for the attempt was the week July 19–26, 1961. All the conspirators were captured and their weapons seized.

The Suicides
Havana, May–June 1961

Higinio Menéndez and Guillermo Caula's group was fairly small. Its members included individuals from various underground groups hit by the DSE at various times. They were united by their hatred of Fidel Castro and had decided that the only alternative left open to them, after the defeats suffered, was to assassinate the prime minister in order to trigger a US intervention in Cuba.

They tried it on two occasions. Once during Castro's visit to a densely populated Havana neighborhood and the other when the leader was dining in a well-known restaurant. Both attempts failed, thwarted by the effective vigilance of his security guards.

Undaunted, however, after receiving a message from the CIA guaranteeing both its backing and a substantial sum of money, they got together and hatched a new assassination scheme.

The idea was a simple one. The conspirators were counting on the complicity of the owner of a service station at the intersection of Rancho Boyeros and Santa Catalina Avenues, on an unavoidable route from the city center to the airport. They would lie in wait there for the approach of the leader's cars and then fire on them with a bazooka. The date selected was the first week of June.

A feverish bout of activity put the finishing touches on the plan. The bazooka and weapons were transferred and the men in place. Everything was ready. The only thing they had not foreseen was the action by the G-2, which, informed of the plan, detained all those involved.

Report of the Department of State Security Headquarters
Havana, July 25, 1961

Information was obtained in recent weeks that a group of individuals were periodically meeting in an establishment managed by Juan Bacigalupe Hornedo, located on the corner of Vento Highway and Estrada Avenue in the Casino Deportivo district.

The most important participants were Higinio Menéndez Beltrán, Guillermo Caula Ferrer, Ibrahim Álvarez Cuesta, Augusto Jiménez Montenegro, Román Rodríguez Quevedo and Osvaldo Díaz Espinoza, individuals who maintained contact with ex-captains Bernardo Corrales and Santiago Ríos, both fugitives from justice. They met in the service station on Rancho Boyeros and Santa Catalina owned by Carlos Pérez González.

Investigations revealed that the group had relations with members of the CIA and made frequent visits to the Guantánamo naval base where they received munitions and instructions on sabotage and assassination attempts on leaders of the revolution.

On June 14, 1961, the group met in the Casino Deportivo land sales office with an individual known as León (Rodolfo León Curbelo), sent to Cuba by the FRD with the mission of assassinating Fidel. In that meeting Juan Bacigalupe, Higinio Menéndez and Guillermo Caula were assigned to the job and given the necessary funds.

Those individuals were given the task of making contact with the chiefs of various counterrevolutionary organizations so they could check out the places frequented by Fidel. On one occasion when Fidel went to the Cucalambé restaurant on 5th Avenue and 112th Street, Higinio Menéndez was seen surveying it with an individual named Antonio and one Josefa Delgado Piñeiro (Fina), who were constantly under the watch of State Security agents.

Through subsequent investigations, it was discovered that "during the meetings Carlos Pérez González and Augusto Jiménez Montenegro were given the task of checking the area located on the stretch of Rancho Boyeros highway between Santa Catalina and Vía Blanca, opposite land occupied by the Ciudad Deportiva."

On July 2, all those involved were arrested and two bazookas with their shells, three M1 carbines, three .45-caliber Thompson submachine guns, two crates of US fragmentation grenades, a radio plant similar to those utilized by the CIA and a large volume of ammunition were found buried at the Rancho Boyeros and Santa Catalina service station.

6

Operation Liborio: "Cuba in Flames"

For Antonio Veciana Blanch, 1959 was a year of great emotion and profound disillusionment. When the revolution triumphed, he was a public accountant working for sugar magnate, Julio Lobo, with aspirations of becoming a prosperous businessman. Unfortunately for him, measures taken almost immediately by the new government had frustrated his dreams. Those measures doubtless cast a disagreeable shadow over his economic plans, and so he began to link up with others disaffected with the new regime. Many of them hoped the US government, as they had done before, would take the action needed to halt or derail the high-speed train that was the revolution and its socioeconomic changes.

Veciana had contact with several prominent figures such as Rufo López Fresquet, minister of the treasury; Felipe Pazos, president of the National Bank; Raúl Chivás, president of the Rail Transportation Corporation; and Manuel Ray Rivero, minister of public works. Almost from the outset, these contacts had encouraged Veciana to develop a dissident movement of malcontents within the government that would try to divide the revolutionary leadership, neutralize the radicals, and put the brakes on their radical reform program.

This proved harder than they anticipated. The revolution was growing more radical and Veciana's associates lost the little power they once held. So, the option they chose was to conspire against the regime. On the recommendation of López, he contacted veteran CIA agent David Phillips, who operated from a public relations office near Havana's busy La Rampa.

After several conversations, Phillips was convinced that Veciana possessed the ability to carry out acts of terrorism, given his marked inclination for violence. They reached an agreement, and a few weeks later Veciana started classes at a branch of the Berlitz Language School, but in subversion, not a foreign language. The classes Veciana attended covered psychological warfare, sabotage, the organization of underground groups and acts of terrorism. He passed the course with flying colors.

Originally, Veciana was instructed to work directly with Phillips, who would be his mentor while he acquired experience in the art of conspiracy. Towards the end of 1960, they received an order from the CIA station in the capital to consider an assassination attempt on Fidel Castro at one of the public meetings he attended almost daily.

They discussed various locations: the university precinct, restaurants, public ministries, plazas, and finally the esplanade that stretched from the presidential palace to Havana's Malecón, the location of many rallies. The palace had an irresistible attraction and they concluded it was the ideal place. A line of buildings extended around the improvised plaza with a large park in its center. Several of those buildings were rented out as homes. Number 29 Misiones Avenue met all the requisite conditions. The meetings were conducted on the palace's north-facing terrace, 50 meters from the selected building.

After various negotiations, Darling Hoost, an agent of US origin acting under contract, rented an apartment on the eighth floor.

At that point, Phillips was recalled to CIA headquarters in Washington to take charge of psychological warfare against Cuba on a continental scale. Veciana was momentarily without contacts and had to postpone the plans.

While he was waiting, Veciana joined Manuel Ray's Revolutionary Movement of the People (MRP). At the time of the Bay of Pigs it was one of the most active counterrevolutionary groups, engaging in many acts of sabotage including the arson attack on El Encanto department store in which Fe del Valle, an exemplary worker, was killed.

After the defeat of the invasion, a new coordinator, Reynold González, took on the MRP leadership and appointed Veciana as its military attaché, in charge of all subversive and terrorist actions.

A few months later, in mid-1961, they heard about Operation Patty. After several talks with its leader, Alfredo Izaguirre, they decided to keep their distance from it, so as not be to compromised if it were discovered, which it subsequently was.

For his part, Veciana continued with his own project. Week by week, weapons were smuggled into the apartment at Misiones Avenue, and he soon had a bazooka, submachine guns, grenades and the uniforms the assassins would use when the order was given.

Death Terrace
The Mayflower Hotel, Washington, DC, July 1961

One day in late July 1961, CIA agent José Pujals Mederos was called to Washington. He had arrived from Cuba a few weeks earlier to report on the progress of Operation Patty and thus had avoided being arrested when the plot was dismantled by the Cuban security forces. Karl Hetsh, his case officer, was waiting for him in the hotel room to which he had been summoned with another US citizen who called himself Harold Bishop (David Phillips), who was to instruct him on a new mission.

In perfect Spanish, with a South American accent, Phillips explained that the task consisted of activating a new project to incite rebellion within Cuba. The work would be relatively easy. He would direct the MRP group headed by Reynold González and Antonio Veciana to conduct an extensive arson campaign and terrorist operations in the country's main provincial capitals and to assassinate Fidel on the north terrace of the presidential palace. This was part of a coordinated plan whereby key elements of the international press would announce to the world that Cuba had plunged into civil war and that the United States would intervene to impose peace.

The remaining task was a little more delicate. This consisted of serving as contact for a small espionage network located in the Cuban air base at San Antonio de los Baños, where a squadron of Soviet-manufactured MIG-15 aircraft, about to arrive in Cuba, were to be installed.

"I don't foresee any difficulties in executing either task. But I think the operation against Castro will be harder," said Pujals.

"Veciana should already have the necessary men," Phillips responded. "He is in contact with the Rescate people and they will facilitate what is needed. Your mission is to give the orders, supervise the operation and coordinate the infiltration of the required equipment. Afterwards you can concentrate on information concerning the aircraft."

A few hours later, on July 28, Pujals, now the CIA's principal link in Cuba, infiltrated the country at a point off the northern coast of Havana province near Puerto Escondido.

Havana, Early August 1961

Two days after arriving in Cuba, Pujals met with Reynold González and Antonio Veciana to give them detailed orders.

According to his later accounts, González did not like the project. He was displeased with recent failures and believed in conserving the organization, using it only for propaganda work in expectation of better times when the US government decided on definitive action. Right now, he felt they were manipulating the MRP, using it as cannon fodder. Veciana was proposing direct action to damage the regime at its weakest points. In the end, after much discussion, they could not agree, and left the decision to an extraordinary meeting of their organization's national leadership.

Pujals did not want to get involved in the dispute. He knew it was not his terrain and he was very clear on the orders he had received. Veciana could solve the problem. He met up with Octavio Barroso, alias César, one of his most important collaborators, who had recruited a dentist lieutenant at the San Antonio de los Baños airbase where they were beginning to assemble the MIG-15 aircraft they had recently received from the Soviet Union. Thus, he would fulfill one of the CIA's top priorities.

The meeting of the MRP national directorate went ahead on a farm belonging to a group member called Amador Odio outside Havana in the small town of Wajay.[1] Various leaders spoke, some in favor and some against the plans being put forward. Finally, Veciana's proposal won the day. Everybody knew where the order had come from and nobody was prepared to stand up to that. Moreover, Veciana confirmed that he had the necessary men and nobody anticipated any direct risk to themselves. Visibly annoyed, González withdrew and let Veciana take care of the details.

"The plan is simple," Veciana explained to those present. "The idea is to sabotage several department stores — Sears, Fin de Siglo,

---

[1]   Amador Odio was the husband of Sara del Toro, who was one of the organizers of Operation Peter Pan, which flew more than 14,000 unaccompanied children out of Cuba. Their own daughters, Silvia and Ana, were linked to Lee Harvey Oswald shortly before he assassinated President Kennedy.

J. Vallés and Ultra — and to blow up the Havana aqueduct and the National Paper Store."

Teams were organized to carry out these actions by placing explosive devices in the various stores, particularly in departments with inflammable material. For the paper store and the aqueduct, the Rescate group had men working in those places who would lay the charges.

The operation was divided into two stages: the first stage included the acts of terrorism, led by José Manuel Izquierdo (alias Aníbal); and the second stage, led by Veciana, was the assassination attempt. This division was based on the assumption that after the planned acts of sabotage had been executed, Fidel would convene a mass meeting at the presidential palace, as he had done previously, providing the occasion to assassinate him.

González's secretary, María de los Ángeles Abach (Mary), who took the minutes of the meeting, asked when the operation would commence and what it was to be called. Veciana told her that the operation was also referred to as "Cuba in Flames" and the campaign of arson attacks would commence on September 20, 1961.

Havana, August 8, 1961

The day dawned cloudy. One of Pujals' first steps in initiating Operation Liborio or "Cuba in Flames" had been accomplished. It was only a matter of periodically reporting on its progress. The only things that bothered him were the constant meetings he was obliged to attend with the underground leaders, because when the acts of sabotage began, G-2 would come down hard on them.

Pujals left the Miramar house in which he was hiding and walked down to 5th Avenue to wait for a taxi, which arrived quickly. In fact, the vehicle's prompt arrival surprised him. Taxis were not usually so readily available that early hour.

"Where to, sir?"

"19th Street between Paseo and A in Vedado, please."

The taxi moved swiftly in that direction while Pujals gazed absent mindedly out the window. Many of the mansions he saw belonged to his old friends, now in exile. He recalled how the government had confiscated his farm in Santa Cruz del Sur. He was distracted from his meditations when the taxi pulled up at his destination. After paying the fare, Pujals walked for a few blocks as a security measure and then turned back the way he had come, heading for an apartment building that he entered, going up to the second floor. Waiting for him was Octavio Barroso (César), the man with the most valuable military information at that moment: the assembly of the Soviet MIG-15 aircraft and the state of training of the Cuban pilots.

"Ernesto, punctual as always! You must have German ancestors," César said, only half joking.

The two of them went out onto the terrace, while Barroso's mother prepared coffee. The subject of the meeting was the activity of two recently recruited agents, Cadet Francisco Crespo and the dentist, Lieutenant José Muiño, who were passing information on the preparation of the Soviet aircraft. The planes were still crewed by Russians, but Muiño had noted that a group of Cuban pilots were about to return from training in Czechoslovakia. Within two months, they calculated, the first MIG-15 squadron would be in full combat readiness.

A knock at the door sent them scurrying to hide in a corner of the terrace. It was a housing inspector in search of information from Barroso's mother. A few minutes later, when Pujals was explaining to his host the need to work only with military agents so as not to expose himself in other kinds of conspiratorial activities, another knock at the door forced them to run for cover again. It was the same housing inspector, who had returned to stress to Barroso's mother that she needed to put in all her housing documents in order to benefit from the Urban Reform Act.

Testimony of Alberto Santana Martín[2]
Havana, September 1993

That morning, August 8, 1961, our chief, Blanco "El Flaco" [Skinny] gave us the task to locate CIA agent Octavio Barroso [César].[3] The only detail we had about him was his mother's address. Around 10:00 a.m. I arrived at her apartment and introduced myself to the woman as a housing inspector, asking her for documents. I was able to observe that there were two men on the terrace who were trying to hide. So, after looking at the documents I left, explaining to the woman that the building was going to be confiscated and she shouldn't pay any more rent until she received fresh instructions.

I went out into the passage and veered around by a window looking on to the wing of the building. From there I could see that one of the men was the individual in the photo I had been given. The other had a holster at his waist. That was the man I was looking for.

I left the building and asked for backup. Shortly afterwards a G-2 patrol came to my aid and we all went up to the apartment. I knocked again, and when the woman answered I explained that I had to ask her some further questions. She opened the door. We raced to the terrace and detained the two subjects, who turned out to be Octavio Barroso and José Pujals, a spy just infiltrated into Cuba. They had a Colt .38 that they did not have time to use.

Pujals immediately confessed to his main mission. He gave details of the meeting with Reynold González and Antonio Veciana and the objectives of Operation Liborio. He only held back the dates and locations of the meetings.

---

[2]   Colonel Alberto Santana Martín was the DSE official who detained terrorist spies Pujals and Barroso.

[3]   Lieutenant Colonel Gustavo (El Flaco) Blanco Oropesa was the former head of Cuban counterintelligence.

From that point we were faced with a veritable nightmare, and we met every night to review any new information. Soon several leads were found, the group was arrested, and the attempt [against Fidel] was frustrated. Barroso and Pujals also named the military spies, who were quickly detained.

Havana, September 1961

The date of September 15, 1961, was picked by Antonio Veciana to pass on the latest instructions to the group in charge of assassinating Fidel Castro. He had called them to apartment 8A, 29 Misiones Avenue, beside the presidential palace.

Present were José Manuel Izquierdo (Aníbal), Bernardo Paradela (Angelito), Raúl Venta del Mazo (Chiquitico) and Noel Casas Vega (El Pelao). They were all men of action, some from the MRP and others from Rescate and the Second National Front from the Escambray.

"This is the bazooka that will ensure our success," Veciana explained to his compañeros.

Raúl Venta del Mazo, who had been trained in the Dominican Republic during the struggle against Batista, got up from his chair, took the bazooka, and approached the window, which offered a view over the northern terrace of the presidential palace. Placing himself in a firing position, he covered the entire objective with the sight. It could not fail. The distance was short enough to make impact with the first shot.

After returning to his seat, Venta del Mazo asked: "And when do we have to get in position? We can't be here indefinitely until there's a public meeting."

"Chiquitico," Veciana replied, "Our people are going to carry out acts of sabotage all over Havana, which I assure you will provoke a meeting. Your task is to fire the bazooka and then to launch some grenades from the window onto the avenue. The grenades will explode in the middle of a mass demonstration, causing terrible confusion and chaos. That will be the moment to flee, dressed in militia uniforms. We can't fail!"

"And when do we take up position?" Angelito repeated.

"The operation commences on September 20 and you must all be in your assigned positions. On the 25th, the whole group will be here. Aníbal will be the last to arrive because he has other tasks. Then we'll see if the mouse falls into the trap."

Report of the Department of State Security (DSE)
Headquarters
Havana, November 1961

September 29 was the day picked to unleash the terrorists' plan. José Manuel Izquierdo (Aníbal) was in charge of distributing the materials. María de los Angeles Abach (Mary) was appointed to sabotage Fin de Siglo [department store], and she would be taken there by Ernesto Amador del Río.

Co-conspirators Dalia Jorge Díaz, José Manuel Izquierdo and someone known as "Kike" went to Mary's house in the morning to distribute the C-4 explosive packs. Alina Hiort was assigned to sabotage the Ultra department store, but she was unable to implement the plan because she was arrested beforehand. A couple from Rescate, who have not been identified, were selected for J. Vallés and La Época stores. The Hotel Capri sabotage was to be carried out by Joaquín Alzugaray, who was given two C-4 packs, while other acts of terrorism involved two bombs, incendiary devices and "live phosphorus," handed over to Raúl Fernández Rivero who was to distribute them within the student sector.

On that day, September 29, Dalia Jorge was arrested at 5:50 p.m. while placing an explosive in the Sears store, as a consequence of the vigilance of employee Élida Salazar.

Testimony of Raúl Alfonso Roldán[4]
Havana, November 1994

According to our investigations, in mid-1959, Antonio Veciana Blanch — a public accountant and employee of the former Banco Financiero Nacional, owned by sugar magnate Julio Lobo — was recruited by David Phillips, a CIA agent located in Havana. That officer, who some years later occupied a high-level CIA post, entered Cuba in 1958 and operated under the cover of David Phillips Associates, a public relations agency located at Office 502, 106 Humboldt Street, Vedado. He lived with his wife and four sons at 21413 Avenue 19A, Nuevo Biltmore, Marianao.

The initial tasks carried out by the recently graduated agent [Veciana] were related to psychological warfare. In late 1960, Veciana joined the recently formed MRP counterrevolutionary organization. Phillips had instructed him to penetrate the group so as to be part of the political bloc that the CIA wanted to promote in the United States under the command of Manuel Antonio [Tony] de Varona.

After joining the MRP, Veciana became its military coordinator, operating from that point under the pseudonym of Víctor. From that date the MRP's terrorist activities increased, with many sabotage operations, including the placing of incendiary devices in La Epoca department store, the Ten Cents stores on Monte and Obispo, the Puentes Grandes paper factory, and an arson attack on El Encanto department store.

In mid-1960 Phillips left Cuba, having been recalled by his chief to take over the propaganda operation against Cuba. He left Veciana in contact with Lieutenant Colonel Sam Kail, military attaché at the US embassy in Havana.

Before leaving, Phillips put his trainee in charge of a delicate mission: an assassination attempt on Commander Fidel Castro. To that end he was given weapons and Apartment 8A, 29

---

4   Raúl Alfonso Roldán led the DSE investigation into this plot.

Misiones Avenue, beside the presidential palace. This apartment was in the name of US citizen Darling Hoost until November 1960, and it was then transferred in December to Cuban Caridad Rodríguez Aróstegui, Antonio Veciana's mother-in-law. The arms to be deployed in the attack were carefully concealed in the false wall of a closet in this apartment.

After the failure of the Bay of Pigs mercenary invasion, Phillips sent an envoy, José Pujals Mederos, to activate the assassination plot, which involved a series of arson attacks throughout Havana to prompt a public demonstration at the presidential palace that would provide the opportunity to commit the crime. Pujals was arrested and provided us with initial information on the plan, codenamed Operation Liborio.

On September 16, G-2 commenced an operation that led to the capture of a group of MRP members who were trying to circulate a false government decree throughout the country, declaring that parents were to lose custody of their children to the state.[5]

As a result of security measures taken in Havana's main department stores, Dalia Jorge Díaz was arrested while attempting to place an incendiary device in Sears, whereupon she confessed and gave away the location of José Manuel Izquierdo.

At that time, President Osvaldo Dorticós's return from a tour of the socialist countries had been announced, and he was to be received by the capital's residents on the esplanade to the north of the former presidential palace.[6] That had been the occasion for the planned attack.

Izquierdo and other accomplices were arrested. Veciana fled the country, abandoning the group in the Misiones apartment before we occupied it. A bazooka, various Czech Model 25

---

[5]   This was the infamous "Patria Potestad" Law, part of a psychological warfare campaign that fueled the panic among some Cuban parents, convincing them to send their children to Miami with "Operation Peter Pan."

[6]   Osvaldo Dorticós was Cuba's president 1959-76.

submachine guns, fragmentation grenades and militia uniforms were discovered in that location.

A few days later, the main leaders of the MRP, including its national coordinator, Reynold González, were captured and a weapons arsenal seized from a safe house occupied by the underground group at 2117 202nd Street, Siboney. The following materials were confiscated: a 60 mm. mortar with eight shells, a .30-caliber machine gun, seven Garand rifles, four Thompson submachine guns and a large quantity of explosive material and munitions.

That was the end of Operation Liborio.

7

Task Force W: "A Chocolate Milkshake"

The buildings housing the old CIA headquarters at Quarters Eye were close to the Lincoln Memorial in Washington, DC. They had belonged to the navy and in the 1950s were fitted out for espionage activities. Many of the buildings had restricted access, particularly those occupied by the chiefs, and the guards who checked functionaries' and officers' passes were backed up by a modern surveillance system.

The CIA was now established in its permanent headquarters in new buildings in Langley, Virginia. Large rooms, spacious offices, sophisticated security systems, radio installations to link up with agents in enemy territory, cafés and spacious parking lots offered even the most demanding members of staff enviable conditions. This had been made possible by two men, who at that time were about to be booted out of the Agency by the president: Allen Dulles and Richard Bissell.

A Special Charm
CIA Headquarters, Langley, Virginia, November 1961

It was a shame, thought Bissell, heading for his office on that cold morning, that he would not be able to enjoy the new building they had designed.

With his university professor's ambling gait, Bissell strode along the glossy corridor to his office. Some of the officials he knew well greeted him reverentially. The new ones, who had heard of his upcoming enforced retirement, gave him the slip so as not to compromise themselves. Such was the bureaucratic optimism of those who thought they were part of a new generation that would rise in the wake of John F. Kennedy, the youthful president.

He pushed open the door to his office and greeted William Harvey, who had been waiting for him for a few minutes in the anteroom. With a quick wave Bissell invited him in, and after depositing several papers he had under his arm on to the desk, he sat in his revolving chair.

"Harvey, I have some news for you. Everything seems to indicate that after Dulles is replaced, I'll be the next victim, and I want to leave the main issues in good hands. Richard Helms is to replace me, and we thought you could be responsible for a new task force, with the mission of reorganizing the Cuba Project, now that Washington realizes it can't escape unscathed from the Bay of Pigs business."

"I don't understand what this purge is about, when right now an operation is being planned to liquidate Castro," Harvey replied.

"The president wants to purge the CIA of his enemies and is using of the Bay of Pigs as an excuse. He was solely responsible for the disaster because he stopped the second bombardment of Cuban airports that would have destroyed Castro's air force. Then he wouldn't give the go-ahead to our naval forces to support the Brigade 2506. The chain always breaks at its weakest link, and so it's Dulles and me. But the Agency is in safe hands. The chiefs might change but it is you, the most long-standing officers, trained in this long war against communism, who make policy and execute operations."

Bissell bent over his desk, picked up some papers and began to explain the new plans. He hoped to remain the CIA's second-in-command for a few months during the handover to Helms, and that would give him enough time to see to all pending matters.

"Operation Mongoose is the codename of the new campaign to overthrow the Cuban regime. In line with General Maxwell Taylor's proposal, it will be a war within the context of the global Cold War strategy on communism. You will reorganize the Cuba task force at headquarters and at the JM/WAVE base in Florida. You will belong to the general staff and will lead Mongoose under the command of General Edward Lansdale, a Pentagon expert on irregular warfare and Taylor's protégé. You'll have to be careful with him, because he's a fantasist hankering after a position in our country's intelligence complex. But, I repeat, our top priority is Fidel Castro's elimination."

"I'm ready for the mission," Harvey replied. "I've met with the participants in the Bay of Pigs operation and I understand their experiences and their errors. I've also met with Edwards and O'Connell to study the reasons for the failure of the Rosselli and Varona poison capsule plan. You can be sure that I'll approach this task just like the ZR/Rifle operation."

With an affectionate handshake, Bissell concluded the meeting. Harvey had understood. He was sure that even outside the Agency, Bissell and Dulles would continue to wield influence.

Report of the Church Commission, *Alleged Assassination Plots...* Washington, DC, November 1975

The Inspector General's [1967] report divides the gambling syndicate operation into Phase I, terminating with the Bay of Pigs, and Phase II, continuing with the transfer of the operation to William Harvey in late 1961.[1] The distinction between a clearly demarcated Phase I and Phase II may be an artificial one, as there is considerable evidence that the operation was continuous, perhaps lying dormant for the period immediately following the Bay of Pigs. . . .

Harvey's notes reflect that Bissell asked him to take over the gambling syndicate operation from Edwards and that they discussed the "application of ZR/Rifle program to Cuba" on November 16, 1961. Bissell confirmed that the conversation took place and accepted the November date as accurate. He also testified that the operation "was not reactivated, in other words, no instructions went out to Rosselli or to others... to renew the attempt, until after I had left the Agency in February 1962." Harvey agreed that his conversation with Bissell was limited to exploring the feasibility of using the gambling syndicate against Castro.

Richard Helms replaced Richard Bissell as DD/P [Deputy Director of Plans] in February 1962. As such, he was Harvey's superior.[2]

CIA Headquarters
Langley Virginia, November 1961

Harvey took one of the elevators in the central building and then walked along one of its large, illuminated corridors until he reached a door labeled Office of Security. He knocked gently and waited for a few seconds until a guard opened it. After a routine identification check, he passed into the spacious office of his colleague Colonel Sheffield Edwards. Approaching Harvey, Edwards explained that Bissell had already brought him up to

---

[1]   The CIA Inspector General's 1967 report on attempts to assassinate Fidel Castro is reproduced in *CIA Targets Fidel*.

[2]   *Alleged Assassination Plots...*, 82-83.

date on the new missions, and that he was at Harvey's service. In a fawning tone, he stated:

"I congratulate you on your assignment as the head of Task Force W, and as far as the reactivation of the poison capsules operation goes, everything is ready to hand over the contacts from my office to yours."

Harvey did not like this individual. His military bearing and his show of efficiency turned Harvey's stomach. Edwards had had the plan to poison Castro in his hands for over a year and had done very little. On various occasions Harvey had tried to pull Edwards out of the operation but his close relations with Colonel King prevented that. "Now everything will be different," Harvey thought. He was commanding the Agency's most important unit, directly subordinate to the DD/P, with resources in the United States itself. This was something that nobody had previously enjoyed in the entire history of the CIA. He was the head of an army that was to initiate a covert war against Cuba that existed only as name. The rest was up to him.

Harvey needed the CIA's Jim O'Connell, who had all the contacts with the gambling syndicate; the men he wanted to manage the operation. He was thinking of pulling Sam Giancana and maybe Santo Trafficante out of the project. Rosselli knew Varona and could resolve things directly with his people. He wanted to send one of Varona's men to Cuba to reorganize the Rescate group and transform it into a large intelligence network that would facilitate the communications needed for the plan. Moreover, that group had recruited many military men from the Carlos Prío government who could organize an armed uprising at any given moment. Harvey and Helms had the idea of organizing Castro's elimination in combination with a program of internal subversion that would give the Pentagon boys a pretext for a military intervention.

Edwards agreed to reactivate the plan to eliminate Castro. Colonel King had already informed him of what was already underway. Harvey picked up the phone and called O'Connell, whom he quickly updated on the mission.

They spent some time discussing certain details. O'Connell had talked with Dr. Gunn, one of the Agency scientists responsible for creating the items to be used against Castro. The first poison capsules they had sent to Cuba just before the Bay of Pigs were difficult to handle and slow to dissolve, but the lab had found a new formula for the manufacture of synthetic botulinum toxin in tablet form, with improved qualities. The new version would dissolve in any liquid and was easier to handle.

The only detail missing was a reliable way of getting the c apsules to Cuba, which could not be sent with an infiltration group. Those people often suffered setbacks, and even if everything went well, they would have to jump ship near the Cuban coast and that could affect the toxicity of the capsules. Moreover, regular journeys between Havana and Miami had been suspended since the Bay of Pigs.

"Let's see if Mr. Varona, who resolved the matter last time, can come up with a proposal," O'Connell suggested. "Another matter worrying me is Mr. Rosselli. I would like you to bear in mind, Mr. Harvey, that this man doesn't work for free. He doesn't want money, but protection against prosecution from Attorney General Robert Kennedy. He's been threatened with deportation on various occasions and that's worrying him a lot."

"Don't worry," Harvey replied. "This is a matter of national security with top priority assigned by the president himself, who will have to control his little brother."

Edwards got up, indicating the meeting was over. Harvey and O'Connell agreed to meet the following week in the Savoy Plaza

Hotel in New York, where they would meet with Rosselli to finalize details.

The new chief of Task Force W left Colonel Edwards' office feeling satisfied. There were many things Harvey now had to do to
take full control of the whole Cuba operation. But one of the main
actions was already underway. In the next few days, he would
meet with Rosselli and define the rules of the game with him.

When Harvey returned to his office, he phoned Ted Shackley,
chief of the JM/WAVE base in Florida, to hear how the actions against Cuba were progressing, and to arrange meetings with exile leaders. He would have a good opportunity to observe Tony Varona
up close and find out what kind of person he was. In Harvey's opinion, the Cubans, like all Latinos, were too laid back and untrust-
worthy. They might claim to have hundreds of men, but it would
subsequently turn out they had barely a few dozen.

Later, when night had fallen on that cold winter's day, he got
in his car and drove to his favorite bar, the Parade, for some drinks
with the sweet girls who made the place enjoyable. Everything was
running smoothly, he reflected, and a little distraction would do no
harm before he immersed himself in the new war.

Miami–Havana, January 1962

Norberto Martínez had been a lifelong supporter of former president, Ramón Grau San Martín, and loyal to his successors in the
Authentic Party, Carlos Prío and Tony Varona. He went into exile
with them when they realized Fidel Castro would not include them
as part of his government and that the Moncada program was a
Cuban form of communism.

Martínez enrolled in the Brigade 2506 in Miami, but his political
mentors advised him to enlist in one of the groups that the CIA was
training for commando operations. The Bay of Pigs defeat trauma-

tized him. He had dreamed of an important position in the government that Prío and Varona would head, but everything collapsed in an instant when the brigade was annihilated. Nevertheless, he continued training with the CIA commandos and was not surprised when, one afternoon in January 1962, Robert, his CIA case officer, called him for an important mission. Martínez was to infiltrate the island to reorganize the Rescate group, whose members he knew very well.The point selected for his infiltration was Santa Lucía in the north of Pinar del Río province. It was a safe place where he could rely on Pedro, a coal miner who had a small boat that would pick him up at sea and bring him in to land.[3]

A few days later Martínez was in Havana where Alberto Cruz Caso, the head of Rescate, met him and hid him in the house of María Leopoldina Grau Alsina (Polita). Once established and equipped with a sound story so that the suspicion of the CDRs would not be aroused, he met with the group's principal leaders.[4]

At the meeting were: María Leopoldina (Polita) Grau and her brother Ramón (Mongo), two founding members of the organization and the niece and nephew of former President Ramón Grau San Martín; ex-colonel Francisco Álvarez Margolles, a nationalized Spaniard who had made a career in the army during the Prío presidency; Rodolfo León Curbelo, the CIA courier; Manuel Campanioni Souza, a former dealer in the gambling room of the Sans Souci cabaret owned by Trafficante; Dr. Carlos Guerrero Costales, who was Prío's physician; and other individuals trusted by the group.

"I have instructions from Tony and the CIA to reorganize the group," Martínez began. "The American government is preparing

---

[3]   Pedro Fernández Díaz was detained in 1964 for his participation in a CIA network of agents in Cuba.

[4]   Committees for the Defense of the Revolution (CDRs) were neighborhood groups created on September 28, 1960, as a citizen's response to the activities of counterrevolutionary organizations.

a final offensive against Castro and we need to create the conditions to ignite the country when that time arrives. Colonel Margolles [a former officer in Batista's army] is to tour the island to organize the interior of the country, creating a group in each province and providing the leaders with means of independent communication. Thus, each one can coordinate their own supplies with a minimum of risk. Here, you need to unite the most trustworthy groups. As soon as everything is organized, the CIA will start to send supplies." Alberto Cruz and the others were in agreement. They all thought a change of tactics was necessary in the wake of the Bay of Pigs failure. The G-2 had learned a lot and had successfully penetrated the underground organizations.

After detailing each person's tasks, Martínez asked Alberto Cruz and Polita Grau to stay behind to discuss another matter.

"Do we still have the Hotel Havana Libre people?" the spy asked.

"Yes, three trusted members of the organization are working there," Alberto replied.

"Good, the Agency wants to activate the poison capsules plan to get Fidel out of the way. According to our information, he still frequently visits the Havana Libre, especially with foreign guests, and that could present us with an opportunity. Who are those men?"

"We have Santos de la Caridad Pérez in the café, and Bartolomé Pérez and José Saceiro in the banquet hall. One is a maître d' and the other an assistant. Any one of them could undertake the mission," Polita Grau affirmed.

"There's only one detail left to work out," Martínez said. "How are we going to bring the capsules from Miami?"

"I reckon Vergara could bring them," Polita interjected.[5] "He's a person we can trust, a diplomat at the Spanish embassy working

---

5   Alejandro Vergara Mauri was the information attaché at the Spanish embassy in Havana from July 1960 to January 1964. Also acting as a CIA agent, he was complicit in a plot to kill Fidel Castro by bringing poison pills to Cuba.

under Caldevilla's orders, and can travel without risk to Miami, collect them and hand them over to me in the embassy. As you know, I'm often there and my visit wouldn't be seen as suspicious."

So, Norberto Martínez's second and most important mission was arranged. A few days later the spy communicated with his headquarters and a CIA vessel picked him up in the same area in Pinar del Río and took him back to the lair.

New York, April 1962

The Savoy Plaza in New York was a luxury hotel with spacious lobbies and several bars and restaurants to satisfy the demands of its regular clientele. Attentive and efficient employees took care of a variety of meetings of businessmen or amorous couples, who chose the place for its discretion.

Such discretion was the reason why William Harvey selected that hotel as an ideal venue for his meeting with Johnny Rosselli, the notorious Chicago Mafia boss. Jim O'Connell, the CIA officer, and Robert Maheu, the Mafia contact man, were also to be there. So the meeting had to be private.

Each of them booked in separately and at the agreed time gathered in the comfortable conference room where they had a minibar and soft armchairs so they could discuss the CIA's prospective plans in style.

O'Connell was the first to arrive, so he could check that everything was in order. A few minutes later Rosselli appeared with his friend Maheu, and finally, like the guest of honor, Harvey turned up in his crumpled dark suit, a pistol in his armpit and a cynical expression on his face.

Harvey quickly took the floor to assert his leadership of the group:

"Mr. Rosselli, the businessmen that I represent believe that the time has come to reactivate the operation to liquidate Castro before the US government triggers its latest plans to overthrow his regime. I can assure you that my representatives are very influential people and are prepared to pay for this job in whatever manner required."

With his actor's face, the dark glasses he never removed even at night, and a slick salesman's smile, Rosselli got up from his chair, and taking a few paces about the spacious room, replied:

"As you are aware, money doesn't interest us. Perhaps some favor at the appropriate moment, but that can be sorted out when required. Your word is enough. In terms of the job, I can see some problems. The capsules you gave us last time were very dangerous to handle and they did not dissolve in any liquid. They will have to be improved if this undertaking is to be successful. Another matter that requires attention is the selection of the men involved. As you know, we have the group of Mr. Antonio de Varona, currently one of the vice presidents of the political front you operate. Certain privileges would have to be given to these people, and above all, they want assurances that their political ambitions will be satisfied once Castro is eliminated. If those details can be resolved, I don't see any problems with executing the contract."

Harvey gave the guarantees that the gangster sought and advised him to leave his associate Sam Giancana and Florida capo Santo Trafficante out of the plan, if that were possible. Rosselli could not make any promises. He knew it was impossible to encroach on the territory of a "family" without its consent, but he decided not to divulge that fact to the Agency men. The final agreement was that they would meet up in Miami with Varona on April 21, 1962, to finalize the details of the operation.

William Harvey testified to the Church Commission that at the time (April 1962) he was acting on "explicit orders" from the chief of CIA operations Richard Helms, and that he requested Edwards to put him in touch with Rosselli.[6] The CIA Inspector General's 1967 Report records:

> Edwards recalls Harvey contacting him in April and asking to be put in touch with Rosselli. Edwards says that he verified Helms' approval and then made the arrangements. Harvey states that he briefed Helms before his first meeting with Rosselli, explaining its purpose and that he also reported to Helms the results of his meeting with Rosselli. Harvey states that thereafter he regularly briefed Helms on the status of the Castro operation. . . .[7]
>
> Harvey's notes show that he and O'Connell went to New York City to meet Rosselli on the 8th and 9th of April 1962. . . .[8]
>
> Harvey recalls leaving Washington for Miami by automobile on April 19. He thought that he took delivery of the pills from Dr. Gunn before leaving. Gunn has no record of any such delivery at that time. . . [REDACTED] does have a notation of delivering four pills (one capsule and three tablets) to "J.O." on April 18, 1962. [REDACTED] reads this as being Jim O'Connell. . . .[9]
>
> Harvey. . . arrived in Miami on April 21, 1962, and found Rosselli already in touch with Tony Varona, the Cuban who had participated in phase one [prior to the Bay of Pigs] . . . . Harvey described the manner in which the lethal material was to be introduced into Castro's food, involving an asset of Varona's who had access to someone in a restaurant frequented by Castro.[10]
>
> When the pills were given to Varona through Rosselli, Varona requested arms and equipment needed for the support of his end of the operation. Rosselli passed the request to Harvey. Harvey, with the help of Ted Shackley, the chief of the

---

6   *Alleged Assassination Plots...*, 83.

7   *CIA Targets Fidel*, 51.

8   *CIA Targets Fidel*, 52.

9   *CIA Targets Fidel*, 54.

10   *CIA Targets Fidel*, 54-55.

JM/WAVE Station [the CIA's Miami base which ran covert operations against Cuba] Harvey procured explosives, detonators, 20 .30 caliber rifles, 20 .30 caliber hand guns, 2 radios and a boat radar [costing about $5,000]. . . . Harvey and Shackley rented a U-Haul truck under an assumed name, loaded it with the arms and equipment, and parked it in the parking lot of a drive-in restaurant. The keys were then given to Rosselli for delivery. . . . Eventually the truck was picked up and driven away. It was returned later, empty. . . . [11]

[In May 1962], Harvey and Rosselli arranged a system of telephone communication by which Harvey was kept posted on any developments. Harvey, using a pay phone, could call Rosselli at the Friars Club in Los Angeles at 16:00 hours. . . . Rosselli could call Harvey at Harvey's home in the evening. Rosselli reported that the pills were in Cuba and at the restaurant used regularly by Castro.[12]

Testimony of Mario Morales Mesa
Havana, September 1993

Operative officers Marcos and Ramón worked on the case in the period when compañeros Demetrio and Eduardo were their chiefs.

The main suspects were: brother and sister Ramón and María Leopoldina Grau (Polita); José Luis Pelleyá Jústiz, Prío's former lawyer; Dr. Carlos Guerrero Costales; Manuel Campanioni, Trafficante's old gambling friend; and several other individuals.

At that time, the activities of the CIA and the counterrevolution were very strong and we used the method of penetrating the subversive groups and networks, but only arresting the main leaders and terrorists, leaving the rest of the conspirators on the streets to allow us to keep up a penetration that would allow us to discover new enemy plots in time.

---

[11]   *CIA Targets Fidel*, 56.

[12]   *CIA Targets Fidel*, 57.

In September 1962, various leaders of Rescate were captured, including its military coordinator Francisco Álvarez Margolles, an ex-colonel in Batista's army who was plotting with other counterrevolutionary groups to execute a subversive plan on a national scale. But we let Polita, her brother Ramón and Alberto Cruz slip out of the net. We thought that through their contacts with the CIA and Tony Varona we would obtain news of other planned operations against Cuba.

By that period the group was already using various means of communication with Miami, including a RR44 radio receiver and encoded letters. They also had access to the diplomatic bags of the embassies of Spain and Italy, as diplomats and CIA agents Alejandro Vergara and Jaime Caldevilla worked in the former, and Massimo Muratori in the latter.

During 1962, the Rescate group divided into various subversive networks made up of handfuls of people with independent means of communication and specific tasks. Nevertheless, the links among the groups were strong and they frequently met at the Graus' house to discuss the work they were doing or to ask for help with a particular task.

In August that year the group reunited, disobeying CIA orders on the separation they were supposed to maintain, for a "counterrevolutionary uprising" planned for that time with Álvarez Margolles as one of its leaders. After its failure, everyone returned to their normal activities, without suspecting that we were on their trail.

In early 1963, we lost contact with the agent we had within the circle of close associates of the Grau siblings, an agent who was one of our main sources of information on the conspirators' activities.

In July 1964, thanks to an error within the CIA, one of our agents established contact with the group of spies communicating through José Luis Pellayá Jústiz, who worked as a representative for the Mexicana aviation company.

We already knew that Pellayá had a specially built communications system, known as AT-3, which transmitted coded messages in just a few seconds, and we were also aware of his contacts with other CIA collaborators, including Henri Beyens, first secretary at the Belgian embassy, Clemente Inclán Werner and Julio Bravo Rodríguez. Through this investigative work the pieces of the puzzle came together, and we uncovered various networks that the CIA had organized in Cuba.

In January 1965, DSE headquarters took the decision to capture all the conspirators and, through the patient labor of the operations section, the plot to assassinate Fidel Castro was also discovered.

This plan had been initiated in March 1961 and, despite its failure just before the invasion of the Bay of Pigs, it was reactivated the following year. In April 1962, the CIA dispatched more poison capsules via Spanish diplomat Alejandro Vergara, this time concealed in a bottle of Bayer aspirin. By then, the whole group was already divided into small intelligence and subversion cells. One of the agents, Manuel Campanioni, offered to find the men to attempt Fidel's assassination.

That was how Hotel Havana Libre employees Santos de la Caridad Pérez, Bartolomé Pérez and José Saceiro were recruited. One was an assistant in the café and the other two worked in one of the restaurants. The poison capsules were handed over to the three of them, initiating the latest plot against Fidel. In June 1962, Polita Grau, desperate because Fidel had not gone to the hotel, proposed an alternative plan, this time to poison Commander Efigenio Ameijeiras so that the FIdel could be targeted while attending his compañero's funeral.[13]

They consulted with CIA headquarters by radio and the plan was approved. Two pistols with silencers to be used in the

---

[13]   Efigenio Ameijeiras Delgado was a founding member of the first July 26 Movement underground cell in Havana, expeditionary in the *Granma* voyage, combatant at the Bay of Pigs, international combatant and brigadier general of the Revolutionary Armed Forces.

attack were dispatched via CIA agent Massimo Muratori of the Italian embassy. A team composed of former soldiers and headed by ex-colonels Álvarez Margolles and Miguel Matamoros Valle picked the site of the ambush on 4th Street and 23rd Avenue in Vedado, along the route that they assumed the funeral cortege of Commander Ameijeiras would pass.

Everything was ready, but the days were passing. August 30, 1962, the date for the planned counterrevolutionary uprising was approaching, and they all understood the importance of decapitating the revolution. But something unexpected occurred. After committing himself and accepting the lethal capsules, the person recruited to poison Ameijeiras — who worked in a café regularly visited by Ameijeiras — changed his mind and moved to another province.

So 1962 passed, as did the first months of the following year. One night, at the end of March 1963, when Santos de la Caridad Pérez was on duty at the Havana Libre café, he saw Fidel Castro arrive, accompanied by several people, and order a chocolate milkshake.

Santos had been given a hard-covered, poison capsule, made for the first phase of the plan, which he placed in the freezer every morning on coming to work. He began to tremble nervously as he started to prepare the milkshake. When he opened the freezer to remove the capsule it broke. He was left dumbfounded as he watched the poison dissolve into the ice in the freezer door. Then, in despair, he had to watch Fidel enjoy the milkshake and then leave the café in perfect health, having escaped yet another homicidal trap laid by the CIA and its counterrevolutionary accomplices.

The entire group was detained in January 1965 and its members confessed their criminal plans in detail. Recalling that case, the phrase uttered by *mafioso* Johnny Rosselli at the Church Commission comes to mind: "Castro seemed to be wrapped in a special charm."

8
.375 Magnum. The Elephant Killer

Richard Helms began his espionage career as a very young man. He was initially in the US Office of Strategic Services (OSS) during World War II, where he acquired fame as an efficient and professional operative. He trained under the tutelage of William "Wild Bill" Donovan, one of the OSS founders, taking advantage of a posting in London to assimilate from his British colleagues the knowledge and perfidy they had perfected over many years.

Later, with the creation of the CIA, Helms had various responsibilities, all of them related to covert action. At first, he was Richard Bissell's aide, and subsequently he headed covert operations when Bissell was sacked by President Kennedy after the Bay of Pigs fiasco.

Among his own kind, Helms was a figure of legend and controversy. All his sentiments, memories and experiences were related to the Agency. He had been made ambassador to Iran in 1973 at the moment Watergate was about to explode, and if someone had asked him how many trips he had made from Tehran to Washington to respond to questions from the Church Commission, he probably would not have remembered.

At one point, Helms was given a $2,000 fine and a two-year prison term for refusing to answer to one of the committees investigating CIA participation in the 1973 coup against President Salvador Allende in Chile. The fine was paid by supporters who organized a public collection and the prison sentence was suspended.

Elegantly dressed, almost always in gray, and carefully groomed, at 40-odd years of age he was at the peak of his profession. Everyone regarded him as the logical successor to John McCone when he retired as head of the CIA.

It was January 1963, and that morning Helms, as head of covert operations, had an important meeting in his Langley office. He had called in the main operatives on the Cuba case to discuss the new policy direction adopted by the Kennedy administration following the October Missile Crisis.

He also had to communicate to the units involved that William Harvey had been replaced by Desmond FitzGerald as the head of Task Force W — in charge of the Cuba case — which from that point was to be subordinated to the recently established Domestic Operations Division under the new name of the Special Affairs Section (SAS). In reality, that decision created an unprecedented force that I have chosen to call the CIA's "Cuban-American Mechanism," which from that point would operate within US territory and even assume certain policing operations. It eventually controlled political policy in Florida and achieved significant legislative and executive power in the United States.

One by one those summoned made their appearance at the meeting: Colonel King, William Harvey, Desmond FitzGerald, Tracy Barnes, Ted Shackley, Samuel Halpern, Howard Hunt, David Phillips, James Angleton and various other officers. After everyone was seated in the spacious conference room, Helms took the floor:

"Operation Mongoose has been discontinued. McGeorge Bundy, the security adviser, has convinced the president to rethink policy on Castro. Attorney General Robert Kennedy is not totally convinced, but for now he does not want to contradict the president's advisers."

He explained that the new task was to draw up strategies that could be adjusted to provide multiple ways of combating Castro. Tightening the economic blockade, developing covert and psychological actions to undermine the Cuban government at vital points, and reorganizing Brigade 2506 for direct military action at a specific moment in time. Meanwhile, ways of forcing a split between Castro and his Soviet allies were being investigated as the Agency sought to take advantage of the conflict that had arisen between Havana and Moscow in the aftermath of the Missile Crisis. If they could isolate Castro from the old Cuban communists and divide his regime, they might invade militarily or force Cuba to the negotiating table under favorable conditions.

He also used the opportunity to inform the meeting that Harvey was to be replaced by Desmond FitzGerald as head of the operative force. This was essential, as sometimes men represent specific strategies, and when these strategies were concluded, they had to go. Everyone looked at Harvey. They knew his explosive nature and understood how uncomfortable he felt. He was the sacrificial lamb, as Dulles and Bissell had been not so long ago. The ex-chief of the Cuba Task Force said nothing. He confined himself to lighting a cigarette. He clearly knew about the decision in advance and had already prepared himself for his demotion. In reality, he had not come out of it too badly. He had been made chief of the CIA station in Rome, and many of the people at the meeting knew of his links to the criminal world, to Johnny Rosselli and Santo Trafficante, in particular. He would be a kind of dual-ambassador in Italy, given that he would be representing both the CIA and the Mafia in its country of origin.

When the meeting ended, Helms asked FitzGerald to stay behind for a few minutes. When they were alone, he said:

"You have to take the necessary measures so that the operations underway continue on track. Castro's elimination continues to be one of our top priorities. It will not be possible to achieve our strategic objectives in Cuba with him alive."

FitzGerald agreed. He understood what he was being told. In his long career as an operative it was not the first time he had faced matters of this nature. He picked up his papers and took his leave of Helms.

Meanwhile, in the anteroom, James Angleton saw to it that he left at the same time as Harvey.

"You seem to be relieved at the way things have played out. Your new destination is a reward. It's as if you are being paid to take a vacation in Europe for a couple of years."

The tremendous tension Harvey had contained during the meeting was now released like a tightly coiled spring. His accumulated rancor against President Kennedy and his disagreement with the administration's line erupted:

"After so much sacrifice, what are we going to say to the Cuban exiles? What are we going to do with all those people in the training camps? Are we going to tell them that from now on we're going to be friends with the Russians and that Castro's a good guy? What's going on, Jim, is that the president got scared over the Missile Crisis. I'm glad to be out of this operation because at least I won't have to explain anything to the Cubans. Those people surrounding Kennedy: Bundy, Sorenson, Schlesinger, Salinger and co., are weak, and they're the only ones allowed to give him advice. We're headed for failure, and if you like, go ahead and tell McCone what I think."

"This guy's baiting me," Harvey reflected as he walked off down the long corridor in the direction of his office. "At least I told him what I thought so nobody can say later they weren't warned."

A Caribbean Adventure
JM/WAVE Base, Miami, February 1963

The recognition of the new winds blowing through Washington in relation to Cuba dropped like a bombshell on the community of US and Cuban spies at the JM/WAVE station in Miami. The resolution of the Missile Crisis in October 1962 did not please them in the slightest. When President Kennedy discovered the rockets in Cuba everyone believed that a military invasion was inevitable, and they all made their preparations to return. The crisis, however, was averted through negotiation and it was rumored that Castro had obtained a promise from the United States that it would not attack the country militarily. Dejection spread through the exile community.

Nevertheless, the exiles found new hope in the exchange of the captured Bay of Pigs assailants during a reception for them and then President Kennedy's speech at the Miami Orange Bowl at the end of December 1962. Furthermore, plans started to move ahead at full steam in 1963. Robert Kennedy met with Manuel Artime, the political leader of the Brigade 2506, and guaranteed him US support for the formation of a new exile army based in Nicaragua, which would launch another attack on Cuba in due course.

The attorney general also met with another CIA protégé: Enrique (Harry) Ruiz Williams, a Cuban American, former Bay of Pigs combatant and Artime's right-hand man. He was to take charge of organizing a strong paramilitary detachment from the Dominican Republic to initiate a guerrilla war in Cuba's easternmost province, where it could use the Guantánamo naval base as a safe refuge. In addition, a new commando group was being trained at a secret CIA base near New Orleans to replace the one captured in

Cuba in the middle of the Missile Crisis. This was called the Mambi Commandos and would be responsible for extermination missions deep in Cuban territory.

Various radio stations were being activated to increase psychological warfare. The special missions group, commandos operating out of the JM/WAVE station, were being fortified with new agents and vessels to pursue their objectives of harassing maritime transportation, supplying subversive networks within Cuba and destroying economic and energy targets.

Finally, there were plans to use the newly created terrorist groups based in the Dominican Republic to attack Cuban representatives in third countries and foreign enterprises attempting to break the economic blockade.

The idea of forcing a split between Fidel Castro and the Soviets and possibly negotiating with Castro, even under favorable conditions, did not please the "covert warriors." They wanted to destroy the Cuban revolution totally. Desmond FitzGerald was pulled in to allay the fears of his men regarding a possible move to the negotiating table.

In his first meeting with the JM/WAVE leaders, FitzGerald employed his strongest arguments. He confirmed that the approved projects would go ahead, with the assassination of Castro as a priority. As he said this, FitzGerald noticed that the disapproval written on many faces had begun to disappear. He grasped that this was a vital issue for those at the meeting.

After stressing that the new projects being discussed were highly classified, FitzGerald detailed an ingenious plan to eliminate the Cuban leader. The plan had two variants. The first would be to persuade James Donovan, the lawyer who negotiated with Fidel Castro for the exchange of the Brigade 2506 prisoners, to give the Cuban leader a diving suit impregnated with a poisonous chemical substance. The second involved placing a seashell containing a powerful charge of plastic explosives in an area where the Cuban leader went underwater fishing.

The JM/WAVE chiefs were satisfied. They only asked if the president had given his approval, to which FitzGerald replied with a smile that they all interpreted as confirmation. This appeased them. They could accept that the changes in the administration's strategy were merely cosmetic ones for the benefit of public consumption. If things were like this, the plan was still on track. Moreover, they had to accept the fact that "he who pays the piper calls the tune."

FitzGerald also had another trick up his sleeve. He had information on the existence of a powerful underground organization in Cuba that was ready to act against the Castro regime. They had sent a message explaining that they were preparing to assassinate the Cuban leader and then stage an armed uprising of all their members throughout the country. At least, that was what their emissaries claimed.

CIA Inspector General's Report
on Plots to Assassinate Fidel Castro
CIA Headquarters, Langley, Virginia, May 1967

At about the time of the Donovan-Castro negotiations for the release of the Bay of Pigs prisoners, a plan was devised to have Donovan present a contaminated skin-diving suit to Castro as a gift. . . . Desmond FitzGerald told us of [the plan] as if it had originated after he took over the Cuba task force in January 1963. Samuel Halpern said that it began under William Harvey and that he, Halpern, briefed FitzGerald on it. Harvey states positively that he [had] never heard of it.

According to Sidney Gottlieb [of the CIA laboratory], this scheme progressed to the point of actually buying a diving suit and readying it for delivery. The technique involved dusting the inside of the suit with a fungus that would produce a

disabling and chronic skin disease (Madura foot) and contami-
nating the breathing apparatus with tubercle bacilli. Gottlieb
does not remember what came of the scheme or what happened to the scuba suit. Sam Halpern, who was in on the scheme,
at first said the plan was dropped because it was obviously
impracticable. He later recalled that the plan was abandoned
because it was overtaken by events. Donovan had already given
Castro a skin-diving suit on his own initiative. . . .

Sometime in 1963, date uncertain but probably early in the
year, Desmond FitzGerald, then Chief of [the Special Affairs
Section] SAS, originated a scheme for doing away with Castro
by means of an explosives-rigged seashell. The idea was to take
an unusually spectacular seashell that would be certain to catch
Castro's eye, load it with an explosive triggered to blow when it
was lifted, and submerge it in an area where Castro often went
skin diving.[1]

The Conspirators
US Naval Base, Guantánamo, Cuba, January 1963

Ricardo Lorié was an experienced CIA agent who had commenced
his counterrevolutionary activities in 1959, a few months after the
triumph of the revolution. He was lucky, as since his initiation he
had worked with people specializing in difficult tasks who, with
the passing of time, had risen up the CIA ranks. Now he had been
selected to work with the New Orleans group that was headed by
Higinio Díaz, his former boss. This group was coordinating the
trafficking of arms acquired by the Agency to the anti-Castro forces
in Cuba.

They had recently sent Lorié on a special mission to the
Guantánamo naval base. His task was to link up with an underground detachment of the MRR operating in Havana under the

---

[1]   *CIA Targets Fidel*, 76-77.

orders of an individual by the name of Luis David Rodríguez González. Through the influence of David Sánchez Morales and his Miami people, Lorié was received with high regard at the base.

Rodríguez's group presented excellent credentials. According to his information, in June 1962 it had planned to assassinate Fidel Castro in Revolution Plaza with an 82 mm. mortar located 300 meters away. The scheduled event in the plaza was suddenly switched to Santiago de Cuba and the plot was averted.

At the end of that year, Rodríguez set up a "revolutionary unit," enlisting the most important groups in the country — including those operating in the Escambray mountains — which he referred to as the Anticommunist Civic Resistance (RCA). He then sent a communiqué to Miami to inform them of its existence, with the express desire to be kept in mind for any CIA plans. That was why Lorié's superiors had decided to send him to the base, to wait for Manuel Cuza Portuondo, Rodríguez's envoy.

The meeting took place as soon as Cuza arrived at the base after a hazardous journey through the minefield surrounding the military enclave at Guantánamo. A detailed assessment lasting several hours satisfied Lorié's curiosity, particularly in the context of a new plan to assassinate Fidel Castro at an upcoming public event. Afterwards, Cuza explained, they would activate their groups throughout the country and create the conditions for "the Americans" landing their troops in order to "pacify the country."

The CIA agent committed himself to sending the arms and explosives requested and handed over a hefty sum of US dollars and Cuban pesos to the "resistance" envoy. When he left, Lorié smiled. He had fulfilled to perfection his instructions, and at the same time, he was in possession of invaluable information: the approximate date of Fidel Castro's death. He could now alert the friends of Trafficante and Carlos Marcello, who would duly pay him for his information. As he saw it, Rodríguez's only demand was the post of government minister in the cabinet to be formed after the collapse of revolution, and his friends would agree to that.

Havana, January 1963

The meeting took place in a relaxed atmosphere. The location lent itself to that: the back room of La Sierra service station, located in the Luyanó district of the Cuban capital. The individuals meeting there were giving the final touches to plans to overthrow the revolution in the coming weeks. They were: Luis David Rodríguez, head of the MRR; Ricardo Olmedo, leader of the Montecristi Group; Juan Morales, representative of the Escambray insurgents; Enrique Rodríguez Valdés, military chief of the Movement for the Recovery of the Revolution (MRR); Jorge Espino Escarles, head of the National Liberation Army (ELN); and Samuel Carballo Moreno, a CIA agent recently infiltrated to supervise and coordinate the plans.

Olmedo detailed the action proposed to execute Castro: "Everything is ready. The .44 Magnum rifle has been hidden by the Guanabacoa United Front (FUG) people in a house in Cotorro. The plan is to take over an attic in one of the buildings facing the university stairway. We think that D-Day should be March 13, because, as we all know, that's the date of the commemoration of the deaths of José Antonio Echeverría and the other presidential palace assailants in 1957. As always, Fidel will be there and he will speak at the event for sure, providing the perfect moment to shoot him. Our men will be wearing khaki and when G-2 arrives to see what happened, it will all be over."

Rodríguez, who was listening attentively, remarked: "That will be the moment to trigger the action. Each one of you must prepare your men, bearing in mind the plan that has been drawn up.

What is fundamental is to seize some strategic positions in Havana and the provincial capitals, have the Escambray people cut off the central highway and ensure that the CIA organizes a good publicity campaign on what is happening in Cuba. That's the pretext the Americans need to intervene."

Everybody agreed. They were not ignoring the dangers they would face. But with support from the US government, the project should be successful. When the men left, Olmedo stayed behind to talk with Carballo. He wanted to firm up certain details for the future and so he asked:

"Carballo, you know I'm going for the big time. I betrayed Fidel, so if we're caught there's no pardon for me. You have contacts with the CIA and Luis David and I have contacts with the former American casino owners. They want the city's most important hotels to be left standing. That's where their interests lie and they want to recoup them. That will be one of my military objectives and I want you to guarantee that, when the Americans arrive, they won't get involved in my affairs."

"Don't worry Ricardo. My bosses are already informed of this. The basic matter now is to eliminate the man and I'll take care of the rest. It doesn't even matter if the uprising isn't so large. The key thing is to have a big shoot-out in Havana in which a good few people die. The scandal's going to be huge. The OAS will intervene and finally it'll be over."

Testimony of Roberto Fernández[2]
Havana, November 1994

Several operative units worked on this case and I headed one of them. We were responsible for investigating the MRR and had information on the moves of Luis David Rodríguez González,

---

[2]   Roberto Fernández was the DSE case officer for the Cuban operation against the Anticommunist Civic Resistance (RCA).

together with Jorge Espino Escarles, to form a new counterrevolutionary unit. They planned an attack on the commander with
an 82 mm. mortar on July 26 of that year [1963] in Revolution
Plaza, to be handled by Braulio Roque Arosamena, but the plot
was foiled when the venue for the day was switched to Santiago
de Cuba.

The agreement to establish the RCA [Anticommunist Civic
Resistance] was signed on September 15, 1962, uniting the MRR,
ELN, Triple A, the Montecristi Brotherhood, the Agramonte
Resistance, Revolutionary Unity, the Guanabacoa United Front
(FUG), the National Central Council and the Second National
Front of the Escambray.

On November 5 of that year, in the midst of the Missile
Crisis, Rodríguez traveled to the Escambray and met with Tomás
San Gil, chief of the armed gangs operating there, obtaining his
integration into the counterrevolutionary bloc.

Through Manuel Cuza he reestablished contact with the CIA
via the US naval base in Guantánamo and agreed to a plan of
action that included an uprising by all the counterrevolutionary
groups in Cuba and Fidel Castro's assassination.

To that end, in line with the plan adopted by the RCA,
Ricardo Olmedo's group organized an attempt on the Cuban
leader on March 13, 1963, when Fidel was to speak from a
platform on the steps of the university.

The weapons had been smuggled into Cuba in March
through various infiltrations coordinated by Samuel Carballo
Moreno, a CIA agent involved in the operation with Rodríguez
and Olmedo.

Several our agents had penetrated the outfit, and given
the imminence of the actions, headquarters decided to act on
March 9. The principal conspirators were detained.

During this action, Rodríguez killed compañero Orlando
López González. He was then struck down by the revolutionary
forces.

Three weapons arsenals were seized. One at 42 Amenidad Street in Havana, another in El Cotorro neighborhood and the last in a house in San Miguel del Padrón, a Havana district. They included two guns fitted with telescopic sights, one of them a .375 Magnum used in elephant hunts; various M3 submachine guns equipped with silencers; radio equipment; a bazooka with shells; and dozens of other weapons.

Not all the counterrevolutionaries were caught, and one group, commanded by Enrique Rodríguez Valdés, activated an alternative plan to assassinate the commander in chief in El Cerro baseball stadium.

The final game in the national baseball series was on April 7, 1963, and the conspirators knew that Fidel would be there. A group of nine men, four of them wearing military uniform and situated in the area where the leader generally sat, would throw hand grenades at him.

The homicide team was Orestes Valero Barzola, Ricardo López Cabrera, Guido Valiente, Esteban Ramos Kessell, Alfredo Farah, Orlando Tacarona, José Cervantes, Honorio Torres Perdomo and Enrique Rodríguez Valdés. The group was arrested before they could carry out the attack.

It appeared that the principal counterrevolutionary groups had been neutralized. A few days later, however, during the second half of May, one of our agents informed us of the existence of an 82 mm. mortar that had not been seized in any of the earlier raids.

It turned out there was a highly classified MRR cell operating in the area of the Monte Street market and headed by Luis Montes de Oca, alias *El Campeón* (the champ). In complicity with Braulio Roque Arosamena, an expert mortar operator trained years earlier in the Dominican Republic, Montes de Oca was planning to reactivate the assassination plot of the previous year, firing on the platform of the central event for July 26, which this time was to be held in Revolution Plaza.

The mortar was seized, and all the group members were detained, with the exception of Roque Arosamena, who went into hiding for some months until he was captured the following year.

This ended the history of the RCA and an assassination conspiracy in which the CIA and the Mafia combined in a joint effort to murder Fidel Castro on four occasions. This operation also signified the dismantling of one of the last counterrevolutionary blocs directed by the CIA in its plans to defeat the Cuban revolution.

Report of the House Select Committee, Investigation of the Assassination of President John F. Kennedy
Washington, DC, 1978

In 1971, [Jack] Anderson [a US journalist linked to the Mafia media and the CIA] once again published information setting forth the retaliation theory [that the Kennedy assassination was linked to conspiracies against the Cuban leaders] in two articles dated January 18 and 19. These articles exhibited more detail, relating that several assassins made it to a rooftop within shooting distance of Castro before being apprehended, that this event occurred in late February or early March 1963, that Robert Kennedy at least condoned the CIA-Mafia plots, and that Rosselli delivered poison pills to be used in killing Castro to a contact at the Miami Beach Fontainebleau Hotel on March 13, 1961. [3]

---

[3]   US House Select Committee, *Investigation of the Assassination of President John F. Kennedy*, Appendix to Hearings, Volume X: Anti-Castro Activities and Organizations, Lee Harvey Oswald in New Orleans, CIA Plots Against Castro, Rose Cheramie (Washington: US Government Printing Office, 1979), 155.

9

An "Autonomous Operation" and Old Friends

Mario Salabarría Aguiar was one of the most active chiefs in the National Police during the 1940s during the Ramón Grau San Martín administration. Under his command, the monstrous Group for the Repression of Enemy Activities (GRAE), a police outfit created in the heat of the Cold War, was a key element in President Grau's efforts to annihilate the workers' and revolutionary movements in Cuba.

In those years, positions in the police force and other repressive forces became highly sought after among elements of the local Mafia who were fighting over the gambling, drugs, contraband and prostitution markets. While all the gangsters had their territory staked out, the moment arrived when disputes for new markets began, in particular, over the key public positions that could offer them protection.

Salabarría, a police commander at the time, was determined to preserve his businesses, and in competition with others of his kind, unleashed a war among the main gangs. This war reached its peak in an infamous battle in the peaceful neighborhood of Orfila, in Marianao municipality, in 1947. Salabarría and his group attacked one of his sworn enemies: Morín Dopico. Dopico was also a police commander, and taking refuge in his home, he put up such strong resistance that the national army had to intervene to stop the warring parties.

Salabarría was sentenced to a 20-year prison term and only after the 1959 revolution was his case reviewed by the courts. He was given parole on account of the time he had served and his good conduct in prison, as prescribed by law.

After leaving prison, Salabarría tried to reinitiate his gangster activities, but found himself in an unfamiliar Cuba. Almost all of his old friends had emigrated to the United States and the new Cuban regime had cleared out of public institutions corrupt individuals, gangsters and embezzlers, cut the drug trafficking routes, and closed down the casinos and brothels. He found himself alone and concluded that the only way open to him was to conspire against the revolutionary government that had given him his freedom.

Operation Rafael
Havana, May 1963

This battle against the revolution was what led Mario Salabarría to agree to meet Alberto Cruz, head of the Rescate anti-Castro group, whom he knew from his days as a member of Congress in the Grau government.

Alberto Cruz had heard of the gangster's situation and had in-depth knowledge of his history as a hired killer and his lack of scruples. Thus, when the demands from CIA headquarters to find a way to assassinate Fidel Castro were stepped up, he thought of Salabarría.

He met with his closest people, including Polita Grau and her brother Ramón, and everyone agreed to offer the killer a large sum of money to carry out the job. They summoned him that May afternoon to the Graus' old mansion on 5th Avenue and 14th Street in Miramar.

They got down to business. Both men were used to dealing frankly with the most delicate subjects.

"Mario, you know I've been against this government from the start," Cruz stated. "Tony Varona is our leader and representative in exile. The organization has worked hard in the last few years against Castro's regime, but it's getting harder and harder to bring together all the forces to combat the communists. G-2 and the CDRs [Committees for the Defense of the Revolution] are making life impossible for us. Recently an envoy from Varona informed us that the CIA was going to take over directing our group and work has been done on a new project to bring down the government. The idea is simple: liquidate Castro and then, using the people we still have within the government, try to take control of it. If that proves impossible, organize an uprising of all the underground groups in the country. The Americans have assured us they will intervene with the navy, if we provide them with an internationally acceptable motive. They've guaranteed there will be no repeat of the Bay of Pigs. So, we thought of you. What do you think?"

Salabarría understood what was being asked of him. It had come up a few days earlier in a conversation with Polita Grau. He had nothing to lose, he reasoned. If the plan was successful, Tony Varona and his boss, Carlos Prío, would remember him and he might even become the next chief of the Cuban police. He responded without hesitation:

"Alberto, you can count on me for anything. I'll need some cash and a rifle with a telescopic sight, if possible, fitted with a silencer. I'll take care of the rest."

The two men made a deal. Alberto Cruz would give Salabarría a few thousand pesos and would ask CIA headquarters for the requested weapon.

JM/WAVE Base, Miami, May 1963

CIA operative David Sánchez Morales was in his new office in the buildings occupied by JM/WAVE, located on land adjoining the University of Miami. He had been made chief of special operations on Cuban territory and the major subversive plans were his responsibility. "El Indio," as everyone called him, was aspiring to destroy the Havana regime through a direct, unrelenting war, using the thousands of exiles under his orders and the vast resources at his disposal in that emporium of terrorism, espionage and subversion.

The task, however, was not simple. It was becoming steadily clearer that the administration's policy was leaning towards pressure and containment and that they were only being utilized for applying pressure, through the approval of selective sabotage. He had thought that after the Missile Crisis the Kennedy brothers might acknowledge the existence of a communist state in the Caribbean as a definite fact. But it seemed that if Castro was to distance himself from the Russians, the White House intellectuals would probably be prepared to pardon Cuba and seek a rapprochement.

In addition, the new SAS chief, Desmond FitzGerald, who had very good relations with Attorney General Robert Kennedy wanted to control everything and was starting to insist on approving ever plan, which meant that Morales had to constantly appeal to Tracy Barnes, head of the Domestic Operations Division, to help him. There was no doubt, he reflected, that the bureaucracy would end up diluting the effectiveness of the war, thus endangering the authority and prestige of the United States.

That was one of the reasons why Morales decided to take some of his own initiatives. He secretly met with Johnny Rosselli and Santo Trafficante. They had been the Agency's "fellow travelers" in various adventures against Cuba and were individuals who could be counted on for an undertaking that would not appear as a CIA operation. According to rumors spreading through the Agency, the president was highly grateful to Sam Giancana, the godfather of La Cosa Nostra, on account of Giancana's contribution to the campaign that took him to the White House.

One of the actions that Morales had recently taken at the request of the mafiosi was the creation of a new "political front," which would sideline the CRC headed by José Miró Cardona. The CRC had been discredited after the fiasco of the Bay of Pigs when Miró had prematurely claimed victory. Now, using Mafia money, Morales had set up the Junta of the Cuban Government in Exile (JGCE), presided over by Carlos Prío and controlled by an obscure junior gangster called Paulino Sierra. Those two were soon joined by the most combative exile leaders, including Orlando Bosch, Antonio Veciana and Manuel Artime.

It was a classic "autonomous operation." The objectives were fixed, the resources handed over, and they would come up with the goods. When the results became public, the Agency would not be implicated in any way. Nevertheless, the Mafia did not want to run unnecessary risks and made its help conditional on the direct participation of one of its captains, Rosselli, who was installed with his associates in one of the training camps at the Florida base. They were discreet and efficient people who could be counted on at the right moment.

That moment soon presented itself. Through one of his agents, Norberto Martínez, who had recently arrived from Cuba, Morales heard of the plans of the Rescate group, headed by Alberto Cruz, including an attempt on the life of Fidel using a hired killer. He quickly got in touch with Johnny Rosselli and Carlos Prío, who were interested in the plan and decided to back it.

Everything had to be properly obscured so that nobody could suspect that the CIA or any other US government agency was backing the conspiracy. Thus, a meeting was organized on a small tourist island in the Bahamas called Bimini, which Rosselli would attend. The JGCE leaders would be waiting for him there and the plan would be an agreement between them alone, although in reality CIA case officers would oversee all the details of the operation.

When the meeting was fixed, Morales phoned the Luces, owners of Time and Life magazines, and former ambassador William Pawley, who were all involved in the anti-Cuba crusade, and informed them of the details of the plan. They would spur the mass media into a huge campaign to discredit Kennedy's policy toward Cuba and would use their influence in the Republican Party to support the latest organization of Cuban exiles, the JGCE, as a viable structure for the next government in Cuba when Castro was defeated.

Bimini Island, Bahamas, May 1963

Robert Plumlee, an experienced CIA pilot, landed his light aircraft on the runway of the little airport serving Bimini Island, not far from southern Florida. On board was Carlos Prío, the former president of Cuba, who was the last of the group to arrive in that holiday paradise. Rosselli, William Carr, aide to Colonel King, and case officer Robert (Bob) Rogers had preceded him.

These men were there for an important meeting with only one item on the agenda: the assassination of Fidel Castro. When everyone was settled on one of the sunny and deserted terraces of the hotel where they were staying, Carlos Prío spoke:

"We've received important news from Havana. One of our underground groups, also operating under the orders of our friends in the CIA, has found the opportunity and the personnel to eliminate Castro. As a result of earlier failures, our Agency friends proposed this meeting to coordinate the details of the operation with the participation of the interested parties."

He explained the information available to him and why Alberto Cruz's group had not used normal CIA channels to transmit the message. They wanted only the "upper echelons" of the Agency and the people crucial to the operation to be in the know. G-2 had many agents in Miami and that was one of the factors that had led to the discovery of earlier plots. So secrecy was essential.

"We need to remember certain things," Bill Carr stated. "It is vital that neither the CIA nor any other US agency should appear to have any involvement in this matter. Acting on our behalf, Rosselli will have the resources required to execute the operation."

"That's correct," Rosselli replied. "We have the human resources that can give Mr. Cruz what he needs."

"In this way we can decentralize the operation," interjected the case officer, "some providing the action and others handing over resources and acting as backup. It's an innovative way of avoiding penetration and information leaks. I propose that we give this operation the codename Rafael."

The sinister meeting concluded with whiskeys and coconuts filled with rum.

Havana, Early July 1963

The supply tasks were successfully completed. The M1 rifle with a telescopic sight was smuggled in through the Spanish diplomatic bag, and the money for the assassination was brought in by CIA agent Arturo Varona Hernández, who handed over 10,000 pesos, two 9 mm. pistols fitted with silencers, two 3.57 Magnum revolvers and two portable radio transmitters to Mario Salabarría.

From that moment, acting alone, Salabarría began to set in motion the plan he had carefully drawn up. When he agreed to take on the operation, he thought of using the flat roof of the National Library for the attack. Later, when it became a solid proposition, he visited the place and found that it was not difficult to gain access to the roof, which overlooked Revolution Plaza. He confirmed that he could position himself there and fire on his victim during one of the regular mass rallies held in the square. There was always the inconvenience of having to neutralize the security guard, but that was something that could be overcome.

When everything was ready, in line with the instructions he had received, he asked for a meeting with Arturo Varona to inform him of the details. They agreed to meet in the Havana Amphitheater at the entrance to the capital's bay. Some children were playing with a brightly colored ball while their mothers, keeping them in sight, strolled along a pathway lined with beautiful flowers. There, in the afternoon sun, the two conspirators talked animatedly:

"I think the best day to execute the plan is July 26, when there will be a celebration in the plaza. I've got everything worked out. I'll park the car close by the library the day before. Then I'll go up to the roof, as I've done on various occasions, and hide there until the next day. When the security guard arrives, I can neutralize him using the pistol with the silencer and I'll have enough time to aim at our man and take him out. What do you think?"

"Fine," Varona replied. "There's only one thing that worries me. How are you going to escape after the shooting? Don't you need backup?"

"No, it's better to do things alone," Salabarría answered. "When the shooting happens, there'll be tremendous confusion. Nobody will guess where it came from, as the weapon is pretty quiet. I already tested it and it hardly made a sound. There will be all the racket of the people marching and rousing speeches from the platform. When security reacts, I'll be far away!"

Report of the Department of State Security (DSE) Headquarters
Havana, August 1965

Our investigations have revealed the following:

1. From mid-1963 to date, through its agents in Cuba, the CIA has attempted to assassinate our Prime Minister Fidel Castro on four occasions. The CIA agents participating to a greater or lesser degree in this plot were: Mario Salabarría Aguiar, Alberto Cruz Caso, María Leopoldina and Ramón Grau Alsina, Miguel Matamoros Valle, Arturo Varona Hernández, Rafael Quintana Castellanos, Bernardo Milanés López, Roberto Caíñas Milanés, Eduardo Llanes García, Roberto Sabater Cepero, Pedro Fuentes Milián, Mercedes de la Paz, Joel Trujillo, Antonio Fernández Rodríguez, Magalys Reyes Gil, Enrique Díaz Hernández, Juan Soto Rodríguez, Félix Rodolfo Valdés Cabrera. Also involved were Antonio de Varona Loredo, Carlos Prío Socarrás, Joaquín Sanjenís and Julio Salabarría Aguiar, all Cubans resident in the United States, and two CIA officers known as Henry and Bill.

2. The four plots referred to were to be executed at:

a/ Revolution Plaza, at the 1963 commemoration of July 26, when the conspirators planned to fire on our prime minister, Fidel Castro, from the roof of the National Library, an action neutralized by security measures that prevented detainee Mario Salabarría's access to the building selected;

b/ Potín restaurant on Línea and Paseo in Vedado, where the detainees planned to fire on Commander Fidel Castro during one of his occasional visits;

c/ Between Línea and 23rd Street on Paseo Avenue, where the conspirators planned a three-car ambush to cut off the vehicle in which the prime minister was traveling and fire on it with submachine guns;

d/ At 5th Avenue intersection in Miramar, where an ambush was planned using a telephone company truck with a .30 mm-caliber machine gun in the back to fire on Fidel's car.

3. Three CIA networks participated in the project described above:

a/ the group headed by Alberto Cruz Caso;

b/ Arturo Varona Hernández's group;

c/ the network organized by Dr. Bernardo Milanés López.

4. The CIA, which planned the project from the outset, periodically exerted control over it. Thus, after Arturo Varona fled to the United States, it recruited Dr. Milanés López in Madrid to act as backup for Operation Rafael, because it needed a man close to Mario Salabarría Aguiar who could exercise effective influence over him. To that same end, in January 1964, CIA agent Joaquín Sanjenís and the US officers known as Henry and Bill gave instructions and provided the means of communication to retain control of the operation, reiterating to Salabarría the order to assassinate Commander Fidel Castro.

5. In the searches related to the detainees, the following weapons were seized: an M1 carbine, four 3.57 Magnum revolvers, two 9 mm. pistols fitted with silencers, two portable radio transmitters and a quantity of bullets.

10
AM/LASH: Rolando Cubela[1]

Immersed in a voluminous file, Desmond FitzGerald was still in his Langley office a little after 9:00 p.m. Working late had become a habit since he took command of Cuban affairs, and that day he was deeply concerned about losing an operative codenamed AM/LASH [Rolando Cubela], the Agency's most important man in Cuba for the last two years.

The previous day he had received an urgent message from agent AM/WHIP [Carlos Tepedino], a former jeweler of Italian descent who had lived in Havana until the revolution came to power.[2] He explained that AM/LASH was currently in Porto Alegre, Brazil, and that he planned to travel to Paris and defect from Cuba.

AM/LASH was one of FitzGerald's main cards against the Havana government: a commander in the Rebel Army, a student

---

[1]   AM/LASH was the CIA cryptogram for this plot against Fidel Castro and Cuban agent Rolando Cubela, who was a former commander in the Rebel Army and the deputy leader of the student-based Revolutionary Directorate that opposed the Batista dictatorship. He held important posts in the revolutionary government.

[2]   Carlos Tepedino (AM/WHIP) was an Italian American who owned jewelry shops in Havana before the 1959 revolution. He was a close collaborator of Santo Trafficante and a close friend of Cubela's. Prior to the revolution, Tepedino had links to the opposition Cuban Revolutionary (Authentic) Party hid Cubela and helped him to go into exile in Miami in 1957. After the revolution, as CIA agent AM/WHIP, he recruited Rolando Cubela and members of the Revolutionary Student Directorate.

leader and former government minister, with access to the top revolutionary leadership.

FitzGerald meditated on his man's history and searched among the files on his desk until he found the information he wanted. With a label reading "FitzGerald Only," the dossier contained all the information on the case that was occupying his thoughts.

In 1953, Rolando Cubela had become friends with Carlos Tepedino, the proprietor of La Diadema jewelers on a main commercial street in Havana. At that time, Cubela was involved in activities against the Batista government, and he participated in 1956 in the assassination of Lieutenant Colonel Antonio Blanco Rico, head of the Military Intelligence Service (SIM).

In early 1957, the FBI located him in Miami, in the Trade Winds Hotel belonging to José Alemán, a close friend and also a Bureau informant.[3] There he reestablished relations with AM/WHIP and it was through these sources that tabs were kept on Cubela and his group's activities. In early 1958, Cubela returned to Cuba with a revolutionary expedition that set up a base in the Escambray mountains, where they commenced guerrilla activities, linking up with Ernesto Che Guevara's troops at the end of the campaign against Batista.

A few months after the revolutionary victory, Cubela suffered a bout of depression, feeling he was being pursued by the ghost of murdered Lieutenant Colonel Blanco Rico. José Alemán, who was in Cuba, found a psychiatrist to help him recover.

In April 1959, information was received from an agent close to Cubela, who had told him that he had talked with Fidel Castro and explained his dissatisfaction with the situation in Cuba. According to the agent, Cubela told him that he was so fed up that if he did

---

[3]   José Braulio Alemán Gutiérrez was the son of José Alemán, the minister of education in the Ramón Grau government (1944-48) who embezzled $20 million from his institution at the end of his term and subsequently relocated Miami.

not leave the country soon, he would kill Castro himself. Around that time, he traveled to Europe and made contact with AM/WHIP who, together with another agent and in the hope of recruiting his friend, warned Cubela about an international communist plot to take over Cuba.

In June of that year, Cubela was appointed deputy government minister, a post he used to help Santo Trafficante to attend his daughter's birthday celebrations while detained in a camp for undesirable foreigners. Subsequently Cubela helped secure Trafficante's release.

In October 1959, he was elected president of the Federation of University Students (FEU) and in that position traveled to a student congress in Mexico in early 1961, where he again made contact with AM/WHIP, who had traveled there with a case officer to complete the process of Cubela's recruitment as agent AM/LASH.

After various conversations between AM/WHIP, the case officer and AM/LASH, it was decided that the latter could support the action planned by Juan Orta Córdova, whom he knew from Havana and who had received some poison capsules from the Agency to kill Fidel Castro.[4] The details of the plan were not revealed, but he was directed to get in contact with Orta, from whom he would receive instructions at the appropriate moment. The idea was that, with his authority within the government, AM/LASH could assume control after Castro was gone.

In the case of failure, or if AM/LASH was unable to defeat the communists, the idea was to get him and Orta out of the country. Initially the operation was scheduled for the last days of March 1961, prior to the Brigade 2506 invasion. The plot collapsed when Orta took refuge in a Latin American embassy, and the escape plan did not take place.

---

[4]   Juan Orta Córdova was secretary of Prime Minister Fidel Castro's office in 1959.

In mid-1962, AM/LASH traveled to Helsinki as part of a Cuban delegation attending the World Festival of Youth and Students, an event organized by the Russians, where he was contacted and his recruitment consolidated, with AM/LASH agreeing to undertake the intelligence tasks agreed.[5]

Desmond FitzGerald closed the dossier without reading it in full. To date, nothing had happened. It was true that the 1962 Missile Crisis had resulted in unforeseen consequences for Fidel Castro's enemies. Many people had thought the United States would attack Cuba and finally overthrow the Havana regime. But none of that occurred and the latest government measures to restrict the activities of the counterrevolution in Cuba had discouraged many people, many of whom had come to the conclusion that there was no solution to the Cuban problem.

FitzGerald got up from his chair and paced around the room. The case still looked promising, as AM/LASH continued to be an important figure in the Cuban government. According to the files, it seemed that his predecessors had treated AM/LASH very superficially. Perhaps he should meet with him personally, FitzGerald reflected. The plan to eliminate Castro and stage a military coup attracted him.

Returning to his desk, he pulled out the note with the information on AM/WHIP and wrote: "Have our man contact him in Paris and sound out his state of mind. We need AM/LASH to be available for the upcoming operation we are preparing."

---

[5]   For more about "Project AM/LASH" and Rolando Cubela, see CIA Targets Fidel, 78-82 and the report of the Church Commission, 86-91 and 174-76.

Excerpts from the CIA Inspector General's 1967 "Report on Plots to Assassinate Fidel Castro"

September 5-8, 1963

Cubela attended the Collegiate Games in Porto Alegre, Brazil, as a representative of the Cuban government. He was met there by [REDACTED] and [REDACTED]. Also participating was [REDACTED], a Spanish-speaking case officer from headquarters, who thereafter acted as case officer for Cubela. [...]

Cubela discussed a group of Cuban military officers known to him, and possible ways of approaching them. The problem was, he explained, that although many of them were anticommunist they were either loyal to Fidel or were so afraid of him that they were reluctant to discuss any conspiracies for fear they might be provocations. Cubela said that he thought highly of [REDACTED] (AM/TRUNK) [Ramón Guín], who was hiding [REDACTED]. [REDACTED] had been sent to Cuba by the CIA to recruit [REDACTED] in place and had done so. [...]

September 16, 1963

Cubela (in Paris) wrote to [REDACTED] (in New York): "I don't intend to see (be interviewed by) your friend again," which you should tell them, "so they don't make the trip. I want to get away from politics completely. . ."

October 3, 1963

[REDACTED] arrived in Paris for meetings with Cubela. [...]

October 11, 1963

[REDACTED] cabled that Cubela was insistent upon meeting with a senior US official, preferably Robert F. Kennedy, for assurances of US moral support for any activity that Cubela undertook in Cuba. [...]

October 17,1963

[REDACTED] cabled the results of a meeting with Cubela

and [REDACTED]. Cubela, in a private conversation with [REDACTED], reiterated his desire to speak with a high-level US government official. [REDACTED] said that basically Cubela wanted assurances that the US government would support him if his enterprise were successful.

October 29, 1963

Desmond FitzGerald, then Chief, SAS, who was going to Paris on other business, arranged to meet with Cubela to give him the assurances he sought. The contact plan for the meeting has this to say on cover:

"FitzGerald will represent self as personal representative of Robert F. Kennedy who traveled [to] Paris for specific purpose [of] meeting Cubela and giving him assurances of full US support if there is change of the present government in Cuba."

According to FitzGerald, he discussed the planned meeting with the DD/P (Helms) who decided it was not necessary to seek approval from Robert Kennedy for FitzGerald to speak in his name.

The meeting was held in [REDACTED]'s house in Paris on October 29, 1963. FitzGerald used the alias [REDACTED]. [REDACTED] acted as interpreter. [REDACTED] was not present during the meeting. [REDACTED] on November 13, 1963, wrote a memorandum for the record of the meeting. It reads, in part:

> "FitzGerald informed Cubela that the United States is prepared to render all necessary assistance to any anti-communist Cuban group which succeeds in neutralizing the present Cuban leadership and assumes sufficient control to invite the United States to render the assistance it is prepared to give. It was emphasized that the above support will be forthcoming only after a real coup has been effected and the group involved is in a position to request US (probably under OAS auspices) recognition

and support. It was made clear that the US was not prepared to commit itself to supporting an isolated uprising, as such an uprising can be extinguished in a matter of hours if the present government is still in control of Havana. As for the post-coup period, the US does not desire that the political clock be turned back but will support the necessary economic and political reforms which will benefit the mass of the Cuban people."

(Comment: [...] FitzGerald recalls that Cubela spoke repeatedly of the need for an assassination weapon. In particular, he wanted a high-powered rifle with telescopic sights or some other weapon that could be used to kill Castro from a distance. FitzGerald wanted no part of such a scheme and told [REDACTED] to tell Cubela that the US simply does not do such things. . . . FitzGerald says that when he met with Cubela in Paris he told Cubela that the US government would have no part of an attempt on Castro's life. . . .

November 14, 1963

[REDACTED] met with [REDACTED] in New York City on 14 November. [REDACTED]'s contact report reveals Cubela's reaction (as told to [REDACTED]) to his meeting with FitzGerald.

"The visit with FitzGerald, who acted in the capacity of a representative of high levels of the government concerned with the Cuban problem satisfied Cubela as far as policy was concerned, but he was not at all happy with the fact that he still was not given the technical assistance for the operational plan as he saw it. [REDACTED] said that Cubela dwelt constantly on this point. He could not understand why he was denied certain small pieces of equipment which promised a final solution to the problem, while, on the other hand, the US government gave much equipment and money to exile groups for their ineffective excursions against Cuban coastal targets. According to [REDACTED] Cubela feels strongly on this point, and if he does not get advice and materials from a US government technician, he will probably become fed up again, and we will lose whatever progress we have made to date."

November 19, 1963

Memorandum for the record prepared by [REDACTED]: C/SAS (FitzGerald) approved telling Cubela he would be given a cache inside Cuba. Cache could, if he requested it, include... high-power rifles w/scopes... C/SAS requested written reports on AM/LASH operation be kept to a minimum.

November 20, 1963

[...] Samuel Halpern and [REDACTED] approached Dr. Gunn for assistance. . . . What they settled upon was Black Leaf 40, a common, easily obtainable insecticide containing about 40 percent nicotine sulfate. Nicotine is a deadly poison that may be administered orally, by injection, or by absorption through the skin. [...]

The plan reached the action stage when Halpern and [REDACTED] contacted Gunn again on the morning of November 20, 1963, and told him that the device for administering the poison (a ballpoint pen rigged as a hypodermic syringe) had to be ready in time for [REDACTED] to catch a plane at noon the next day. . . . [H]e succeeded in converting a Paper-Mate pen into a hypodermic syringe that worked. He said that the needle was so fine that the victim would hardly feel it when it was inserted — he compared it with the scratch from a shirt with too much starch. He delivered the workable device to [REDACTED] the following morning and retained two of the later prototypes. . . .

November 22, 1963

[REDACTED] arrived in Paris in the morning of November

22 and met with Cubela late that afternoon. [REDACTED] states that he showed the pen/syringe to Cubela and explained how it worked. He is not sure, but he believes that Cubela accepted the device but said that he would not take it to Cuba with him. [...] Cubela said that, as a doctor, he knew all about Black Leaf 40 and that we surely could come up with something more sophisticated than that. . . .

[REDACTED] reiterated the assurances given Cubela by FitzGerald of full US support if a real coup against the Castro regime were successful. Cubela asked for the following items to be included in a cache inside Cuba: 20 hand grenades, two high-powered rifles with telescopic sights, and approximately 20 pounds of C-4 explosive and related equipment. Cubela suggested the best place for the cache was on the *finca* (farm) managed by his friend, [REDACTED] . . . . As they were coming out of the meeting, [REDACTED] and Cubela were informed that President Kennedy had been assassinated. Cubela was visibly moved over the news. . . . The contact report does not state the time nor the duration of the [REDACTED]-Cubela meeting, but it is likely that at the very moment President Kennedy was shot a CIA officer was meeting with a Cuban agent in Paris and giving him an assassination device for use against Castro. [REDACTED] states that he received an OPIM cable from FitzGerald that night or early the next morning telling him that everything was off. We do not find such a cable in the AM/LASH file. There is a record in the file that [REDACTED] was due to arrive back in Washington at 18:10 hours, November 23. . . .

December 1, 1963. FBIS [Foreign Broadcast Information Service] reported that Cubela returned to Cuba from Prague.[6]

---

[6]   *CIA Targets Fidel*, 87-95.

The 1975 US Senate Commission (the Church Commission) investigating plots to assassinate leaders of foreign governments reported the following:

(iii) Providing AM/LASH with Arms

CIA cables indicate that one cache of arms for AM/LASH was delivered in Cuba in March 1964 and another in June. An entry in the AM/LASH file for May 5, 1964, states that the case officer requested the Technical Services Division to produce, on a "crash basis," a silencer which would fit an FAL rifle. The contact report of a meeting between the case officer and a confidante of AM/LASH states that AM/LASH was subsequently informed that it was not feasible to make a silencer for an FAL rifle. [...]

Documents in the AM/LASH file establish that in early 1965, the CIA put AM/LASH in contact with B-1, the leader of an anti-Castro group.[7] As the Case Officer explained to the Inspector General:

> "What had happened was that SAS had contrived to put B-1 and AM/LASH together in such a way that neither of them knew that the contact had been engineered by CIA. The thought was that B-1 needed a man inside and AM/LASH wanted a silenced weapon, which CIA was unwilling to furnish to him directly. By putting the two together, B-1 might get its man inside Cuba and AM/LASH might get his silenced weapon-from B-1."

A CIA document dated January 3, 1965, states that B-1, in a lengthy interview with a case officer, said that he and AM/LASH had reached firm agreement on the following points:

1. B-1 is to provide AM/LASH with a silencer for the FAL; if this is impossible, B-1 is to cache in a designa-

7   Cuban State Security identified "B-1" as Manuel Artime Buesa, leader of the counterrevolutionary group MRR.

ted location a rifle with a scope and silencer plus several bombs, concealed either in a suitcase, a lamp or some other concealment device, which he would be able to carry and place next to Fidel Castro.

2. B-1 is to provide AM/LASH with escape routes controlled by B-1 and not by the Americans. The lack of confidence built up by the Bay of Pigs looms large.

3. B-1 is to prepare one of the western provinces, either Pinar del Rio or Havana, with arms caches and a clandestine underground mechanism. This would be a fallback position and a safe area where men and weapons are available to the group.

4. B-1 is to be in Cuba one week before the elimination of Fidel, but no one, including AM/LASH, will know B-1's location.

5. B-1 is to arrange for recognition by at least five Latin American countries as soon as Fidel is neutralized and a junta is formed. This junta will be established even though Raúl Castro and Che Guevara may still be alive and may still be in control of part of the country. This is the reason AM/LASH requested that B-1 be able to establish some control over one of the provinces so that the junta can be formed in that location.

6. One month to the day before the neutralization of Fidel, B-1 will increase the number of commando attacks to a maximum in order to raise the spirit and morale of the people inside Cuba. In all communiques, in all radio messages, in all propaganda put out by B-1 he must relate that the raid was possible thanks to the information received from clandestine sources inside Cuba and

from the clandestine underground apparatus directed by
"P". This will be AM/LASH's war name.[8]

Report of Cuba's Department of State Security
to the US Congress commission on the assassination
of President Kennedy.[9]
Havana, November 1978

Rolando Cubela Secades was born in 1932 in Cienfuegos. Later
he moved to Cárdenas in Matanzas province where he began
his studies. On completing his studies, he entered the University
of Havana, where he played an active part in the struggle against the Batista dictatorship and became military chief of the
Revolutionary Student Directorate (DRE), being detained on
several occasions for activities related to that movement.

At the end of 1956, after participating in the execution of
Blanco Rico, Batista's military intelligence chief, he went into
exile in Miami, taking refuge in the motel run by José Alemán
Gutiérrez, a friend from Havana who had become an FBI agent
and who would have a key influence on his future conduct.

At the beginning of 1958, he returned to Cuba on an
expedition to promote an uprising in the Escambray mountains,
fighting there until the revolutionary triumph in 1959. He was
promoted on account of his conduct to the rank of commander
of the Rebel Army.

In 1959, he was made deputy secretary of government and
later, in October, he was elected president of the FEU after

---

8   *Alleged Assassination Plots...*, 89-90.

9   This report was prepared by Cuba's Department of State Security in
     response to a request by the 1978 US Select Committee of the House
     of Representatives investigating the assassination of President John F.
     Kennedy and Martin Luther King, Jr. The author of this book (Fabian
     Escalante) directed this Cuban investigation that examined the files of
     anti-Castro exiles and terrorist groups which revealed their links to the
     plot to assassinate President Kennedy.

defeating his opponent in a hard-fought election. Reckless and licentious behavior characterized his life that year. He constantly frequented bars and nightclubs, spending time with friends who began to criticize the revolutionary government's measures. Cubela expressed his disagreement with the direction in which the revolution was going within that circle, verbally attacking Fidel Castro for being, in his view, the main protagonist of the country's misguided sociopolitical development.

Cubela was a voluble, unstable and ambitious man with a false concept of friendship that prevented him from seeing the defects of the people around him. Also inconsistent in his political ideas, which varied according to his emotional state, he turned against the revolution and its leaders. His conduct and personal characteristics were known, but because of his revolutionary history he was not perceived as a danger and was able to act with relative impunity for several years, until in 1965 information was received corroborating his involvement in conspiratorial activities. An investigation was initiated that uncovered part of the plot, for which he was sanctioned the following year.

The information that activated our investigation came from Paris. On April 9, 1965, it was communicated by a reliable source that Cubela was conspiring against the revolution. It emerged that he was handling large sums of money, frequenting nightclubs and luxury restaurants, and had made several trips to Paris, Madrid and Switzerland, where he was constantly visited by Jorge Robreño and Carlos Tepedino, two known CIA agents. The source insisted that Cubela was involved in a conspiracy to assassinate Fidel Castro.

Subsequently, the activities of Cubela and his close friends were monitored for nearly one year. It was established that he was in contact with Cuban exile groups in the United States, France and Spain, and it also emerged that this contact was linked to a CIA plan to assassinate Fidel Castro and to defeat the revolutionary government in Cuba.

All the information at that time was related to the central aspects of the plot reorganized by the CIA at the end of 1964, when a meeting was arranged in Madrid between Cubela and its agent B-1 — none other than Manuel Artime Buesa, head of a mercenary brigade being trained in Nicaragua to instigate a military coup once the Cuban leader was assassinated.

It was necessary to reconstruct the entire plot from its beginning in order to unravel the conspiracy. In the light of information declassified in the United States, the puzzle was gradually put together and we discovered a large volume of material in our files that had previously been unclear or had not been seen as linked to the Cubela case until that point.

In August 1960, during a visit to Switzerland, Cubela met with CIA agent AM/WHIP [Carlos Tepedino], an old friend from Havana, who invited him to spend a few days in Rome. On that occasion, while they were lunching in a restaurant, another acquaintance of Cubela's showed up, also a CIA agent, who described in great detail the communist penetration in Latin America and the related dangers for Cuba in that context.

At the beginning of 1961, Cubela visited Mexico to participate in a solidarity event. From there he got in touch with Tepedino again, and the latter turned up accompanied by a US officer, described by Tepedino as an expert on communism. The objective was to recruit Cubela, and there is evidence of his possible participation in a conspiracy organized by the CIA and the Mafia to assassinate Fidel Castro prior to the Bay of Pigs invasion.

In March 1961, Cubela and Juan Orta decided to defect and requested help. CIA headquarters agreed to prepare an exfiltration operation for both of them, which was subsequently suspended because information reached them that G-2 was aware of it.

As head of the prime minister's office, Juan Orta was the person proposed by the Mafia to poison Fidel with capsules sent by the CIA. Orta and Cubela had known each other from at least 1959 and both of them had been in contact with Santo Trafficante, the Mafia delegate in Cuba up until that year. By this time, Cubela was a recruited agent or one "in the process of being recruited" by the CIA. He had already affirmed his disposition to eliminate Fidel, which was known to the CIA; he had an important position within the revolutionary government; he was a commander of the army; and he was at the center of a group of resentful people prepared to follow him in any adventure against the Cuban regime.

Shortly after Cubela's return from Mexico — from March 20 to mid-May — he regularly visited Casablanca on the banks of the bay of Havana, even staying overnight on occasion in a boathouse there. Information given by different people on the movements of Cubela and persons in his company aroused suspicion that he was planning an illegal exit by sea.

After making some repairs, he left a vessel there, which according to one of the visitors "could get him to Florida in four hours." Concealed on board were various weapons, including Garand rifles. The people who frequented the place had long conversations with Cubela, who also received telephone calls from different provinces, particularly Las Villas. Cubela looked nervous, agitated, "as if he was waiting for something," according to one of the sources.

Finally, another unconfirmed piece of information from that time notes that on March 28, 1961, counterrevolutionary Margarito Espinosa, a fugitive from justice, stated that "Cubela was one of the men he was counting on to overthrow Fidel."

The interest in exfiltrating Orta and Cubela at the end of March 1961 could have been related to the assassination plot concocted by the CIA and the Mafia to decapitate the revolution before the mercenary invasion [in April 1961]. They probably realized that Cuban State Security was aware of their plans, because the exfiltration was aborted and Orta took refuge in a Latin American embassy.

Then it became clear that the only reasonable motive for getting Cubela out of Cuba had to be his involvement in something very important that would make his exfiltration worthwhile right after his return from Mexico. Only a conspiracy that placed him in imminent danger could have warranted a plan of that nature.

On September 8, 1962, Cubela traveled to Paris where he stayed for one week, meeting with Carlos Tepedino who, as always, offered his protégé a well-earned vacation with all expenses paid.

A few weeks after returning to Cuba, Cubela visited a mountainous area in the Escambray region of Las Villas province with a group of 20 men. He stayed there for two or three days and then left, leaving behind his entourage, whose members remained in the area for two weeks without incident, despite the fact that it was frequented by insurgent bands.

That was not the only time Cubela had visited the region, which was the former theater of his guerrilla actions, where he enjoyed a degree of support from the *campesino* community.

In mid-June of that year Cubela left Cuba for Helsinki to attend the World Festival of Youth and Students. Shortly before this, he sent a message to Tepedino arranging to meet up with him in Europe. On July 30, Cubela met with Tepedino and his case officer in Helsinki and informed them that he intended to defect. The officer persuaded him to return to Cuba to direct a US-backed plot to overthrow the Cuban government.

A semantic error by the recruiter almost led to the collapse of the undertaking. When he proposed the "assassination" of Fidel Castro, Cubela rejected the idea. He was not opposed to the act itself, but the choice of the word. For discussion purposes, "eliminate" was a more acceptable expression.

There were further meetings in the following days, held in Copenhagen and Stockholm to conceal Cubela's relationship with the CIA from the other members of the Cuban delegation, who remained in Helsinki. During that period, a plot was agreed. It included sabotage operations against strategic objectives in Cuba as well as the assassination of veteran communist leader Carlos Rafael Rodríguez, the Soviet ambassador and "Fidel and Raúl, if necessary."

Cubela stayed in Paris with Tepedino from August 14 to August 23, 1962, in order to receive training in various fields, including two of vital importance: secret writing techniques and demolition.

New talks on the assassination of Fidel took place between Cubela and his case officer and, as quoted by the CIA Inspector General, the officer reported, "Have no intention [to] give Cubela physical elimination mission as requirement but recognize this [is] something he could or might try to carry out on his own initiative."[10] Cubela remained in Paris until August 29, 1962, when he returned to Havana.

A few weeks later Cubela went to the Dos Arroyos area of the Escambray and visited the city of Placetas in the foothills of the mountains. There he met with *campesinos*, former collaborators with his guerrilla force.

In October 1962 he left the Rebel Army.

After his detention he said of that period: "I was beginning to feel unstable again and tried to seek refuge by traveling abroad, as I had done on previous occasions. But this time my intention was more definite as I was thinking of remaining in France."

In 1963 he began to work as a doctor in the Commander Manuel Fajardo Hospital in Havana, and in August, as he had planned, he prepared a journey to Brazil which he viewed as a permanent departure.

He had been invited to the University Games in Porto Alegre in Brazil and there he renewed contact with Tepedino, to whom he voiced his desire to emigrate and establish himself in France. Some days later he was visited by "a Spanish-speaking

---

[10]   *CIA Targets Fidel*, 86.

case officer" who tried to persuade him to continue within the conspiracy. He failed to bring Cubela around, but they agreed to another meeting in Paris for a more detailed review of the matter.

While Cubela was in Brazil in September 1963, JM/WAVE was executing an important operation in Cuba under the codename AM/TRUNK, which consisted of recruiting various officers from the Rebel Army that the CIA believed it could hook. Among them was ex-commander Ramón Guín Díaz, one of Cubela's closest friends, who would subsequently be an active participant in the CIA plans to assassinate Castro.

That same September José Luis González Gallarreta arrived in Madrid as a diplomatic attaché. A few weeks later, he was recruited by James Noel, head of the Madrid CIA station. Gallarreta, who came from a bourgeois Cuban family that owned a liquor import company, was one of Cubela's associates, who had studied in the United States and then at the University of Havana, where he had linked up with Cubela.

According to Cubela's statement, when he arrived in Paris in September 1963, he met with Tepedino — who was waiting for him — and reiterated his idea of remaining in France. Tepedino convinced him to talk with a "second Spanish-speaking officer, because if he wanted to enter and live in the United States, that person could help him."

This new "Spanish-speaking officer," subsequently identified by Cuban security as [Chicano CIA officer] David Sánchez Morales, was then second in command of JM/WAVE, the largest CIA operative base in the world. He was also David Phillips' officer when the latter was working as an undercover agent in Havana in the late 1950s.

According to his statement, on that occasion Cubela insisted he was not prepared to waste his time on uncertain future projects, and that if he was to continue in an operation of that nature, he needed backing at the highest level from the United

States. He proposed a meeting with Robert Kennedy, the brother of the US president.

Morales traveled to Washington where Richard Helms, deputy director of the CIA, decided that Desmond FitzGerald, chief of the SAS, should meet with Cubela using the cover of a US senator representing Robert Kennedy, and offer him the guarantees he wanted. On October 29, FitzGerald, Morales and the first Spanish-speaking officer attending the case met with Cubela in Paris and discussed the future with him.[11] [Cubela] was flattered and satisfied by the guarantees offered and finally agreed to renew his involvement in the conspiracy.

The plan had two parts: first, the assassination of Fidel, and second, a coup d'état instigated by Cubela's collaborators, backed by a US mini-invasion carried out by a brigade of Cuban mercenaries who were training in Nicaragua under the command of Manuel Artime.

Cubela insisted on the need for resources to implement the plan. He wanted a telescopic sight and a silencer (for a FAL rifle he owned) deposited in Cuba, as well as other weapons and money. Finally, they made a deal and FitzGerald assured him that his request would be met. They would send what he had asked for through Ramón Guín, agent AM/TRUNK, who had a farm on the northern coast of Matanzas province. The meeting was over.

From that point there was a period when, without any apparent justification, for one reason or another Cubela was prevented from returning to Cuba. He had booked a flight to Havana via Prague for November 19, but a fresh request from the officer made him put off his journey. The officer explained that he needed to consult with Washington in order to confirm certain details related to the deposit in Cuba. Finally, Cubela was called in for a meeting in the late afternoon of November 22.

---

[11]   When Cubela identified David Sánchez Morales in his statement, he explained that another Spanish-speaking officer attended him, whom he thought was a Puerto Rican, possibly Néstor Sánchez, who was mentioned in the 1967 CIA Inspector General's Report..

The case officer was waiting for him, and according to Cubela's statement, tried to give him a fountain pen that could fire projectiles, another with a needle for injecting poison and a radio transmitter. Disconcerted, Cubela categorically rejected the items, explaining that they were not what was agreed, as he had always emphasized that any attempt he made against Fidel had to be effected at a prudent distance in order to preserve his life. It was at that precise moment that a phone call came through informing the case officer of the death of President Kennedy.

Cubela was shocked by the news and the officer explained to him that Kennedy's death could change all the plans, and that Cubela should not return to Cuba until he had checked things out with Washington. They made their farewells and a few days later, disobeying the order, Cubela decided to return to Havana via Prague on November 28, 1963. The abrupt departure of his case officer had plunged him into uncertainty about the project's viability. Nevertheless, a few weeks later, the CIA reestablished contact through Ramón Guín, and offered him the necessary guarantees. Two consignments of weapons and military equipment were sent to him via infiltration groups that smuggled them into Cuba.

The plan Cubela was trying to set in motion was the same: to organize an ambush for Fidel Castro at the summer residence of the Council of State in the resort of Varadero. He would wait for Castro there in order to assassinate him, and afterwards would attempt to take control of the new government that would be formed, or at least play a significant part in it.

The months went by and the plot failed because Castro did not fall into the trap. Cubela despaired and sought another opportunity to escape from Cuba and relocate to Europe. That opportunity presented itself when, in November 1964, he was invited by the International Union of Students to a meeting of its executive committee in Prague. From there he traveled to Paris on November 25, where he made contact with Carlos Tepedino, to whom he confided his wish not to return to Cuba. The same episode was to be repeated. The same Spanish-speaking officer appeared and, with Tepedino, convinced Cubela to continue being part of the plot [to kill Fidel Castro], this time with a new variant: the CIA proposed to formally disassociate itself from the assassination.

The new plan was that Cubela should meet with Manuel Artime and the two of them would coordinate the plans: one the assassination, and the other, in the midst of the predicted chaos created by the leader's death, an invasion and the installation of a provisional government that would request US and OAS aid, thus legitimizing a military invention.

That meeting finally took place in Madrid at the end of December. On one side, Cubela and Tepedino, and on the other, Artime, Howard Hunt — his case officer — and James Noel. Various CIA agents connected to both as aides and confidants were also present, including Jorge Robreño, José Luis González Gallarreta, Alberto Blanco, Cucú León and Bichi Bernal.

Cubela and Artime met on various occasions in the Spanish capital, where little by little the plan was consolidated. Cubela was to prepare a new ambush in Varadero and Artime to initiate a naval campaign on Cuban coastal targets to "raise the people's morale" until the crime was effected.

Afterwards Artime and his men would take Punta Hicacos, the peninsula where the Varadero resort is located. Several Central American countries had committed their support to Artime in the event of Cubela and himself forming the government junta that would seek aid and assistance. The plan was to be initiated in June–July 1965.

Once again Cubela asked for the telescopic sight and silencer for his rifle. Artime mobilized the specialists in JM/WAVE to acquire the sight and manufacture the silencer, which were finally handed over.[12] Everything was agreed, and everyone

---

[12] The silencer was tested on wasteland in Miami by Anis Feliafel, one of Artime's aides.

was left to implement their part in the plan.

Cubela returned to Cuba on February 28, 1965, with the accessories he had requested for his rifle. He had agreed that Robreño would remain in Madrid as a link with Artime, while Blanco and Gallarreta would return to Cuba some weeks later to act as his aides in the assassination attempt. Several weeks passed; by May none of Artime's promises had yet materialized.

That was the month scheduled for the attacks on Cuban coastal targets. Cubela maintained contact with the CIA through AM/TRUNK and on various occasions insisted on the need for Artime to fulfill his part of the deal. Meanwhile, he and his aides positioned themselves in the house they had selected in the Varadero resort, from where they would target their victim. They had prepared a story that Cubela was on medical leave due to stress and needed a prolonged vacation. Thus, his lengthy stay in that place would not arouse suspicions.

In June — given the imminence of the attack — CIA headquarters circulated a telegram to its European stations explaining that for security reasons they should suspend all contact with Cubela's group, which was not to be trusted on account of numerous indiscretions it had committed.

It also silenced radio messages sent to agent AM/TRUNK so that when the assassin compromised the United States there would be no evident connection with the crime and no compromising documents. In any event, the telegram could explain to anyone interested that, effectively, Cubela was a contact who had been abandoned due to his co-conspirators' indiscretions.

With that cable, which Cubela and his group never knew about, everything was concluded. It was an internal matter, only existing in the archives in case it had to be utilized one day establishing the defense of "plausible denial."

Cubela's ambush failed again. Fidel Castro only rested when he could, not when he wanted to. The months went by and Cubela and his group came up with an alternative attempt.

An important date was approaching: the commemoration of the 1957 assault on the presidential palace by a revolutionary group attempting to execute Batista.[13] Fidel attended the event every year and was usually the final speaker. That would provide an occasion on which they could shoot him. The conspirators had an apartment at 455 N Street on the corner of San Lázaro, from where the platform erected on the university stairway was perfectly visible. Thus, everything was agreed: March 13, 1966, would be the date for the assassination of the prime minister.

After that decision was made, Cubela sent a message to Alemán Gutiérrez in Miami, asking him to inform the CIA of the change of plans and activate US backing for the plan. But Cubela omitted some important details. He made no mention of abandoning the coup plan and the insurrection in the Escambray mountains. He had arranged his own escape by recruiting a fisherman on Jaimanitas beach to the west of the capital to take him to the United States after effecting the crime.

The days went by rapidly for the conspirators, who were unaware that the authorities were following their every move. On February 28, 1966, exactly 12 months after his return from his last trip abroad, Cubela was arrested along with all his co-conspirators. Operation AM/LASH — an attempt to assassinate Fidel Castro and overthrow the Cuban revolution spanning more than five years — was dismantled.

The detention of Cubela and his group marked the conclusion of one of the most extensive and important subversive actions planned by the United States against the life of the Cuban leader and the revolution.

This plan had all the ingredients that have characterized US aggression against our country for more than 60 years: attempted

---

[13]   On March 13, 1957, José Antonio Echeverría led a group of students in an armed attack on Batista's presidential palace. The attack failed and the assailants brutally killed.

assassinations, terrorism, mercenary invasions, planned coups, psychological warfare and alliances with the Mafia.

11
The Condor in Chile

David Phillips was waiting impatiently outside Richard Helms's office. He had been urgently summoned for a meeting with the director and presumed it was related to an important mission. He reflected that he had come a long way from the day when he was recruited as a covert agent in Chile and from his time as a spy in Havana working under the cover of a publicity agency in the late 1950s.

Responsibilities in Mexico and then the Dominican Republic, when it was decided to oust the Constitutionalists under Colonel Francisco Caamaño Deñó, trained him as a highly qualified professional within the Agency.

Despite their best efforts, the CIA had not met with the success they had anticipated in their fight to contain communism in Latin America. The region's geopolitical map in that year of 1970 did not accord with the efforts they had expended. In spite of rigid US policies and the fact that soldiers trained in the United States controlled many national governments, in Chile, where Phillips had begun his career, social instability was growing. The Socialist Party Senator Salvador Allende was once again a candidate in the presidential elections and intelligence estimates gave him a slight majority. The Chilean left was very powerful and could actually win this time.

The secretary interrupted his thoughts: "The director says you can go in," and a few seconds later he was facing the chief. A conceited man with a cold and penetrating look, immaculately dressed and courteous, Helms was a CIA legend, having commenced his activities as a spy in the far-off days of World War II in London, where he acted as a link between the OSS and the British MI6.

The conversation between the two men moved directly to the issue that had prompted the meeting. Helms wanted Phillips to take charge of the task force being formed to prevent Salvador Allende winning the Chilean presidential elections. He would not have to give up his responsibility at the head of the Cuba section because, without a doubt, the Cubans and their leader Fidel Castro were backing the communists throughout the hemisphere, especially in Chile.

Senator Allende was the socialist leader who had contested elections on several occasions at the head of a left-wing coalition. He was also a consistent friend of the Cubans. It was Allende who received the survivors of Che Guevara's guerrilla force in his country when they escaped across the border from Bolivia. He was likewise the principal instigator of solidarity campaigns with Cuba. Informants confirmed that one of the first measures he would take if he won the election would be to reestablish relations with Cuba.

While he thought they had come very late in the day, Phillips understood his orders. Washington's strategies had led to much lost time and, at this stage, only a coup could prevent a left-wing triumph. He had predicted it on various occasions. Given he had spent his youth in Chile, he was well placed to grasp the direction in which Chilean politics was hurtling, but he could not turn down the task. He therefore assured Helms that he would do everything possible to block Allende's presidential aspirations.

Some hours later, in his office, Phillips mentally reviewed the troops he could count on for his new mission. The Cuban exiles would have to be the cornerstone of the plan. The Operation 40 group was in Miami, captained by Joaquín Sanjenís. Then there were Orlando Bosch's men, who had created a new political front to combat "Castroism" on a continental level. Luis Posada Carriles, Orlando García, Ricardo Morales Navarrete and various associates were in Caracas holding important positions within the political police. His veteran agent Antonio Veciana had been in Bolivia since the campaign against Che Guevara and his army of internationalists, and he was currently in charge of the psychological warfare program that the CIA had drawn up against the revolutionary movement in the Americas.

In addition, Phillips had excellent relations within the Chilean right-wing press, which would be needed to create a base for the subversive project through a solid campaign of psychological warfare, with the aim of discrediting the Popular Unity party that had nominated Salvador Allende, pressuring the armed forces and preventing victory for the Marxist left.

Meditating on the responsibilities he has assumed, a shiver ran down his spine when he realized that averting the possibility of a second Cuba in the hemisphere depended on his mission. Fidel Castro would certainly not let the opportunity to support Allende go by, and Chile might even become the first Latin American country he would visit.

Phillips got up from his armchair and contemplated the darkness of the night through the window. If that visit occurred, Chile would become Castro's tomb. On various occasions in the past he had prepared assassination attempts on the Cuban leader, but for one reason or another, they had all failed. In Chile it would be different. Maybe he would be unable to prevent Allende's triumph, but one thing he was sure of was that if Allende did win, it would provide the long-awaited opportunity to eliminate Fidel Castro.

Phillips began to call his agents in the various Latin American capitals, summoning them to a meeting to receive his instructions. He would send the Operation 40 group to Argentina to direct the commando groups responsible for unleashing war against leftists to the streets and communities on the border with Chile. The Caracas groups could offer training for the political activists and terrorists who would go on the offensive against the communist party, and Veciana's men could take care of the anti-Allende propaganda directed at Chile and its neighbors, explaining the threat to regional peace and stability implicit in a leftist victory.

A sense of power overcame him. He was about to enter into combat and this time he could depend on a president, Richard Nixon, who was eager to confront the Russians and international communism.

The Flight of the Condor
Miami, Spring 1971

Phillips's men were meeting again, this time in a safe house in Miami. After being convened by Phillips they had worked hard but had been unable to prevent Salvador Allende's electoral triumph. Despite all their efforts, including their October 1970 assassination of General René Schneider, chief of the army, in an attempt to provoke an intervention by the armed forces, Allende had won.

It was the first time since 1959 that an openly socialist, left-wing politician had won a general election, albeit with a small majority, and this set a precedent that had to be destroyed, even if the US government had to risk all its authority and prestige in achieving it. Ways of destabilizing the new Chilean government had to be found. All available resources would be mobilized, campaigns would be organized throughout the Americas, and the communist threat would be played up to the full.

As usual, David Phillips chaired the meeting. The rest settled themselves around the table. Antonio Veciana, Joaquín Sanjenís and Frank Sturgis were on his left, and on his right, Luis Posada Carriles, Ricardo Morales and Orlando Bosch. After a brief description of the Chilean political scene, Phillips outlined President Nixon's decision to get rid of Allende's constitutionally elected government and, in addition, to take advantage of a possible visit to that country by Fidel Castro — Phillips had confidential information that it was going ahead — to eliminate him.

Everybody had assumed this would be the US approach from the day Allende assumed the presidency. His statements of solidarity, his visit to Havana, and above all, the recent presence of a Cuban security agent — associated on other occasions with Fidel Castro's security — at the Cuban embassy in Chile, all pointed in that direction. This confirmation was what they had been waiting for, and all of them rushed to propose options for Castro's assassination.

Phillips had to intervene to call the meeting to order. The CIA had a plan, which consisted of taking advantage of two of the most insecure points of the visit. The first, when Castro would emerge on to the balcony of La Moneda Palace to address a crowd that would undoubtedly come to welcome him, providing an opportunity to fire on him from one of the rooms of the Hilton Hotel, whose balconies faced in that direction. This plan was somewhat similar to the attempt planned years before on the northern terrace of the presidential palace in Havana.

If the opportunity did not present itself then, Castro would be sure to give a press conference at the end of his tour and could be shot at that time. They had the idea of concealing a revolver inside a video camera. Two duly accredited journalists could smuggle it into the press room with the complicity of police officers on guard at the venue and use it to kill Fidel. Afterwards, the same Chilean police agents implicated in the operation would detain the assassins, get them out of the place, and prevent Castro's agents from executing them.

The idea seemed like a good one to everyone. Nevertheless, Veciana wanted to go over certain details. He thought it improbable that anyone could escape from the action at the press conference, and moreover, he considered the assassins' escape unnecessary. "Wouldn't it be better to make an agreement with the police to kill the assassins so as to cover up any possible traces?" he asked.

Phillips regarded him with a satisfied expression. Antonio Veciana was one of his first-rate agents. Phillips had recruited him in the early years after the revolution in Cuba, and since then he had become one of his finest instruments. Intelligent, passionate and calculating, he was always at hand when a frontline operative was needed.

He could not hide from those men the most interesting details of his plan. It had another component. Posada Carriles's group would fabricate a file to remain within the Venezuelan Police Department that would reveal the two men selected for the attempt on Castro as informers for Soviet intelligence. When the assassins were killed, the investigation would lead directly to Venezuelan police archives, thus exposing Castro's assassins as Soviet agents.

Caracas, Venezuela, September 1971

After the Bay of Pigs fiasco, Luis Posada Carriles enlisted in the US forces to participate in another invasion of Cuba set for mid-1962. He was sent to a training camp and there was selected to take an intelligence course in Fort Jackson. Along with other Cubans, he was to be part of the new secret police that would clear the country of communists while the US troops set about conquering towns.

That plan failed when Kennedy negotiated a way out of the Missile Crisis at the end of that same year, leaving him jobless. The men of Operation 40, as his group was called, did not abandon him and he therefore established himself in Venezuela.

The skills Posada Carriles had acquired soon led him to investigative work and he joined Venezuela's Directorate of Intelligence and Prevention Services (DISIP). Of course, none of that was by chance. His friends in the Caracas CIA station gave him the backing he needed and thus he rose to become one of the chiefs of that repressive agency by 1971. His field of action was related to the communist movement and the activities of the Soviet and Cuban intelligence agencies. In particular, he took on the case of a Soviet press correspondent accredited in Caracas who appeared to be a KGB representative.

His relations with the émigré Cuban community were strong and from time to time he did small favors for his former compañeros-in-arms. On various occasions he had concealed the presence in Venezuela of persons wanted by the US courts for having "served justice" on an individual who had publicly expressed a desire for an improvement in relations between Cuba and the Cuban community in the United States. Posada Carriles was determined that the exile movement, especially in Miami, could not be allowed to soften or be penetrated by Castro's agents.

One of his closest friends was Cuban American Lucilo Peña, an important businessman who had been recruited to the terrorist training camp in the Dominican Republic in 1964 when the CIA decided to form a team of men to execute the Agency's dirty work in its war on Cuba.

In the end, all the terrorists had become businessmen, as in one way or another they wound up heading cover enterprises that the CIA had organized in order to carry out its Latin American activities. All of them had become rich, one of the results of the "holy war" they had waged for more than 10 years. Some of the businesses were questionable, but it was a fact that they facilitated resources to continue the battle against communism.

Drug trafficking was at the core of those flourishing enterprises. In 1968, Antonio Veciana became an important adviser to the Bolivian national bank. That gave him the cover to gain access to coca leaf producers. For his part, Posada Carriles controlled all the air traffic from a phantom CIA company operating in South America. It was easy to use that channel to smuggle drugs into the United States and everyone benefited, including the Agency chiefs. It was drug trafficking that had provided the money for the anti-Cuba campaigns on the continent and for advising various police agencies anxious to dismantle revolutionary organizations in their respective countries.

For those reasons, when Phillips proposed the mission to assassinate Fidel Castro in Chile, Posada Carriles and Veciana were keen to oblige. If the Cuban leader died, the revolution could not be sustained, and that would allow them to convert the country into a transit point for drug trafficking to the United States. Business and political interests would advance hand in hand.

Fabricating the supposed Soviet agents who were to assassinate Castro in Chile was the responsibility of Posada Carriles's group. Agents' reports, doctored photos and instructions supposedly received from the Soviets would be planted in the rooms the patsies occupied in Caracas en route to Chile. This would help the DISIP demonstrate in its subsequent investigations that the Cuban assassins were agents of Moscow. The idea was similar to that utilized in the assassination of President Kennedy, when a huge propaganda operation was mounted to demonstrate that Lee Harvey Oswald was a Cuban and Soviet agent.

The Posada Carriles group was also in charge of seeking accreditation as Venevisión journalists for the two assassins, a task that was easily accomplished. The complication lay in fitting the revolver into the video camera that they would carry, with which they would make the fatal shot. Using Lucilo Peña's contacts, though, this was also accomplished.

When Phillips, Veciana, Sturgis, Hemming, Rodríguez, Bosch and Sanjenís arrived in Caracas to finalize the plan, everything was ready. They had heard through a reliable source − a general in the Chilean police − that Castro was to visit that country in early November of that year.

La Paz, Bolivia, Late October 1971

The city airport was unusually busy. That day the national folkloric ensemble was returning to the country after a successful international tour and many fans had turned up to welcome them home. In one of the halls, a tall, slim man with a close-trimmed mustache, aged around 40, was waiting expectantly. The Caracas-constructed video camera, fitted with a revolver, and other arms, including a powerful rifle with a telescopic sight and a silencer, were also due in on that flight.

The idea was Antonio Veciana's. His contacts in Bolivia had made it possible to load the equipment in Caracas, the folkloric ensemble's last stopover, and pick it up in La Paz with the aid of the customs authority, which had lent itself to tasks more complicated than this one on many other occasions.

The plan was ready. He was in charge of coordination on the ground. Two alternatives had been planned for the assassination of Castro and the room in the Santiago de Chile Hilton had been reserved. The Cubans would themselves take care of the press conference when it was called.

Nevertheless, he would also take advantage of the assassins' press accreditation to seek alternatives. The task could perhaps be moved forward. To that end, he directed the fake journalists to join the press caravan accompanying Castro throughout his visit. Whatever the case, this would be useful as they would get to know the bodyguards, who might let them get close enough to shoot when the moment arrived.

The most complicated detail was the execution of the assassins once they had shot the Cuban leader. The first plan was to pick them up in a car and then kill them in a safe place, giving credit to the efficiency of the national police force. In the alternative plan, their security agent contacts within the Chilean police force could take them out in the press conference room itself, thus frustrating certain action on the part of Castro's security.

One very important aspect was the need to not arouse the suspicions of the killers. They were no novices in their field, and the slightest suspicion could result in their desertion.

These thoughts were running through Veciana's mind that morning in the Bolivian airport when a man approached him and muttered a few words. Both of them walked in the direction of the parking lot. There they found the weapons in a van. Everything was ready and Veciana would soon be transporting them himself on the highway to Santiago, where he would leave them in a previously arranged safe house. Then he would wait for the killers and inform Phillips, who was coordinating the operation from another safe house. Phillips was in contact with the Chilean police and had responsibility for the execution of the phony journalists when they had completed their task.

Prensa Latina News Agency Report
Santiago de Chile, November 10, 1971

Tonight, Cuban prime minister Fidel Castro, greeted Chilean workers and affirmed that his encounter with President

Salvador Allende was a great victory for the peoples of Chile and Cuba, and thus for Latin America.

The Cuban leader spoke with a group of national and foreign journalists who managed to enter the front garden of the residence of Mario García Incháustegui, the Cuban ambassador to Chile, a few minutes after Fidel, accompanied by President Allende, had arrived from the airport.

Commander Fidel Castro spoke informally on various international problems and replied to questions related to Peru, Bolivia and Uruguay.

When he was asked what meaning he attributed to his visit to Chile, he said: "It has to be analyzed from a moral and revolutionary standpoint, and from that point of view it is of great significance. Our two countries have engaged in many struggles and have both been dominated by imperialism. The meeting has importance not because of us, the protagonists, but on account of its historic value."

He added: "This is a victory for the peoples of Chile and Cuba and thus of Latin America. One already has the sense of a revolutionary America. History is beginning to change in a distinctive manner. Perhaps this meeting can be best evaluated by the US imperialists themselves."

The prime minister said he did not know how long he would be in Chile and expressed his desire to meet with workers in the saltpeter, copper and coal mines and other rural workers. He added that his interest in these sectors was personal and social as well as political.

In conversation with the journalists, the revolutionary leader had words of praise for Chile and the Chileans. At the end of his first statement on Chilean soil, Commander Fidel Castro commented that he also had invitations to visit Algeria, Hungary, Bulgaria and the Soviet Union in the near future.

While it has not been confirmed, the Cuban leader is expected to offer a press conference tomorrow after a visit to President

Allende in the presidential palace.

Report of the Department of State Security (DSE) Headquarters
Havana, November 1979

From the end of 1970, the CIA was planning to assassinate Commander Fidel Castro when he visited Chile. According to information, we received the operation had a budget of $50,000 and its leaders were Cuban counterrevolutionaries, Antonio Veciana Blanch, Luis Posada Carriles, Orlando Bosch, Lucilo Peña, Joaquín Sanjenís, Marcos Rodríguez, Diego Medina, Secundino Álvarez and Félix Rodríguez, as well as US citizens, Frank Sturgis, Gerry Patrick Hemming, a Bolivian resident called Nápoles, and US operative David Phillips.

The plot originally contained two alternatives that could be carried out in Chile, plus two further attempts in Lima, Peru, and Quito, Ecuador, given the stopovers programmed for Commander Fidel Castro's return to Cuba.

The assassination plot was hatched in meetings in the cities of Miami, Caracas, La Paz and Santiago. The first option was to carry out the attack from a room in the Hilton Hotel adjacent to the presidential palace, the venue for the first of our prime minister's appearances in that country.

When that plan failed due to the participants' cowardice, the second option was put into action. Earlier, in Caracas, journalist credentials from the Venevisión channel had been given to Cuban counterrevolutionaries Marcos Rodríguez, from Orlando Bosch's group, who had very short, graying hair, olive skin, glasses, and was of regular height, and Diego Medina from the Second National Front of the Escambray, who was short, with thick hair, painted nails and olive skin.

Both were trained in precision shooting and to handle the television camera that contained the .38-caliber revolver with which they would fire on Fidel in his final press conference in Chile.

This latter attempt failed because the assassins pulled out, perhaps realizing they would never get out of the place alive. In fact, Rodríguez and Medina obstructed the plot from the outset. Medina claimed that a cousin of his who lived in Cuba was part of Fidel Castro's bodyguard and might recognize him at any moment. Rodríguez, for his part, simulated acute pain that doctors diagnosed as possible appendicitis. This led them to hospitalize him, thus giving him an excuse to back out of the action.

In fact, one of the principal reasons the plot was neutralized was due to the strict security measures taken by our men, who demonstrated to the enemy at all times — as they later affirmed — that any attempt on the life of the commander would be fatal for the individual who risked it.

Investigations confirmed the complicity of the Chilean police corps. According to our informant, General José María Sepúlveda was in charge of facilitating the assassins' entry into the venue of Fidel's press conference. He was also responsible for executing the assassins once the fatal shot had been fired.

We also knew that counterrevolutionaries Luis Posada Carriles and Lucilo Peña, both resident in Venezuela, had thought up a scheme to fabricate false evidence linking Rodríguez and Medina to Soviet intelligence officers in Caracas. The objective was to make it seem that the assassination of our prime minister had been the work of the Russians, acting to remove Fidel from the regional scene out of their displeasure with his support for the revolutionary movements in Latin America.

Before the failure of the Chile plot, through counterrevolutionary Amaury Frajinals in Miami, Phillips and his group contracted Eusebio Ojeda, ex-captain of the Second National Front of the Escambray, to position himself on the terrace of Lima airport in Peru with two explosives experts known as Horacio and Marcelo. They were to wait for the arrival of Fidel's delegation on its return from Chile in order to attack it with two grenades. After agreeing to the plot, the two experts disappeared and could not be found. Posada Carriles then volunteered to assassinate Fidel when he landed at Quito airport in Ecuador on the final stopover of the flight back to Cuba.

This last plot involved recruiting brothers Guillermo and Roberto Verdaguer, proprietors of an Ecuadorean airline, in order to have them conveniently place one of their planes in the terminal area, providing cover for Posada Carriles and another accomplice by the name of Osiel González to fire on Fidel as soon as he appeared at the door of his aircraft.

The plan failed when the Verdaguer brothers refused to carry out the action, arguing that they would be caught and their business ruined.

One significant detail of these criminal plans is the origin of the weapons to be used. In all cases they were supplied by a contact in Dallas, Texas. That was where Veciana coordinated the transfer of weapons on various occasions, through a Cuban woman called Hilda.

12
New York and Miami: Alpha 66

In 1979, 19 years after his first visit to New York, Fidel Castro was returning there to participate in the 34th session of the UN General Assembly, this time as president of the Nonaligned Nations Movement, an organization that had recently concluded its Sixth Summit in Havana. Cuba's prestige and authority had grown in spite of the US blockade and the aggression and hardships suffered. Fidel's international stature had also grown as the undisputed leader of countries in the Global South.

The news of Castro's visit shook the counterrevolutionary émigrés to the core. Cuba's triumphs embittered them, the image of a combative Fidel Castro reminded them of the Bay of Pigs disaster, and the Cuban leader's visit to the United States was a provocation that they were not prepared to endure.

Years had passed, but Castro remained an obsession for Antonio Veciana, whom he saw as having destroyed his life and that of the men of his generation. The battle against him had consumed Veciana's youth. Before he left Cuba in the 1960s, he had attempted but failed to assassinate Fidel. Later, when Castro visited Chile, he failed again. On this occasion, however, Castro would be in the United States itself, Veciana's own territory, this time he would not escape.

Veciana was in his comfortable house located in the area of Miami known as Little Havana. Before him was a letter informing him of Fidel's visit, and for a few minutes his thoughts went back through the years to the last day he met his case officer, David Phillips, in a greyhound racetrack parking lot on Flager Street.

Phillips was very annoyed that somebody had blown the whistle on the cocaine racket that the two of them had been running from Bolivia to Colombia for several years. He recalled how, with a piercing stare, Phillips had explained that the police were about to arrest him and that he, Veciana, must take full responsibility so as to avoid involving the Agency in the scandal. Phillips acknowledged Veciana's loyalty and the services he had lent and told him that they would not abandon him. An arrangement had been made with the relevant authorities so that Veciana would only serve a few months in prison term, for which he would be paid $250,000. At the end of the day, Phillips said, Veciana had no other option if he wanted to stay alive, as it was impossible to predict the reaction of their Mafia associates who would inevitably be arrested if the Cuban confessed.

He recalled the days of Watergate, of the Church Commission, and finally, his 1978 interrogation by the House Select Committee investigating the Kennedy assassination. His statements there had almost cost him his life. It was a slip-up, he thought, mentioning the existence of Phillips to investigator Gaetón Fonzi, even though he only referred to Phillips' alias Harold Bishop.[1] He had then fallen into an acute depression. The CIA was highly discredited by the Congressional exposé of many of their dirty dealings. The investigators' threats to include him in investigations into the assassination of the US president and the prospect of long months in prison for the drugs venture had finally loosened his tongue.

Since then, he had discreetly distanced himself from his counterrevolutionary colleagues, claiming that the FBI was watching

---

[1]   Gaetón Fonzi was an investigator with the 1978 US House Select Committee Investigation of the Assassination of President John F. Kennedy and author of *The Last Investigation* (Thunders Mouth Press, 1993)

him and that his movements in Dade county were restricted, which was in fact true.

Nevertheless, he had great respect in the Cuban émigré community. Andrés Nazario Sargén, the leader of Alpha 66 — the organization Veciana had founded when he arrived in Miami — always consulted him about every action, and that satisfied his vanity. That was why he thought of Sargén for the new idea circulating in his mind. He would call him, Veciana thought. "Now let's see if the old guy can hang on to his pants."

The Softball
Miami, September 1979

There were two covered armchairs in the little room, one green and the other red. Blown-up individual photos of smiling young people adorned the walls. The chairs were separated by a small table at which Antonio Veciana, the host, was having an animated conversation with Andrés Nazario Sargén.

"Our friends have sent me a letter informing me of Fidel's upcoming visit to New York," Veciana began. "They're sure that after his victory in the recent Nonaligned Nations Movement summit hosted by Havana, he'll come to the United States to rub their faces in it.

"They always have reliable information. Anyway, it's logical. But I wonder why they're persisting with the idea after such a long time. The CIA people have been hit hard and President Carter has put a chief admiral in there, who, as I've heard, favors technical rather than human sources.

"Nevertheless," Veciana continued, "our people still hold key positions. They're getting ready for the elections, when Carter is going to get a kick in the ass. And something happening to Fidel on US territory would hasten Carter's exit; a president who can't even offer security to a foreign leader. It's also obvious they don't want to be seen to be involved, and that's why they've passed the information on to me. They want us to do their dirty work as usual. What's happening is that our interests are converging again. Imagine if Fidel were to be blown into a thousand pieces in the middle of New York."

"What have you got in mind?" asked Sargén.

"Nothing concrete for now. I'm just thinking that it would be good if you could get hold of a sufficient quantity of C-4 explosives through your contacts and maybe think about some of our compañeros who might be prepared to park a car along Fidel's route from the Cuban UN Mission building. We could so something along the lines of the Orlando Letelier hit. Remember Allende's foreign minister who the Novo Sampol brothers and that little American CIA guy blew away in the middle of Washington?"

A smile lit up Nazario Sargén's face.

Department of State Security (DSE) Headquarters
Havana, September 1979

The prospect of Fidel's trip to New York put everyone in the DSE on edge. It was a period of escalating terrorism against Cuban representatives and officials located abroad, particularly on US territory, where the Cuban mission to the UN had been the target of many bomb attacks and constant threats on its personnel. By that time there had been more than 20 acts of terrorism in the New York area against the Soviet and Venezuelan missions to the UN, six attacks of the same kind on the Cuban mission, and the murder of Eulalio Negrín, a Cuban American who was advocating the normalization of relations. One year later Cuban diplomat Félix García was assassinated and an attempt on the ambassador, Raúl Roa Kourí, was foiled.

Those terrorist acts stemmed from the counterrevolutionaries' desperation and reflected their decline, although that did not make them any less dangerous. In fact, they continued operating on US territory with a high degree of impunity. These groups' historical links with the CIA provided them with sophisticated training in subversion and access to arms, explosives and modern technical devices for their actions. According to reports from the FBI itself, at that time, the Cuban counterrevolutionary groups were the most dangerous network operating in the United States. Moreover, they were linked to organized crime, drug trafficking, and intelligence agencies that, as in the case of the Chilean National Intelligence Directorate, utilized them to eliminate their opponents in the United States itself.

Various specialist security teams traveled to New York to study conditions in the various venues and the routes the Cuban president would probably have to take and to organize the necessary arrangements with the UN and US authorities in charge of protecting foreign dignitaries.

In the midst of this hectic activity, we received information that the counterrevolutionary organization Alpha 66 was planning to attack Fidel in New York. This group, set up by the CIA in 1962, had devoted itself for several years to attacking Cuban vessels and those from other countries trading with Cuba. In fact, they operated as armed pirates until international pressure forced them to pull back. So they turned to terrorizing sectors of the Cuban community in the United States that did not share their position and to maintain a line in blackmail that served as a source of enrichment for the leaders. The CIA also used Alpha 66 on many occasions as a psychological resource to divert the attention of Cuban security and force it to invest resources in averting possible attacks that never materialized. It was originally thought that this projected attack was part of that strategy. Nevertheless, being professional, a plan was drawn up to verify the information.

One of our officers located in Miami was given the mission to make contact with the informant. As the source was not considered entirely trustworthy, it was decided that our agent would approach the woman on her way to work, while taking particular security measures.

Testimony of Officer Omar
Intelligence Directorate, January 1995

I located myself at a convenient café that afforded me control of the exit of her building and the parking lot through the window, as I didn't know whether she would leave by foot or in a car. My idea was to follow her in my car if she did the latter. It wasn't difficult to identify her because, as you say, she's a beautiful woman who attracts attention. I saw her open a red VW but she appeared to have forgotten something and went back into the building, which allowed me time to approach her in the parking lot. I thought it was a quieter and safer place to park alongside her car and when she arrived, I gave her the password in a totally natural way. She was clearly shocked, and her reply was that we were crazy. Laughing, I said I guessed that wasn't really her reply. She smiled and said: "Go to hell!" We went in her car because I didn't want it left there in case the family saw it and got worried about her, and neither did I want to leave her alone at any moment. I indicated a route that gave me a chance to countercheck and detected no sign of enemy activity.

She says she got the information from her father, whom Nazario had approached for money, telling him that it was for an attempt on Fidel's life they were going to make in New York and that they needed explosives. She also talked about it with one "Robertico," last name unknown, a new guy in Alpha 66 who arrived from Cuba not long ago where says he had been in prison. This Robertico is in love with her and told her that the explosion was going to be heard in Miami. She doesn't give much credence to this man because he's a braggard, but she is worried by a comment her father made along the lines that this time it's for real, which is unusual because he doesn't have any faith in Nazario and avoids him because he spends his whole life hitting people up for money.

I directed her to sound out her father with the excuse that she was worried about innocent people dying and him being linked to something like that, and to approach Robertico to find out his real participation in it. She was a bit reluctant about the latter because she says the guy's a sleazy idiot, and she's not prepared to have a thing with him. I clarified that nobody was asking her to do that; that she should reject him sexually as she has done up to now, but not totally cut off ties, and encourage his bragging.

I stressed the importance of her mission and the responsibility she had, and I went over with her the guide that you sent and had her learn it off by heart. I then destroyed it in her presence so that she would realize the serious nature of things and acquire good habits. She asked me how she could get in touch with me and I told her that if she had anything urgent, she should call Eastern Airlines and reserve a flight to Caracas in the name of María Portales on the 20th or the 27th of this month, and then I would locate her. I know it's a risk, but I had no other alternative.

She seems to be an immature but well-intentioned girl and came across as sincere and intelligent. I am going to direct Q-24 to check out this information in detail and communicate with you. I will approach her again by surprise next week even if there's no urgency.

Information provided by agent Q-24

I talked with Nazario [Sargén]and learned they are preparing an attack in which they will launch a grenade at the car taking Fidel from our UN mission to the UN building. It would seem that it is not being organized by Alpha, although Nazario is asking for money from everyone and wants to claim success for it if it comes off. Alpha 66 is possibly supplying the men and the car they will use. Nazario told me of a man and a woman living in Union City, which would mean they could avoid using Miami people. I suppose the car would have New York or New Jersey license plates for the same reason and would have to be hired with false documentation, a stolen car or one of those old cars bought for cash that don't need any papers.

Nazario told me they had economic problems in terms of buying the explosives, but I doubt that's the case. He's probably saying that to get money. I told him I could get him a clean car through a friend, thinking that if we had control of the car we could control the operation. He said he thought Veciana already had one but if there was any need he'd call me.

I don't believe we have sufficient control through Nazario because Veciana is compartmentalizing everything. I don't have any reason to see Veciana directly, but I will talk to [REDACTED] about what Nazario told me to see if he'll introduce me to Veciana. [REDACTED] must know something because of his access to explosives and his relationship with Veciana. It's important to see him because if he's in the know, then so is the CIA. I know for a fact that Nazario has talked to various people about this, so I don't think there's any problem in transferring the information to the US secret services so that they can neutralize the operation.

In the context of the visit, it was decided to proceed with the move of the Cuban UN mission to from the old mansion on 67th Street and 15th Avenue to a building on Lexington Avenue and 38th Street. This building offered the possibility of accommodating the delegation more cheaply and with better security. Located just a few blocks from the UN building itself, in the center of downtown Manhattan, this area is one of the most central, densely populated and busy areas of the city.

The consequences of blowing up a car loaded with explosives in a place like that were unimaginable. It would kill not only Fidel but accompanying Cuban officials and security personnel as well as dozens of US secret service and police officers, along with many of the thousands of people passing through the area, who would inevitably wait out of curiosity to see the Cuban president's convoy pass by. No political rationale could justify such an act; even for the Cuban security professionals, who had confronted the counterrevolutionary groups' wildest plots and had witnessed arson attacks on stores full of people, attacks on humble fishing vessels and even the sabotage of a passenger plane in full flight, the idea was incredible. This plan went beyond the conceivable, but it was a fact. Something had to be done — and it was done.

Testimony of Division General Fabián Escalante Font
Havana, January 1995

I was working in my office when a friend called to tell me that two Cuban journalists from the weekly *Juventud Rebelde* magazine had recently returned from a visit to Florida, where they had been researching the Cuban community there. The study was sponsored by the Center for International Policy at the Johns Hopkins University, headed by Wayne Smith, former chief of the US Interests Section in Cuba.

Journalists Hedelberto López Blanch and Ignacio Hernández Rotger spent almost three weeks in Miami and interviewed various people from the Cuban exile community. My conversation with them flowed easily. I explained the work that I was doing and they told me of an interview they did with Antonio Veciana, with whom they had struck up a casual conversation in a restaurant.

The journalists told him they were from Cuba and were interested in facts rather than motives, and he told them his story. Of course, he told them only part of it and nothing in relation to the CIA, his case officer David Phillips, acts of terrorism against Cuban targets in third countries, expeditions against Cuba, drug trafficking, the adventure in Bolivia, or all the counterrevolutionary activities in which he participated over more than 30 years.

Interview with Antonio Veciana[2]
Miami, October 1994

I already sensed that the revolution was very strong and as a practical man I knew we weren't winning, so my strategy was to kill Fidel, and I tried to do so on three occasions.

First: I rented Apartment 8A on Misiones Avenue before the [1960] Urban Reform Act was implemented. I needed a special weapon and I went to the US embassy to ask for it. Sam Kail was chief of intelligence. I told him who I was and that he could check me out. He asked me what I was after and told me that he was going to the United States and, when he returned, he would give me an answer. When he came back, he told me that he couldn't and didn't want to have anything to do with me. I told him that if Castro was killed the United States would be blamed anyway. He reaffirmed that he didn't want to know anything about it, and that his country couldn't be linked to the action. I told Bernardo Morales about it and he told me he had a bazooka.[3] At first, I put my mother-in-law in the apartment, although I never told her what I was planning to do. The attempt failed, as the people who had to do it thought I was crazy or

---

2   This interview with Antonio Veciana was conducted in Miami in October 1994 by Hedeberto López and Ignacio Hérnandez for the Cuban journal *Juventud Rebelde*.

3   Bernardo Morales was possibly the Chicano CIA official David Sánchez Morales.

stupid. I had placed two men in the apartment, one was Bernardo Paradela. He thought the gas produced by the bazooka might lead to an explosion in the apartment, and the operation failed because the others also backed out using the excuse of the gas, although initially around 50 to 60 people were prepared to do it. Orlando had obtained uniforms and machine guns.

Second: Chile. Somebody within the Chilean government, who I still can't name, told me six months beforehand that Fidel was going to Chile [in 1971]. I trained two individuals, both dead now: Diego Medina, killed in Santa Marta (Colombia) for peddling drugs, and Marcos Rodríguez. We trained them in Venezuela as photojournalists. I was a boxing promotor and stole passports from various boxers. The training lasted for about three months. They went to Chile a month beforehand and managed to get the credentials to enter La Moneda [the presidential] palace. The equipment was bought from the *Venevisión* channel. You know money can buy anything. The plan was to kill Fidel at a large press conference of around 30 journalists in the hope that the act would get major coverage in the international media. That scenario was chosen because Castro's security agents couldn't operate there and it had to be a moment of less tension. There were two men, but only one of them was supposed to fire. Both the guys involved asked for life insurance for their families in the event of anything happening to them and that was granted.

Soon after Fidel arrived in Chile, Diego Medina ran away to Peru, but the other guy could and should have done the job. Marcos Rodríguez attended Fidel's first press conference, but, as planned, and to give Fidel's security people more confidence in him, he didn't carry the weapon. After that Marcos got himself admitted to hospital claiming he had appendicitis. When I went to see the doctor, he told me that although the patient was suffering from chronic appendicitis, it wasn't a case for an urgent operation and could wait for months or even years. Nevertheless, Marcos insisted on an operation and after talking with him again, I told the doctor to go ahead with the operation and that I'd take care of the cost. So neither of the two men attended the second press conference. They called me the "spider captain" because I was the one who supplied the weapons, found the locations, but by pure coincidence didn't take part in the actions. That time they didn't kill Fidel because they didn't have the balls.

Third: In Miami I met up again with Juanita, a crazy girl, but not too crazy. I remembered her from the underground movement because she saved my life once in Jaimanitas. I met up with her again in the United States, and we planned to eliminate Castro during his visit to the United Nations in 1979. I was the one who was going to check it out and follow Fidel's car right from the airport. I would do so with a walkie-talkie. We chose to use a contact detonator disguised as a softball with little Cuban and July 26 flags on it, when the crowd was gathered near the UN to welcome Fidel. I would advise her of which car he was traveling in, and when he arrived, she would throw the ball. Given the crowd and the confusion, Juanita would easily be able to escape.

But in this case, there was an infiltration by the US secret service. They took me to an office and threatened to put me in the electric chair. They placed me under surveillance to intimidate me. Then I thought I could be the bait for the secret service and somebody else could execute my plan of action. That didn't work out because Juanita, who should have thrown the ball, backed out at the last minute. I always tried to provide an escape route for the people who took part in these actions. If I had gone there would have been some action. I haven't been a man of average rather than exceptional courage. To tell the truth, I don't have the balls. I was always arguing with the CIA and the FBI. They think they're more capable because they have far more resources, but some of the attempts they planned were really dumb, like those with cigars and [poison] pens.

The *Marielito* Infiltrators
Alpha 66 Offices, Miami, March 1982

Nazario Sargén leant back in his swivel chair, which, beside the mahogany desk, was one of the few remaining pieces of furniture in his rather bare office. He recalled the good times, when the CIA — the same CIA that now demands receipts for everything — would hand over any amount of cash without question. Now they were really stingy.

In the following days he would plan an infiltration into Cuba of one of his much-publicized "commandos." How different everything was! Previously, they would almost give such "commandos" a public send off from the main street of Little Havana. Now he had to put up with the man from the CIA reprimanding him for a statement reported in the Miami Herald about an imminent operation in Cuba by his group. You can't work this way, he told himself. The blame for all of this lay fair and square with President Kennedy, who decreed that everything the Cubans planned against Cuba had to be approved by government agencies. That's why he got what he deserved.

He recalled the days when CIA case officers supported any autonomous operation, their only concern being achieving the goal of getting Castro, by any means! Far from improving with age, the CIA had become an inert bureaucracy. They now asked for original documents and copies and full explanations for everything. He had recently got approval to send two "sacrificial lambs" on a mission to kill Castro in Cuba. In return, the two Cubans, who had arrived illegally in the United States as *Marielitos*, would receive a few dollars and hopefully get the Miami police off their backs.[4]

The two Cubans were waiting in the anteroom of the office of the Alpha 66 leader, Nazario Sargén. They knew that returning to Cuba was dangerous, but they were desperate. They found themselves being constantly harassed by Miami police — perhaps because of their color or, more likely, because they didn't speak English. They certainly did not consider the four supermarket robberies they had committed in that city meant that they should be deemed as serious criminals and therefore compelled to go every other day to the police station near the rough boarding house where they lived.

At the time of the Mariel boatlift in 1980, they had been prisoners in Cuba's Combinado del Este prison, and an associate gave them the letter. If they asked to leave the country, the government would grant them permission. And that is how they made it to the United States. But they still seemed so far from that promised land they had imagined.

On arriving in Miami, Luis had gone straight to California, where he got work picking apples; but his hands almost froze in that damn job. Later, he returned to what he knew best: selling cocaine in schools. Then, one fine day, a police raid sent him back to Miami, where he was unemployed. The Cubans there were quite different and had no sympathy for the recent arrivals. The *Marielitos* found themselves despised by the more established Cuban-American community.

Finally, Nazario Sargén admitted the two future heroes into his office. There were no speeches or pressure. He explained the plan

---

[4]   The *Marielitos* were part of a mass boatlift of some 125,000 people, who left Cuba from the port of Mariel (just outside Havana) with approval of the government to emigrate to the United States between April 15 and October 31, 1980. Some of the *Marielitos* had recently been released from Cuban jails and mental health facilities and deemed "undesirables" by US authorities who sought to send them back to Cuba.

for them to sneak into the country near the city of Matanzas, close to the large Antonio Guiteras power plant, where they would be met by a group of his men. They would give them everything they needed and would explain the plan to assassinate Fidel Castro and Ramiro Valdés, the minister of the interior.

After chatting for a while, he observed them closely. Their names, Luis and Rogelio, were as common as thousands of other Cubans, but he had a hunch that the future of these unhappy souls would be tragic. The only thing the CIA was interested in, and the reason they requested his services, was a public relations campaign on the supposed human rights situation in Cuba of which Ronald Reagan was so critical. Surely the G-2 would catch them in a matter of hours, this would soon become public knowledge and the CIA would have the evidence needed for its propaganda.

And that is exactly what happened. In the first week of April, the Cuban government announced it had detained two heavily armed men, Luis Llanes Águila and Rogelio Abreu Azcuy, in the vicinity of Matanzas. When the men who were supposed to meet them did not turn up, as Sargén had promised, the infiltrators threatened some local inhabitants. One of the locals happened to be in the Territorial Militia and managed to arrest the infiltrators and hand them over to the nearest police post. Once again, Nazario Sargén, the "historic" leader in exile, had "dispatched" two of his compatriots.

Testimony of Division General Fabián Escalante Font
January 1995

I recall that, in April 1982, information reached DSE headquarters about an infiltration — people coming into the country illegally. A small rubber raft had been found half-buried on the coastal reefs, and rumors about the infiltrators spread among the population living near the Antonio Guiteras power plant, on the outskirts of Matanzas.

On that day, Commander Ramiro Valdés, then minister of interior, called me to share the details and ask me to travel with him to the location and assess the importance of the operation, which was clearly carried out by the enemy. Shortly afterward, I picked him up in my car and we drove quickly towards Matanzas. As we approached the location, we noticed several police officers on the highway who were continuously calling through megaphones, urging the infiltrators to hand themselves in. By that time, it was known that one of the men came from the town of Alquízar. So, one of the police in charge repeatedly called out: "Hand yourself in, Alquízar. You're surrounded." This made us all laugh.

Commander Ramiro spoke to the ministry staff in charge of the operation. All the necessary measures were taken, and it was only a matter of time before the infiltrators were caught. Before long, a local *campesino* appeared at the improvised command post, leading two men with their hands tied. Trying to escape the cordon, they had gone to the *campesino's* house, hoping he would hide them. This was a mistake. The *campesino* was a member of the militia, and when he discovered who they were, he took out his machete, disarmed them and handed them over to the police.

This is how the adventure of these two Marielito mercenaries ended, two Cubans who were also victims of media manipulation. Armed to the teeth, planning to assassinate Ramiro Valdés and Fidel Castro on the highway between Havana and Matanzas, the assistance Alpha 66 chief Sargén had promised them on arrival for their mission never materialized. No one ever showed up.

13
The Saturnino Beltrán Commando Unit

For several months, the Cuban and Nicaraguan intelligence services had known about the relocation of the Contras' base of operations from the airport in Aguacarte, in Olancho Department in
Honduras, to the Ilopango airport in San Salvador, El Salvador.
Headed by Félix Rodríguez Mendigutía, a group of CIA experts
had arrived in Ilopango to lead the operation, tasked with
equipping the counterrevolutionary forces in the interior of
Nicaragua, for which they had several Douglas C-47 and Fairchild
C-123 cargo planes.

The Salvadoran dictatorship's security forces and the US Army
in El Salvador had given the green light to the mission. Within
a few weeks they had put at its disposal several safe houses, the
necessary vehicles and a hangar at the airport that could be used as
a military hardware and munitions dump for the materiel coming
from Honduras and the United States.

At the discretion of Lieutenant Colonel Oliver North, a
high-ranking official in the US National Security Council, a large
group of CIA agents of Cuban origin were responsible for various
aspects of the anti-Sandinista operation. Among them were
Rafael Quintero, alias Chichi, who was the link between North
and the commando unit in El Salvador; Colonel Luis Orlando
Rodríguez, who acted as deputy chief of the US military mission
in El Salvador; Mario Delamico, assistant to General Humberto
Regalado, chief of the Honduran army; Colonel Reynaldo García,

the US Army adviser in Honduras; René Corbo, the unit's representative in Costa Rica, who was tasked with the operation of an air strip at the El Murciélago ranch on the Costa Rica–Nicaragua border; and Mario Rejas and Ubaldo Hernández Pérez, advisers from the Nicaraguan Contra group UDN-FARN, which carried out incursions into southern Nicaragua from Costa Rica. The other members of the group were Felipe Vidal, Frank Castro, Frank Chanes, Luis Rodríguez, José Dionisio Suárez and Alvin Ros, all of whom were based in Nicaragua. From there they ran shell companies responsible for covering up drug trafficking and gunrunning for the Nicaraguan Contras and money laundering, the proceeds of which were later used to finance the ballooning costs of the war against the Sandinista government in Nicaragua. In addition, Ramón Milián Hernández served as the link between the CIA unit and the Colombian drug lord Pablo Escobar, head of the Medellín cartel and CIA "collaborator" par excellence.

It was probably during the last few days of 1984 that the group of Cuban terrorists based in El Salvador learned from Félix Rodríguez about Fidel Castro's imminent visit to Managua, Nicaragua. In the second week of January 1985, Fidel would attend the swearing-in ceremony of Commander Daniel Ortega, until then the coordinator of the Government of National Reconstruction established in 1979 after the overthrow and expulsion of the dictator Anastasio Somoza. It was a unique opportunity to assassinate the Cuban leader and not one to be passed up.

After tossing aside various plans, they developed an option that would have a good chance of success. The idea was to bring in a Russian-made C3M missile and wait for the announcement of the arrival of the plane carrying the Cuban leader. All they had to do was select a house close to the route that the plane would take on its approach to the airport and, at the right moment, launch the missile. Fidel would then be history.

They quickly got in touch with their associates in Miami and directed them to set up a front "organization" made up of Cuban and Nicaraguan exiles, who would announce to "the world" the union of these two exile groups. For this, they could count on their old collaborators at the Nuevo Herald, the Spanish-language sister publication of the Miami Herald, and several of the key Miami-based radio stations. The idea was to allow the assassins to operate behind a political and media smokescreen so that later they could easily get away and their tracks would be erased in the counterrevolutionary cesspool of drugs and organized crime into which the exiled entrepreneurs had converted Miami.

The Commando State Security headquarters
Managua, Nicaragua. January 1985

The information had been received a couple of weeks earlier, probably at the end of [1984], and it came from a trusted source based in Miami. The source informed them of the setting up of a joint commando unit — named "Saturnino Beltrán" after a Nicaraguan killed accidently at a training camp in the Florida Everglades — made up of Nicaraguans opposed to the Sandinistas and counterrevolutionaries of Cuban origin. The source linked the upcoming swearing-in of president-elect Commander Daniel Ortega to Fidel Castro's attendance at the inauguration ceremony. The counterrevolutionaries thought this was a golden opportunity to assassinate the Cuban leader, and they promptly submitted their plan for consideration by the head of the CIA in that city.[1]

The idea that got a quick stamp of approval was to shoot down the plane carrying Fidel as it began to prepare for landing. To

---

[1]   MIAMI OR MANAGUA???? A month later, at the end of 1985, the details of the plan, and the involvement of the cell led from El Salvador by Félix Rodríguez Mendigutía, became known.

this end the CIA, would hand over in Honduras a Russian-made surface-to-air missile that would have to be smuggled into Managua and fired by two Nicaraguan Contras who had been trained in its operation.

The security services of both Cuba and Nicaragua analyzed what information they had about potential threats to the Cuban leader on his trip to Managua, and a joint working group was established headed by a Sandinista leader called Vincente — an experienced combatant in the dirty war unleashed by the United States against the Nicaraguan people more than three years earlier. Vincente, or "El Negro," as he was affectionately known by everyone, had been an active participant in the struggle against the Somoza dictatorship. Of average height, about 25 years old and demanding by nature, he had a cool head that enabled him to make the right decisions under pressure.

Despite a great effort, little had been achieved in terms of expanding on the information supplied by the source. The key conspirators had safely left for Honduras, and nobody could be found who might add anything new. The details of the information they did have were reviewed again. It all seemed credible, but unfortunately important pieces of the puzzle were missing. Nothing was known about the would-be perpetrators, nor about the safe houses they would use, or even the likely locations from which they intended to launch the missile.

There was a real danger for the planes coming from Cuba that crossed the Caribbean Sea, entered Nicaragua at the elevation of Puerto Cabezas on the Atlantic coast and flew a diagonal route to the great Lake Nicaragua. They would then descend, bearing north. They would thus begin their preparations for landing by flying over Managua from north to south, making them easy targets for a missile.

The date of the inauguration ceremony was rapidly approaching. It would take place in the square with the monument to Carlos

Fonseca, the founder of the Sandinista National Liberation Front [FSLN] who had died in combat in the struggle against Somoza; nearby was the Managua cathedral and what was once the Congress building, in the very center of the city, prior to its near-total destruction in the 1972 earthquake.

By this time Cuban intelligence knew the names of some of those involved. The person in charge, who was also the head of the Nicaraguan Contras, was Adolfo Calero Portocarrero, a veteran CIA agent. He was backed up by several people of Nicaraguan and Cuban origin: Orlando Valdés, Manuel Reyes and Roberto Milián Martínez.

On January 5, the intelligence working group met, this time with the guerrilla commander Lenin Cerna Juárez — head of Sandinista security — in attendance. They once again went over all the available information in minute detail. They also analyzed the reports of agents who had infiltrated the Contras, in Nicaragua as well as in Honduras, and they could not confirm a single revealing fact.

The finishing touches to the security arrangements for the festivities were being made. Everything revolved around the security of the numerous dignitaries and personalities who would attend the event. There were no weak links in the security detail that had been assigned, but anyone armed with a C3M-type missile of Russian manufacture could hit the Cuban plane as approached Sandino Airport.

Everyone agreed there was only one way to prevent an assassination attempt. That same day the Nicaraguan foreign ministry drafted a diplomatic note to the US government that would be delivered in Managua and Washington simultaneously. The note denounced the plan without revealing everything that was known about it and gave the impression that more was known than was actually the case. The Reagan administration would be held responsible for any incident or action that occurred during

President Ortega's inauguration, including any attack against Fidel Castro. The note made it clear that if anything happened all the details of the plot would be made public, including those not included in the note. The diplomatic countermeasure appeared to have the desired effect.

Meanwhile, the flight path of every leader attending the inauguration was studied in detail and the Cubans decided to use three of their Ilyushin 62M aircraft to mislead the enemy, who could not be certain which of these planes carried Fidel.

In this way, despite the risk, the Cuban leader defied yet another criminal attempt on his life and attended the inauguration ceremony of Commander Daniel Ortega, the first president to be elected by the people of a free, Sandinista and sovereign Nicaragua.

14

Twilight of an Obsession

From the early 1990s, Fidel Castro began to travel overseas more frequently. As a new era dawned in Latin America, numerous progressive heads of state were elected and Fidel was invited to visit many of their countries. European governments and others also requested his attendance at important events. In this situation, the hitmen of the so-called Cuban American National Foundation (CANF) began to look for new opportunities to assassinate Fidel on one of his visits abroad, something they knew would be almost impossible to carry out in Cuba.

Formed in the early 1980s during the administration of Ronald Reagan, CANF had emerged as a lobby group to pressure Washington politicians into passing new laws and regulations against Cuba in Congress. These measures were aimed at shoring up the discredited economic, political and cultural blockade imposed by the United States in 1962, which was beginning to show cracks in the UN itself. [1]

CANF's sinister plans were soon exposed as being not merely political and that behind the public facade of a security apparatus for the protection of its leaders was a mechanism for subversion, terrorism and criminal activities. Notorious terrorists gathered in its shadow, the real aim of which was to target Cuban interests,

---

[1]   In November 1992, for the first time the United Nations General Assembly voted in favor of a Cuban resolution condemning the 30-year US economic blockade of the island.

functionaries and leaders anywhere on the planet. The CIA made discreet, periodic payments to the CANF to cover its expenses through foundations set up for this purpose.

The first attempt against Fidel Castro was scheduled to take place in Spain during his visit to Galicia; a group of hitmen was led by Mario Salabarría and Marcos Tulio Beruff. Later attempts were made in Brazil, Venezuela, Cartagena in Colombia, Bariloche in Argentina, Venezuela's Margarita Island, the Dominican Republic and, finally, Panama in 2000. These plots always the same group of would-be assassins: Roberto Martín Pérez, Gaspar Jiménez Escobedo, Luis Posada Carriles, Santiago Álvarez, Ramón Orozco Crespo, José Hernández, Guillermo Novo Sampol, Pedro Remón Crispín, Ramón Font, Francisco Eulalio Castro and several other collaborators. These same people tried time and time again, at the behest of the United States or on their own initiative, to assassinate the Cuban leader, never accepting their historic failure.

One of the most dangerous plots, however, one which had every chance of success — was undoubtedly that planned for November 18, 2000, in Panama City during the 10th Ibero-American Summit. The idea was to place 35 pounds of plastic explosives in the amphitheater of the local university to be detonated by remote control during a solidarity event that Fidel would attend, an event organized by students and the community. But the assassins failed to factor in the efficiency of the Cuban intelligence services, which discovered the plot in time. On touching down in Panama, the Cuban president publicly denounced the criminal plot that had been set in motion, named its leaders and explained where they had planned to go into hiding.

The terrorists were detained within a few hours and that despicable plan was revealed to the world, thanks to Fidel's denunciation and the actions of the Panamanian authorities. Luis Clemente Posada Carriles, Guillermo Novo Sampol, Pedro Remón Crispín and Gaspar Jiménez Escobedo were arrested.

Official declaration of the Cuban president, Fidel Castro
November 17, 2000

On arriving at this historic Latin American territory of Panama, I would like to greet its patriotic and brave people, who are now the lawful owners of the Panama Canal and run it better than those [i.e. the United States] who did so until very recently. In the name of Cuba, which benefits from its services as do all the peoples of the world, I thank you.

Like the other Latin American heads of state, I have come here to participate in the 10th Summit in a spirit of contributing to its success for the benefit of our peoples and, especially, the interests and prestige of Panama.

However, I am duty bound to inform you that, as on other occasions when I have traveled to these summits, terrorist elements organized, financed and directed from the United States by the CANF, which is a tool of imperialism and the far right in that country, have been sent to Panama to assassinate me. They are in this city right now and have smuggled in arms and explosives.

I am denouncing this now, rather than prior to departing, so that it does not occur to anybody to imagine that any danger or threat could intimidate the Cuban delegation. We have no concern whatsoever for the security of our delegation, the members of which are astute, experienced and veterans of the struggle against ambushes, treacherous plans and other acts of aggression by imperialism and its allies. But numerous delegations and heads of state and of government are participating in this meeting and, while the Panamanian authorities have worked painstakingly to ensure everyone's security, we know that the terrorists plan to shoot or detonate explosive charges where they think it will serve their purposes. In carrying out such actions, they have no concern for multi-passenger vehicles the heads of other delegations might be traveling in, or where those leaders might be meeting.

The leader of this group of terrorists, to whom the leaders of CANF entrusted with the mission, is the infamous Luis Posada Carriles, a cowardly and utterly unscrupulous man who was behind the downing of the Cubana Airlines aircraft as it took off from Barbados on October 6, 1976, with 73 passengers on board. He was assisted in this by some Venezuelan mercenaries. After escaping from a Venezuelan jail in August 1985, Posada Carilles participated actively in the provision of arms for the dirty war against the Nicaraguan government, an operation directed from the White House that gave rise to the Irangate scandal. He has been responsible for terrorist attacks on hotels in Havana using mercenaries from El Salvador and Guatemala.

During the Fourth Summit, held in Cartagena, Colombia, on June 14 and 15, 1994, they were about to fire on us as we toured the old city in a procession of horse-drawn carts organized by our hosts. [The Nobel laureate novelist] Gabriel García Márquez accompanied me on this tour. I would have had, in this case, the honor of dying with such a brilliant writer.

The CANF gang, which planned another attack on [Venezuela's] Margarita Island where the seventh summit was to be held on November 8 and 9, 1997, was intercepted by a US Coast Guard cutter on suspicion of drug smuggling when their vessel sailed close to Puerto Rico. They confiscated the arms found on board, including two semiautomatic 50 caliber guns with telescopic sights, infrared light and a 1,500-meter range that could be used in daytime or at night. As we know, the group's members were acquitted in a spurious and fraudulent trial that took place on the colonized island [of Puerto Rico].

Posada Carriles arrived in Panama recently on November 5 [2000] with forged identity documents and made no attempt to disguise himself. He has accomplices in Panama that he depends on and trusts absolutely. Given his criminal record, [the Cuban government] had to go public with this denunciation.

In our view the authorities of the host country have a duty to track down the terrorist chief and his accomplices and prevent them from fleeing through any airport, checkpoint or port, arrest them and put them on trial in the appropriate courts for violating national and international laws.

They will no doubt do their utmost to uphold the honor of their country and ensure the success of the summit, which have been put at risk by international criminals who have acted with outrageous disdain and contempt for the Panamanian authorities and people. Our delegation is willing to provide them with the information we have.

We also ask for the cooperation of the Panamanian people to contact the authorities with any information that may contribute to the arrest of the terrorists. We are supplying the press with recent photos of Posada Carriles with a plea that they be published.

We hope the Panama summit is an unqualified success despite these criminal plans.

Epilogue

The war against Cuba continues and the enemies of the Cuban revolution have persisted in their plans to eliminate its leaders. Sometimes using an ambush or sophisticated poisons, or more recently by slandering the revolution, its leaders and their example. It suffices to read the reams of declassified US documents on covert operations against Cuba. Yet there is still an attempt to cover up, with a veil of half-truths and lies, all those incidents in which US government agencies tried to assassinate leader of the Cuban revolution by every available means.

Thus, included here are references to several additional texts that support the facts presented in this book, all of which confirm the calculated criminal nature of these US government actions.

Beginning in 1961, the CIA created a department with the code name ZR/Rifle with the purpose of eliminating political leaders deemed to be hostile to the United States, among whom Fidel Castro was a prominent example. Responsibility for these activities was masked by the rubric of "plausible deniability." This concept was complemented at the time by another euphemistically called "autonomous operations" in an effort to hide the CIA's direct participation in dirty wars; this has served as a working doctrine for the key terrorist groups of our times. What do both these concepts, forged in the heat of war against Cuba, really mean?

The 1975 US Senate Committee headed by Senator Frank Church investigating plots to assassinate foreign leaders acknowledged the "concept of 'plausible denial'" was "designed to protect the

United States and its operatives from the consequences of disclosures, [and] has been expanded to mask decisions of the President and his senior staff members. A further consequence of the expansion of this doctrine is that subordinates, in an effort to permit their superiors to 'plausibly deny' operations, fail to fully inform them about those operations."[1]

Senator Church's report concluded: "The original concept of 'plausible denial' envisioned implementing covert actions in a manner calculated to conceal American involvement if the actions were exposed. The doctrine was at times a delusion and at times a snare. It was naïve for policymakers to assume that sponsorship of actions as big as the Bay of Pigs invasion could be concealed."[2]

The 1979 report of the US House Select Committee examining the assassinations of President J. F. Kennedy and Martin Luther King, Jr., outlined the guidelines for the "autonomous operations," approved by the National Security Council in 1963:

> [Such operations must] be executed exclusively by Cuban nationals dedicated to the idea that the overthrow of the Castro/Communist regime must be accomplished by Cubans inside and outside Cuba working in concert. If the effort to overthrow the Cuban regime became too costly in human lives, the United States would withdraw financial support and would not consider resumption at any future date. All operations had to be mounted outside the territory of the United States. If ever charged with complicity, the US government would publicly deny any participation in the groups' activities. US presence and direct participation would be kept at an absolute minimum. An experienced liaison officer would be assigned to each group to provide general advice, funds and material support.[3]

1   *Alleged Assassination Plots...*, 11.

2   *Alleged Assassination Plots...*, 277.

3   Report of the Select Committee on Assassinations, US House of Representatives, 95th Congress (Washington: US Government Printing Office, 1979), 77.

In the introduction to his 1967 report on plots to assassinate Fidel Castro, CIA Inspector General, J.S. Earman noted:

> This reconstruction of Agency involvement in plans to assassinate Fidel Castro is at best an imperfect history. Because of the extreme sensitivity of the operations being discussed or attempted, as a matter of principle no official records were kept of planning, of approvals, or of implementation. The few written records that do exist are either largely tangential to the main events or were put on paper from memory years afterward. William Harvey has retained skeletal notes of his activities during the years in question, and they are our best source of dates.[4]

So why, some 60 years after those events, do they still try to obscure the facts about most of them? Why has the US government only declassified an insignificant number of documents about the plots on the life, image and ideas of Fidel Castro?

This book describes only some of these plots in detail, but almost all of them are listed in the chronology, clearly showing that Cuba's claims are not imagined or part of a media campaign. We have evidence of 167 assassination plots, the instigators of which were detained and sanctioned, and a further 467 conspiracies that were uncovered and thwarted in the planning phase.

In international gatherings and discussions with US analysts and experts, I have heard and felt obliged to refute arguments such as, "If there were only eight plans to assassinate Fidel, why make such a fuss?" Are eight plots to assassinate a person not a serious crime, especially when, as in this case, we are talking about the leader of a country? Why has the most powerful nation in history stooped to using these terrorist methods? Was the plot uncovered in Panama in 2000 in a crowded university theater not potentially a terrible crime?

---

4   *CIA Targets Fidel*, 23.

Based on the conduct of the US government, the answer is "no." Instead they protected Luis Posada Carriles and his accomplices, who returned with impunity to Miami, under the discreet protection of US authorities.[5]

We believe this book provides an accurate, detailed account of these macabre plans in an era when US imperialism sees its role as the global cop and when the doctrine of preemptive strikes has been added to the philosophical lexicon of the US government.

Meanwhile, Cuba will continue resisting and exposing all plots against our revolution. Its enemies will be unable to destroy the still-imperfect society we are creating, just as they could never kill Fidel.[6] They persist in repeating the same mistakes. The history of Cuba, of Latin America, is and will always bear witness to this.

---

[5]   Luis Posada Carriles was initially imprisoned in Panama for his role in this plot to bomb the university in Panama but later pardoned and released.

[6]   Having stepped down from his posts in the Cuban government some years before, Fidel Castro died peacefully at the age of 90 on November 25, 2016.

Chronology of the Crimes

1959–2000

This chronology includes two categories of homicidal plots: those that reached the stage of practical action before being discovered and those that were neutralized at a preliminary stage. The first category includes cases made public in the United States as a result of reports by the CIA and other agencies that have been declassified in recent years, and which were also investigated by Cuban State Security.

The result is a list of 167 assassination plots whose perpetrators were detained and punished by the courts or reported to the relevant authorities in third countries, and 467 conspiracies that were uncovered in the planning phase — without including those attempts never made public or not uncovered by the Cuban authorities — in the first four decades of the Cuban revolution. There are no historical precedents for this persistent effort.

Directly or indirectly, the United States has been responsible for these murderous plots. On the occasions when they were not directly planned by US government agencies, the hand or money of certain US agencies was often still present. In those that occurred independently, the idea was fomented in the minds of the killers through US propaganda campaigns urging the elimination of Cuba's leaders.

The information presented here demonstrates the responsibility Washington bears for these criminal plots that were an integral part of US plans to overthrow the Cuban revolution. Readers can see how both objectives — the assassination of Fidel Castro and the destabilization of our society — were pursued simultaneously as part of the US government's Cuba Project. Attempts to destroy the revolutionary unity achieved over many years of struggle, which Fidel Castro forged and promoted, are continuing. It is supposed that with Fidel gone this unity will collapse, and Washington will finally achieve its objectives.

The chronology below provides the essential details of the 167 conspiracies uncovered by the Cuban security services in which weapons were seized and the conspirators sentenced by the Cuban courts and of others uncovered through official reports declassified in the United States. We trust this will serve to document irrefutably how the United States, the most powerful nation on Earth, has attacked the sovereign nation of Cuba. We also hope that this exposé might help to prevent similar US policies and the repetition of such despicable acts being perpetrated anywhere else on the planet where conflicts arise or opposition to Washington's imperial might emerges.

1959

January: A plot to assassinate Fidel Castro in the Sierra Maestra, organized by FBI agents and the Batista dictatorship, was uncovered. US citizen Alan Robert Nye was captured December 25, 1958, by rebel combatants; he confessed his intension and named the instigators of the plot. His plan was to infiltrate the guerrilla movement and then ambush its leader. He was caught in possession of a Remington .30-06 gun with a telescopic sight and a .38-caliber revolver. In early 1959, Nye was tried and sentenced by the Cuban courts.

March: On the initiative of Rafael Leónidas Trujillo, the Dominican dictator, and Batista, with the consent of the US authorities, Rolando Masferrer, an ex-chief of the death squads in pre-revolutionary Cuba, planned to assassinate Fidel Castro in an ambush in the vicinity of the presidential palace in Havana. The operative group consisted of Obdulio Piedra and Navi Ferrás, who, on being discovered, fled the country for the United States.

Mid-1959: Frank Sturgis (Frank Fiorini), an agent contracted by the CIA, planned to assassinate Fidel Castro by taking advantage of a meeting in the Cuban air force headquarters, which he had infiltrated. The conspiracy, approved by James Noel, head of the CIA station in the US embassy, was to place a bomb in the military installation. Pedro Luis Díaz Lanz, chief of the air force, and Gerry Patrick Hemming, a US mercenary, were also involved in the operation. The plot failed due to security measures in place at the chosen location.

December: Colonel J.C. King, head of the Western Hemisphere Division of the CIA, proposed to his boss, Allen Dulles, the assassination of Fidel Castro as the most expeditious means of defeating the Cuban revolution. A few weeks later his proposal was authorized by the CIA high command.

November 1959–February 1960: A counterrevolutionary group headed by Major Robert Van Horne, military attaché at the US embassy in Cuba, organized a plot to assassinate Fidel Castro during a visit to the residence of Commander Ramiro Valdés, head of Cuban State Security. The plot was neutralized by agents infiltrated into the group. The conspirators included US citizen Geraldine Shamma, Fernando López, Pablo Márquez and Homero Gutiérrez.

1960

April: On his return from an exploratory trip to Havana, Howard Hunt, a CIA officer assigned to the newly created Cuba Task Force, proposed the assassination of Fidel Castro as the only way to defeat the revolution. In the same month, a plot to assassinate Fidel Castro, directed from the United States by Manuel Artime Buesa, a protégé of Howard Hunt, was dismantled. On that occasion the plan was to shoot the Cuban leader at the University of Havana. The operation was commanded by Juan Manuel Guillot Castellanos and Rafael Quintairos Santiso, who were arrested two years later for their activities in the service of the CIA and confessed these plans.

August: Galo Martínez Chapman, Fernando Mancheco González, José Martínez Gómez, Alfredo Curí Abdo, Amancio Abeleiras Pérez and Reinaldo Ruíz Cortinas organized a conspiracy to provoke an armed uprising in the central region of Cuba in order to defeat the revolutionary government. As part of the plan, they agreed to make an attempt on the life of Fidel Castro when he left his office in Havana, and carry out various acts of sabotage, terrorism and subversion.

September: In conjunction with elements associated with the Mafia, the CIA made various plans to assassinate Fidel Castro while he was in New York for the 15th session of the United Nations. The conspirators plotted to place two boxes of cigars — one containing a powerful poison and the other explosives — in the hotel room the Cuban leader was to occupy.

When that plot failed due to lack of cooperation from the local police, they tried to put thallium salts in Fidel's shoes to cause his beard to fall out, and to induce him to smoke an drug-impregnated cigar so that, during a televised interview, the drug would make the Cuban leader appear ridiculous.

Walter Martino, a US gangster and brother of a casino operator in pre-revolutionary Havana, tried to assassinate Fidel Castro during an event in Central Park by placing a powerful explosive device under the speaker's platform. This plot was discovered and deactivated by the New York police.

October: Colonel Sheffield Edwards, chief of the CIA Office of Security, coordinated with Mafia capo Johnny Rosselli to send to Havana professional killer Richard Cain, who was to assess the options to assassinate Fidel Castro. In the Cuban capital, Cain contacted counterrevolutionaries Eufemio Fernández and Herminio Díaz, former henchmen of the Mafia capo Santo Trafficante, who were to support him in the operation. The plan was to shoot Fidel from a moving car. After an exhaustive assessment of possible locations at which to execute the action, they canceled the plan on account of Fidel's tight security measures.

Indalecio Pérez, Rafael Pérez Campa, Carlos Rivero and Manuel Suárez were arrested while they were preparing an armed ambush of Fidel Castro in the vicinity of the presidential palace in Havana. This was part of a plot that included an assault on the 14th police precinct in Havana, as well as acts of sabotage and an armed uprising in the Escambray mountains.

Another group of people incited by the US embassy in Havana organized an attempt on the life of Fidel Castro in the vicinity of Revolution Plaza. The conspiracy was averted with the detention of Arturo Amaya Gil, Alfonso Armas Orozco, Alejandro Collazo Izquierdo, José García Lavado, Armando Junco Brizuela, Roberto Morffi González, Juan Nardo Echevarría and José Velasco.

November: An attempt hatched by the CIA was averted with the detention of counterrevolutionaries Armando Cubría Ramos and Mario Tauler Sagué, who had infiltrated Cuba from Florida via Punto Hicacos, Matanzas province, under the orders of CIA agent Eladio del Valle Gutiérrez. Weapons, grenades, a remote-control device and six detonators were taken from them.

A plot to assassinate Castro in the vicinity of the National Institute of Agrarian Reform was instigated by Elpidio Brito Gómez, César Valdés Moreno, Ocilio Cruz Sánchez and Luis Puentes Rodríguez, who were all arrested.

December: A conspiracy to kill Fidel Castro on a bridge close to the Baracoa airport in Havana province was uncovered. On two occasions a group of men set up an ambush by placing a powerful dynamite charge to explode as the Cuban leader's car passed by, blocking the highway with a vehicle, and waiting with sawn-off shotguns to fire on their target. José A. Martí Rodríguez, Francisco Pujols Someillán, Javier Someillán Fernández and Roger Hernández Ramos were arrested.

A counterrevolutionary group was captured preparing to ambush Fidel Castro's car near the presidential palace. Orlando Borges Ray, Pedro René Hernández, Laureano Rodríguez Llorente and Emiliano Reinoso Hernández were detained, and arms and explosives were taken from them.

Directed by the CIA station in the US embassy, agent Vladimir Rodríguez (El Doctorcito) planned the assassination of Fidel Castro from a building on the corner of Línea and Paseo Avenues in Havana. A gun with a telescopic sight was to be used to fire on the target when he entered the Potín restaurant. The plot was neutralized, the gun seized, and its instigator captured.

A team of CIA agents infiltrated from the United States was captured trying to place a powerful plastic explosive device in the drains of a central Havana avenue. The plan was to detonate it by remote control when Fidel Castro passed by. Julio Antonio Llebra Suárez, César Fuentes, Jorge Ulises Silva Soubelette and Ronald Condom Gil were arrested, and the explosives seized.

1961

January: CIA agents Frank Sturgis and Marita Lorenz plotted to poison Fidel Castro as part of a conspiracy planned with US Mafia elements. The crime was to be executed in the Hotel Havana Libre, taking advantage of a visit there by the prime minister. According to Sturgis himself, the plot was abandoned at the last minute due to the danger involved.

Another CIA and Mafia plan to poison Fidel Castro involved recruiting Juan Orta Córdova, then head of the prime minister's office, who was an old associate of the Havana casino bosses during the 1950s. Orta Córdova was to carry out the plan in Castro's office or his residence. It failed because he got cold feet.

Guillermo Coloma, Ernesto Bordón Basconcillos, Francisco Salazar de la Aceña and other counterrevolutionary elements attempted to promote an armed uprising to defeat the revolution. Coloma and Bordón traveled to Miami and made contact with CIA agent Eladio del Valle, from whom they received money and precise instructions to assassinate Fidel Castro and commit other acts of terrorism. On returning to Cuba, they were arrested at José Martí International Airport where plans, photos and documents were taken from them.

March: A CIA-organized a plan was to ambush the Cuban leader in the vicinity of the home of Fidel's secretary, Celia Sánchez. Mario Hidalgo Garcel, Julio Berdote González and Carlos Suárez Roque were detained for this conspiracy, and arms and explosives were seized.

The CIA and the Mafia plotted to assassinate Fidel Castro using poison capsules sent to Tony Varona's group in Havana. The plan was to poison the Cuban leader during one of his regular lunches in the Pekín Chinese restaurant in the busy Vedado district. The planned executor, one of the chefs, took fright at the dangerous nature of the action and sought exile in an embassy. The principal conspirators included Alberto Cruz Caso, María Leopoldina (Polita) Grau Alsina and Rodolfo León Curbelo, who were arrested some years later.

Rafael Díaz Hanscom, the designated civil coordinator of the internal counterrevolutionary front, was infiltrated with other agents into Cuba on March 13. Díaz Hanscom's missions included unleashing Operation Generosa, a vast terrorist plot to attack the country's main energy installations and placing a powerful incendiary device in the National Housing Institute meeting room, given that a meeting had been called there by Fidel Castro for March 27. The plot was frustrated with the capture of Díaz Hanscom and his accomplices.

May: Policemen José Álvarez García, Antonio Castro Cárdenas, Cándido Torres Pérez and Rafael Prío plotted to assault their own headquarters — that of the National Revolutionary Police. Subsequently, utilizing police patrol cars, they planned to position themselves on one of the access roads to the presidential palace to await the arrival of the Cuban leader, when they would throw several hand grenades. On being arrested, they admitted they were influenced by radio broadcasts from the United States calling for the elimination of Fidel Castro.

June–July: Three criminal acts were plotted by a counterrevolutionary group acting under CIA instructions via veteran agent Tony Varona, leader of the CRC, who ordered the following actions: an ambush in a residence located in the Biltmore district of Havana known to be regularly visited by Fidel Castro; an ambush in the Cucalambé restaurant in Marianao; if the earlier ambushes failed, another was planned to take place at the junction of Santa Catalina and Rancho Boyeros Avenues, firing from an open jeep with a bazooka and hand grenades.

Arms were seized and conspirators Juan Bacigalupe Hornedo, Higinio Menéndez Beltrán, Guillermo Caula Ferrer, Ibrahim Álvarez Cuesta, Augusto Jiménez Montenegro, Román Rodríguez and Osvaldo Díaz were detained.

July: A conspiracy to assassinate Fidel Castro organized by the CIA had been set in motion in January, in which notorious terrorist Félix Rodríguez Mendigutía was initially to participate. On this occasion, brothers Mario and Francisco Chanes de Armas selected two alternative locations for committing the crime: one in Santa María del Mar, east of the capital; the other at the residence of Celia Sánchez.

The first attempt failed because Fidel did not go to there on the day chosen for the ambush. A few weeks later, they tried to forcibly enter a warehouse located 50 meters from the target residence and station themselves there with a gun equipped with a telescopic sight. A few days before the action, the weapons were seized and the instigators, the Chanes brothers, José Acosta, Orlando Ulacia, Ramón Laurent, Ángel Sánchez Pérez, Félix Tacoronte Valdés, Roberto Cosculluela Valcárcel and Alfonso Díaz Cosculluela were arrested.

The same month, counterrevolutionaries José Díaz Quintana and Higinio Martín Castro were arrested preparing to fire on Fidel Castro from the Naroca building at the intersection of Línea and Paseo Avenues. Both individuals had previously carried out acts of sabotage in different parts of the capital.

In yet another plot, the CIA planned to assassinate Fidel and Raúl Castro during commemorative events for July 26 in Havana and Santiago de Cuba. This plan was connected to an act of provocation at the illegally occupied Guantánamo naval enclave, which would create a pretext for direct intervention by the United States. All the plotters were detained, including CIA agent Alfredo Izaguirre de la Riva, the main leader. Weapons and military equipment were seized in different parts of the country.

Another counterrevolutionary group planned to assassinate Fidel Castro during the July 26 event in Havana's Revolution Plaza. The action consisted of tossing hand grenades at the platform when the leader was making his speech. Principal mastermind, Alfredo Gómez, was arrested and various weapons were taken from him.

August: Silvio Salvio Selva and Alberto Junco, two men belonging to the Christian Democratic Movement (MDC), planned to ambush

Fidel Castro during his visit to a house in Vedado.

A plot was organized to assassinate Fidel Castro during one of his visits to the Ministry of Foreign Affairs. The plan was to fire on him from the window of an office opposite the ministry. When this plan failed, another was drawn up to be executed at an event in Revolution Plaza. Plotters Julio Peón and Julio Díaz Argüelles were arrested.

September: The Rescate group plotted the assassination of Castro during a public event to inaugurate several residential apartment buildings for workers. The plan was to launch hand grenades at Fidel. Francisco Álvarez Margolles, mastermind of the plot and an ex-colonel in Batista's army, was captured.

October: A major plot to assassinate Fidel Castro was set in motion by the CIA. The previous year an apartment had been rented close to the northern terrace of the presidential palace, from where the Cuban leader addressed public gatherings. Counterrevolutionaries secretly smuggled arms into the apartment and the action was decided for early October, taking advantage of a public welcome for President Osvaldo Dorticós on his return from an overseas tour. The operation was directed from the United States by CIA officer David Phillips and controlled in Cuba by his agent Antonio Veciana Blanch. The plot failed when its organizers fled the country. The weapons were seized and some of the conspirators detained, including Dalia Jorge Díaz, Manuel Izquierdo, and Reynold González.

1962

January: A counterrevolutionary group tried to poison Fidel Castro with cyanide in the Carmelo restaurant in Vedado. All the conspirators were detained, including Pedro Forcades Conesa, Aldo Cabrera Heredia, Eduardo Pérez García, Rubén Fernández Florit, Rafael Llanos Rodríguez, Manuel Pérez Pérez and Eusebio Quesada López.

March: Members of the National Liberation Front concocted a plan to assassinate Fidel Castro that consisted of placing an explosive device in the pylons of the bridge over the Quibú River in Marianao. Heriberto Fernández Aguirre, Felipe González Cruz and Alberto Rodríguez Roque were arrested when it was discovered they had access to the explosives.

Using his job as a worker at the Baracoa air force base, aviation mechanic Humberto Noble Alexander tried to place a bomb in the aircraft used by Fidel Castro for his domestic trips.

April: William Harvey, chief of Task Force W and responsible within the CIA for the Cuba Project, and Johnny Rosselli, a Mafia capo, handed over to Tony Varona in Miami a bottle of poison capsules especially manufactured for the elimination of Fidel Castro. Utilizing Alejandro Vergara, the Spanish diplomat accredited in Havana, the capsules were sent to the Rescate group headed by Alberto Cruz Caso and María Leopoldina Grau, who were to give them to their accomplices in the Hotel Havana Libre so that they could poison the leader's meal. The plotters, in two of the main restaurants, waited for more than 12 months for an opportunity, without success.

CIA agent Juan Guillot Castellanos plotted to eliminate Juan Marinello Vidaurreta, then rector of the University of Havana, in order to subsequently assassinate Fidel Castro at his funeral. The plot was neutralized with the capture of Guillot and the leadership of his organization.

Another armed ambush of Fidel Castro failed in the vicinity of Revolution Plaza. Detained in relation to the plot were Raúl García, Pedro Julio Espinosa and José García Vázquez.

May: Under CIA directions from the US naval base in Guantánamo, the assassination of Foreign Minister Raúl Roa García was plotted with the aim of then eliminating Fidel Castro at Roa's funeral. The individuals involved were equipped with hand grenades and automatic pistols. The plot was linked to other subversive actions in the rest of the country. All of the conspirators, headed by Jorge Luis Cuervo Calvo, then grand master of the masonic lodge, were captured.

June: Under CIA supervision, a group headed by Bernardo Corrales, Elsa Alfaro and Servando Sánchez plotted to assassinate Fidel Castro by means of a bazooka fired from a building neighboring the home of Celia Sánchez. The conspiracy failed due to security measures which made it impossible to smuggle in the bazooka.

Those involved were later detained.

July: A plot to kill Fidel via an ambush with fragmentation grenades in the vicinity of Revolution Plaza was foiled with the arrest of Servando Ovies Fariñas, Abel Joaquín Costa Martínez, Felipe Becerra Espinosa and Rodolfo Montes López.

Directed by the CIA, Luis David Rodríguez, Ricardo Olmedo Moreno and Braulio Roque Arosamena planned to assassinate Fidel Castro by firing at him with a mortar located near Revolution Plaza during the event commemorating July 26. The plot failed because the event was transferred to the city of Santiago de Cuba.

August: A bloc of counterrevolutionary organizations supported by the CIA planned a military uprising with the aim of destabilizing the country. The central element of the conspiracy was to assassinate Fidel Castro during an activity in the Karl Marx Theater. Guillermo Reyes Viaba, Tomás P. Ruíz Santana, Evelio Hernández Soto, Jesús Lazo Otaño, Otto Rodríguez Díaz, Félix Martín Nicerán, Félix Soto Sánchez, Leonel Hernández Mendez, Mario R. Estrada Alonso, Raúl Jorge León, José González Poladura, José Estrada González and Félix Sotolongo Morejón were detained.

Another attempt on the life of Fidel Castro was hatched by the Anticommunist Civic Resistance (RCA), which, under the direction of the CIA, hoped to instigate a general uprising by its groups to facilitate US intervention in Cuba. An ambush of the Cuban leader's car was organized in a central avenue of Havana. The plan was to hit the car with several fragmentation grenades. The operation was frustrated and the principal conspirators, Amaranto Torres, Ernesto Castillo and Ángel Custodio Portuondo, were captured.

September: Members of the Junta de Liberación Anticomunista, Frente Interno de Liberación and the Unión Nacional Democrática plotted to simultaneously execute acts of sabotage, assaults on units of the Revolutionary Armed Forces, and an attempt on the life of Fidel Castro on a busy Havana avenue. Delio Torres Hernández, Manuel Morales Jerez, Celio Armenteros Aruca, Eugenio Julián Jan, Ricardo González García, Mercedes López Fleites, Rafael

Cruz Casio and Rafael Rojas Martí were arrested.

Various members of the 30 November Revolutionary Movement plotted to assassinate Fidel Castro in the vicinity of Revolution Plaza. The detainees included Mario Ortiz Toledo, Manuel Pino Silva, Alberto Gálvez Alum, Elio Pardo Tabío and Heliodoro Grau.

Rafael Enrique Rojas Varela was detained by members of the commander-in-chief's bodyguard when he attempted to kill the leader on a public street.

End of 1962: Acting on CIA instructions, the Rescate group, headed by Tony Varona and Alberto Cruz, planned to poison police chief Efigenio Ameijeiras in order to bring about Fidel's attendance at his funeral, when an armed commando group would assassinate him.

1963

January-March: Desmond FitzGerald, CIA head of Cuban affairs, planned the assassination of Fidel Castro using a diving suit impregnated with bacteria. US lawyer James Donovan, who was doing business in Cuba and had access to Fidel, was to deliver it. The plot failed when Donovan refused to cooperate. FitzGerald planned another homicide attempt that consisted of placing an exotic shell prepared with a powerful explosive charge in the area where Fidel went underwater fishing. The plot failed as they were unable to place it in the appropriate spot.

March: The RCA, directed by the CIA from the US base at Guantánamo and supported by the Mafia, planned an armed uprising throughout the country to be initiated by the assassination of Fidel Castro at a March 13 activity at the University of Havana. The conspiracy was discovered and all the participants detained, including principal leaders Luis David Rodríguez, Ricardo Olmedo Moreno and Jorge Espinosa Escarlés.

Members of the so-called United Army in Arms planned to fire on Castro from an apartment close to the baseball pitch located within the grounds of the Department of State Security (DSE). Evelio Montejo Quintana, Francisco Amigó O'Farrill and brothers Marcos and Delfín Martín González were arrested.

The Rescate group had an opportunity to poison Fidel Castro with one of the capsules sent by the CIA when the leader went to the Hotel Havana Libre cafeteria while one of the conspirators, Santos de la Caridad Pérez, was working there. His task was to place the capsule in a chocolate milkshake, but he failed because the capsule broke when he removed it from the freezer where it was hidden.

April: A group from the Movement for the Recovery of the Revolution (MRR) planned to assassinate Fidel Castro during a baseball game in El Cerro stadium. The operation consisted of throwing eight grenades at the leader. Arrested for that conspiracy were Enrique Rodríguez Valdés, Esteban Ramos Kessell, Alfredo Egued Farah and Ricardo López Cabrera.

May: The Revolutionary Anticommunist Internal Front, directed from the United States, plotted an attempt on Fidel Castro's life at the May Day event in Revolution Plaza. They were also to carry out various acts of sabotage on the Havana aqueduct, the El Naranjito electricity plant, La Rampa movie theater and other public buildings. Pedro Hernández Álvarez, Enrique González, Francisco Cepero Capiró and Indalecio Ferreiro Varela were detained.

June: The Revolutionary Movement of the People (MRP) plotted an attack on Fidel Castro with a street ambush as well as acts of sabotage and subversion at key points in the Cuban capital. Carlos García Vázquez, Mariano Fernández Suárez, Pedro Julio Espinoza Martínez, Julio Hernández, José Marrero Frank, Horacio Arquímedes Ocumares Leyva and Armando Cuesto Constantino were detained. Blocks of C-3 explosive, homemade bombs, a .45-caliber submachine gun, fragmentation grenades and various pistols were taken from them.

July: The National Liberation Movement set up an ambush for Fidel Castro when he visited a Havana residence where veterans of the Moncada attack were gathered for a modest ceremony to commemorate that event. Enrique Falcón Beltrán, Ramón Soria Licea, Eliecer Senra Ramírez and Antonio Senra Lugueira were detained.

Operation Rafael, a CIA-sponsored project to assassinate Fidel Castro during the July 26 commemoration in Revolution

Plaza, was set in motion. The CIA sent the conspirators a gun with a telescopic sight and a silencer. Mario Salabarría and US intelligence agents Alberto Cruz Caso and Arturo Verona took part. The plan was thwarted by security.

A group from the MRR planned to assassinate Fidel Castro at the July 26 festivities. Their plan was to fire an 82 mm. mortar at the presidential platform from the patio of a neighboring house. Luis Montes de Oca and Braulio Roque were arrested.

July–September: Hatched on US territory by Cuban terrorist Orlando Bosch and Mafia associate Mike McLaney, a plot to bomb Fidel Castro's residence in Cojímar was devised. The plan failed when the bombs were seized in a raid by the FBI and the subjects were detained. They were subsequently released as a result of CIA intervention.

August: A planned uprising by counterrevolutionary groups belonging to the Civic Resistance bloc was averted. The project included an assassination attempt against Fidel Castro, for which they had several high-precision weapons. Arrested were Palmiro Bartolomé Santiago, Miguel Argueo Gallastegui Zayas, Gilberto Amat Rodríguez, Héctor Ballester Fernández, Honorio Torres Perdomo and others.

September: A counterrevolutionary group planned to attack Fidel Castro with hand grenades during a public event on the 28th to mark the anniversary of the CDRs in Revolution Plaza. The plan was frustrated and Ángel Mesa Puentes, Dositeo Fernández Fariñas and Roberto Porto Infanzón arrested.

An assassination attempt was foiled during the events celebrating the creation of the CDRs. Members of the so-called Frente Interno de Unidad Revolucionaria and the Triple A planned to place an explosive device in the drains underneath the podium mounted for the event. One of the conspirators was the engineer in charge of Havana's water and sewerage systems. Explosives supplied by the CIA were seized, and Federico Hernández González, Pierre Quan Diez de Ure, Francisco Blanco de los Cuetos, Jesús Rodríguez Mosquera, Orlando de la Cruz and Luis Arencibia Pérez were arrested.

October–November: Desmond FitzGerald met with Rolando Cubela in Paris to coordinate a planned coup in Cuba and the assassination of Fidel Castro. On the same date that President Kennedy was assassinated, November 22, 1963, a CIA case officer gave Cubela a hypodermic syringe filled with a powerful poison with which to kill the Cuban leader during an event planned for December of that year. The plot failed because Cubela got cold feet.

December: A CIA network made up of Bernardo Lucas Milanés, Roberto Caíñas Milanés, Adela Nagle, Loreto Llanes García and others planned an assassination attempt on Fidel Castro during his visit to the Potín restaurant. The plan was to intercept the leader's fleet of cars when they stopped and to open fire on them with automatic weapons. After several weeks of surveillance, the operation was abandoned when Fidel Castro failed to show up.

The National Liberation Army (ELN) planned an attack on Fidel Castro during a public event at the University of Havana. The plan was to concentrate a group close to the podium, and when the Cuban leader arrived, to throw hand grenades at him. Roberto Ortega, Ciro Rey and José Águila were arrested.

1964

January: A group from the ELN plotted to assassinate Fidel Castro during an event marking the fifth anniversary of the triumph of the Revolution in the plaza. The plan was to take by force one of the apartments at 1423, 1425 and 1427 Zapata Avenue, from where the presidential podium could be seen. Once there, they would fire on him with three rifles with telescopic sights. The plan was discovered, and its participants arrested, including Rafael Mir Peña and Manuel Santos Martínez.

Bernardo Milanés López returned from Madrid after discussing and agreeing with CIA agent Joaquín Sanjenís on a plan of action that included the assassination of Fidel Castro. The plan consisted of organizing an ambush on 5th Avenue in Miramar with a telephone company truck that would carry a .30-caliber submachine gun in the back. When Castro's cars approached the truck, its rear doors would be opened and the occupants would fire on the Cuban leader. The plot was uncovered and Mario Salabarría, Roberto Sabater, Bernardo

Milanés and other conspirators were arrested.

March: Individuals belonging to the National Alliance of Anticommunist Coordinators, made up of the Anticommunist Civic Resistance, the Agramonte Resistance and the Internal Government of Anticommunist Liberation, plotted to activate a huge subversive plan throughout the country that included an attempt on the lives of Fidel Castro and Blas Roca. The conspirators organized their actions in the vicinity of Revolution Plaza as the leaders were heading for their offices. Luis Casanovas Morales, Arturo Flores Zamora, Roberto Torres Alfonso and others were detained.

May: A group belonging to the 1422 Military Unit conspired to take its installations by assault, seize its weapons and subsequently organize an uprising. The plot included the assassination of Fidel Castro, who they would draw to the unit by making certain economic demands. The plot was discovered and its participants arrested, including José M. González Castellanos, José G. González Carmenate, Cándido Ruiz Palencia and Narciso Baró Serrano.

Members of the Internal Anticommunist Front planned to ambush Fidel Castro in Puente Cabrera in Marianao. The plot consisted of firing automatic weapons from previously selected locations. The operation was discovered and the plotters, Manuel Fordán Diéguez, Ricardo Solana Zayas de la Paz, Armando Prieto Puig, Jorge García Rodríguez, Pedro Lemagre Zárate and José Villamil Arias were arrested.

August: A group from the ELN plotted to assassinate Fidel Castro in an ambush with automatic weapons at the intersection of Presidentes and Zapata Avenues. In order to acquire the weapons, they planned to assault a Revolutionary National Militia garrison. Gregorio Mena Perera, Miguel Tomey Peláez and Pedro Aguilos Montoy were arrested.

September: Members of the Internal Liberation Front plotted an attempt on Fidel Castro's life in the home of Celia Sánchez, after previously attempting it at the intersection of Zapata and Carlos Manuel de Céspedes Avenues in Vedado. They were equipped with a Czech 7.62 mm. submachine gun and several hand grenades. Francisco Muñoz Antunes, Nemesio Cubillas Pérez, Juan Vailac Valdés, Ángel Arencibia Bidau, José Montano Meneses and Manuel Torquemada Tendero were detained.

A plot to assassinate Fidel Castro by launching hand grenades at him when he was in the presidential box at the World Youth Baseball Series was uncovered. Alberto Grau Sierra, the brothers Reinaldo and Valentín Figueroa Gálvez, and Felipe Ramos Rodríguez were arrested, and three submachine guns and grenades were taken from them.

1965

January: From the United States and with CIA approval, the MRR, headed by Manuel Artime and Nacín Elias Tuma, plotted the assassination of Fidel Castro during the commemorative event for the triumph of the revolution. They recruited one of the leaders of the MRR in Cuba, whom they took to Florida for training. When everything was in place, they infiltrated him back into the country on December 23, 1964. The plot failed because the supposed leader was Abel Haidar Elías, an agent of Cuban State Security who had penetrated the counterrevolutionary organization. Rifles with telescopic sights and other weapons were seized.

March: Members of the ELN conspired to assassinate the Cuban prime minister at the home of Celia Sánchez or in that of Commander René Vallejo, Fidel's aide. Orlando Travieso Peña, Tomás Gilberto Guerrero Matos, Justo González García, Iluminado García Pérez and Modesto García García were arrested.

June: A group from the Democratic National Front plotted to assassinate Fidel Castro at the event for the anniversary of July 26 in Santa Clara. To that end, they stole a FAL rifle and various pistols from a military unit. Ramón Medina Machado, Alejo Álvarez Santana and Santiago Apóstol Gómez Gutiérrez were detained.

July: Elements from the Revolutionary National Unity plotted to assassinate Fidel on the corner of 21 and L Streets in Vedado. They had a .45-caliber Thompson submachine gun. Enrique

Abreu Vilahu, Julio Ruiz Pitaluga and Carlos Sánchez Hernández were arrested.

CIA agents planned an attempt on Fidel Castro's life during his visit to an agricultural project in Los Arabos, Matanzas province. The same network devoted itself to acts of espionage and sabotage. Roberto Ramos Rodiles, Antonio Alonso Soca, Rolando Quevedo Negrín, José Pellayá Jústiz and Mirta Beatriz Pérez López were detained and two US-made M3 submachine guns were taken from them.

August: A US Defense Intelligence Agency network acting in Cuba under the command of agents Benjamín Acosta Valdés and Antonio Ramírez Méndez plotted the assassination of Fidel Castro. The conspiracy consisted of a planned commando operation of 30 armed men on the residence of Celia Sánchez. León R. Martínez Gómez, Felipe Hernández García, Raúl Hermida Lafita, Juan A. Morera Suárez, Enrique Fernández and others were arrested. The US agents managed to escape from the country.

September: Members of Rescate planned an attempt on Fidel Castro's life at the commemoration of the anniversary of the CDRs, for which they had blocks of C-4 explosive. Roberto del Castillo Fernández, Salvador del Castillo Atkinson and Lorenzo Medina were detained.

December: Members of the ELN plotted to fire an 81 mm. mortar at the home of Celia Sánchez when Fidel was there. Elio Diáz García and Sergio Romero were arrested.

1966

January: An attempt on the life of Fidel Castro was plotted for a conference bringing together representatives from the international revolutionary movement in Havana. Various machine guns were to be used in the attack. The plot consisted of an assault on the Hotel Havana Libre where the Cuban leader was to make an appearance. Guillermo Valdés Sosa, Amado Santana Correa and Carlos M. Vidal Fernández were arrested.

The Democratic National Front planned to kill Fidel Castro during an event in Revolution Plaza. They had in their possession

10 pistols as well as fragmentation grenades. Luis Fernández Rodríguez, Raúl Martínez Lima, Ricardo Padrón Acosta, Aurelio Gascón Díaz, Luis Mitjans González, Mario Valdés Cárdenas, Francisco Palomino Castillo, Felicio Valdés González, Sabino Villar Suárez and Jesús González Ramos were arrested.

Counterrevolutionaries Víctor Rodríguez Landerer and Giraldo Suárez Martín, who had organized an ambush of the prime minister in the vicinity of the presidential palace, were captured. The chosen location was the Fausto movie theater building on Prado and Colón, where Suárez Martín worked as an administrator.

February: Rolando Cubela Secades (the CIA agent AM/LASH) and a group of his collaborators were arrested while plotting an attack on Fidel Castro during an event at the University of Havana planned for March 13. Subsequent investigations revealed that Cubela and his associates, in conjunction with the CIA, had previously planned to ambush Fidel's vehicles when he visited Varadero. On the cited occasions snipers were positioned in the selected locations, but Castro did not appear. The dates concerned were March–April 1964 and June–July 1965.

March: Members of the counterrevolutionary groups MRP and the Revolutionary National Union plotted an attempt on Fidel Castro's life at the baseball stadium in El Cerro. The plan was to throw fragmentation grenades at him as he entered the stadium. The weapons were seized and counterrevolutionaries Juan Pereira León, Juan Valdés López and Oscar D. Sáenz Rodríguez were arrested.

April: Members of the counterrevolutionary organizations MRP and the United Western Front planned to assassinate Fidel Castro during a visit he was to make to the Emergency Hospital on Carlos III Avenue in the Cuban capital. The conspirators hid in a corridor of the hospital armed with a submachine gun and a pistol awaiting the Cuban leader, who, on that occasion, did not go to the institution. Roger Reyes Hernández and Jorge de la Torre were arrested.

Gustavo Gil Hernández was arrested for planning an attempt on Fidel Castro's life with fragmentation grenades on the highway leading to the Liberación sugar refinery in Cuatro Caminos, in Havana province.

May: A CIA special missions group was captured infiltrating the coast near Havana with the objective of assassinating the Cuban president, Osvaldo Dorticós, in order to attract Fidel Castro to his residence and then kill him. The members were surprised by the Cuban militia and fighting broke out. Terrorists Herminio Díaz García and Armando Romero were killed and Antonio Cuesta Valle and Eugenio Zaldívar detained.

Rodobaldo Hilarión Fariñas Lumpuy was arrested while preparing an attack on Fidel Castro in the El Cerro baseball stadium. His plan was to throw two fragmentation grenades.

June: A counterrevolutionary group plotted to assassinate Fidel Castro when he was crossing a bridge in the Biltmore district, Marianao. The plan was to fire on him from the cover of nearby shrubs. The main organizer, Francisco Díaz Valdagil, was captured and an M3 submachine gun seized. The other conspirators managed to escape to the United States.

July: Members of Alpha 66 and the Christian Democrat Movement (MDC) planned to assassinate Fidel Castro by throwing fragmentation grenades at him in El Cerro stadium while he was receiving the Cuban delegation to the Central American Games in Puerto Rico. Francisco Bernal González, Pedro Gervasio Pérez Jorrín and others were arrested.

September: An attempt to assassinate Fidel Castro in Cojímar was foiled. The plan was to ambush his vehicle and throw fragmentation grenades at him from motorcycles. An additional plan was to assault various police units and subsequently to stage an uprising in the mountains in Havana province. Guido Farmiñán Fernández, Rodolfo Sierra Cabrera, Vicente Rodríguez Molina and José Alfonso Calderon were detained.

October: Members of the Brigade Battalion organized a plot on Fidel Castro's life in an ambush on Paseo Avenue. This route was frequently used by the Cuban leader. The conspirators possessed various guns and pistols and also had an apartment in one of the buildings in the area. Ramón Luis Arias Cuña, Narciso Oseguera Rodríguez and Pantaleón Rivera Rodríguez were detained.

1967

July: An ex-sergeant in Batista's army, Pascual Peña García, planned a solo attempt to kill Fidel Castro, plotting to shoot him with a Czech machine gun in the vicinity of the headquarters of the Cuban Communist Party. He was arrested and his weapon seized.

September: Several individuals from the Anticommunist National Group plotted to shoot Fidel Castro with automatic weapons during his visit to a farm in the Aguacate neighborhood. José Paradela Ruiz, Rodolfo Suárez Sardiñas, Roberto Milián Sánchez and Alfonso López were arrested.

November: An attempt on Fidel Castro's life was planned during the inauguration of the national baseball series in El Cerro stadium. The plot consisted of positioning a man next to the main electricity cable to interrupt the electricity supply, and at the same time, to throw fragmentation grenades at the Cuban leader's box. José Acosta Corona, Marcelo Ramos González, Segundo Rodríguez Pérez, Isidro Benavides Segura and Reinaldo Barrios Romero were detained.

1968

March: Oscar Rafael Planas Madruga and Juan Sánchez Gómez plotted to assassinate Fidel Castro during his visit to a genetics institute in Havana province. They were in possession of weapons and hand grenades for the attack. Both conspirators were arrested and their weapons taken.

A group of counterrevolutionaries planned to assassinate Fidel Castro and then flee from Cuba to the United States. The conspirators were watching the access roads to the home of Celia Sánchez. Julio Pedrosa Gómez, Norberto Vega Salas, Felipe Israel Cruz Saavedra and José Buenaventura Ruiz Hidalgo were detained.

April: A plot was hatched to assassinate Fidel Castro during his visit to the Nazareno genetics institute in Santiago de las Vegas. The counterrevolutionaries made a careful study to ascertain the number of cars in the leader's entourage, as well as access routes and suitable locations for an ambush. Digno Pereira,

Valentín Fernández and Pedro Chang were arrested and two M3 submachine guns seized.

May: A plot to assassinate Fidel Castro in an ambush on a street he used to travel to the government offices failed. The conspirators possessed various weapons and were studying the selected location. Santiago Oliva Ramos and Berto Gutiérrez were arrested.

Nemesio Rafael Rodríguez Amaro plotted to assassinate Fidel Castro during his visit to the Chullima shipyard in the bay of Havana. He made contact with criminals who agreed to supply the weapons for a sum of money, but without warning they fled the country before the date of the planned crime.

Individuals resident in Florida contracted Bartolomé Hernández Quintana and Antonio Muñoz González in Havana to assassinate Fidel Castro during one of his trips around the capital. They were arrested and their weapons seized.

Pedro Luis Sabina plotted to assassinate Fidel Castro during a visit to his aide, Commander René Vallejo. He staked out the house on various occasions and obtained a .45-caliber pistol.

June: Members of the Democratic National Front conspired to assassinate Fidel Castro in an ambush in a Havana avenue. They had four .22-caliber pistols with silencers and rockets poisoned with cyanide. Desiderio Barreto Martínez was detained for this action, while the others involved escaped to the United States.

Onelio León Zayas and Luis Monzón Painé planned an attempt against Fidel during one of his regular trips around Havana. Monzón Painé was a demobilized officer of the Ministry of the Interior and possessed information on the leader's itinerary, as well as various automatic weapons. Both individuals were detained.

July: Desiderio Conrado Pérez and Ramón Salazar Román conspired to assassinate Fidel Castro during one of his visits to Villa Clara. They were detained and their weapons taken.

Members of the Montecristi Group plotted to assassinate the Cuban leader during one of his visits to Quivicán. The plan was to intercept his vehicles and fire on him with automatic weapons. Justo Páez Santos and Mario Llorens Hernández were detained.

Rafael Domingo Morejón Recaña was arrested for plotting to

assassinate Fidel Castro during the event celebrating the July 26 anniversary in Santa Clara. Morejón had decided to shoot him from the crowd, a suicidal act for which he was equipped with a .45-caliber pistol.

Marcos Ortiz González also planned to assassinate Fidel Castro during the same event. He selected one of the access routes to the plaza where the event was to take place. He was arrested and his pistol seized.

August: Members of the 30 November Revolutionary Movement plotted an attempt on Fidel Castro's life with two snipers from the ranks of Batista's army. Pedro Pablo Montes de Oca Martínez, Bernardo Montero González and Eladio Ruíz Sánchez were detained and their weapons seized.

Marcial Mirabal, Flor Damaris Garlobo Pérez and Daysi Valdés Sánchez were arrested on the discovery of a conspiracy to assassinate Fidel Castro during the commemoration of the July 26 anniversary in Santa Clara. The operation consisted of firing on the leader from the public area with .32-caliber pistols. The conspiracy was frustrated as they were unable to reach the selected location in time and did not have the required view of the podium.

September: Carlos Alberto Mata Escobar, Rigoberto Castro Gutiérrez, Juan Antonio Loureiro Padilla and Roberto Osvaldo Catá Gómez plotted to assassinate Fidel Castro on a main avenue in the capital and then flee to the United States. They also planned various acts of terrorism to coincide with the attempt. The location selected was the Alcoy Bridge in San Miguel del Padrón. All those involved were arrested.

October: CIA officer David Phillips organized a plot to assassinate Fidel Castro from the US naval base in Guantánamo. The plot consisted of infiltrating a heavily armed commando unit that would organize an ambush in the vicinity of Manzanillo, Oriente province, the location of an event to celebrate the centenary of the struggle for Cuban independence. The operation failed as the men could not be infiltrated.

November: Argeo Hernández Durán, Emilio Montes de Oca, Antonio Torres, Pedro Matute and Juan Moreno were arrested in the vicinity of the residence of Fidel Castro when they were checking the movements of the Cuban leader. Under interrogation they confessed that they were plotting to assassinate him. They had a rifle with a telescopic sight, which was seized.

1969

February: Hugo Rojas del Río, David Hernández Tiant and Miguel Finlay Villalvilla, members of the Internal Government of Anticommunist Liberation group, were detained conspiring to assassinate Fidel Castro with a fragmentation grenade.

March: Félix Olivera Castillo, a member of the National Internal Front, was directed by his organization in the United States to prepare an assassination attempt on Castro. He devoted himself to studying the routes he took. At the moment of his arrest he was found awaiting a vessel from Florida bringing him a gun with a telescopic sight and various pistols.

Counterrevolutionary Agustín Rivero Rodríguez, a member of the MRR, decided to make an attempt on Fidel Castro's life with a pistol that he owned, during a speech by the leader in El Cangre, Havana province. He was arrested.

Salvador de la Torriente and Rayné Hernández, individuals belonging to the Agramonte Resistance, plotted to kill Fidel Castro at a public event in Havana province. To achieve their objective, they planned to approach the stage and then attack him with knives.

April: Mario Ramón Echevarría Camejo, Juan Hermida Salinas and Eugenio Ledón Aguilar were arrested for plotting an attempt on Fidel Castro's life. The action was to be carried out when the leader was touring agricultural projects in the area. Various small arms prepared for the attack were seized.

Luis Acosta González and Francisco Hernández were arrested for plotting the assassination of Fidel Castro during his visit to an agricultural project in the town of Quivicán in Havana province. Various fragmentation grenades were taken from them.

June: Following instructions from Armando Fleites, leader of the Alpha 66 organization located in the United States, Guillermo del Carmen Álvarez Teijeros planned to assassinate Fidel Castro during one of his tours around Havana. He had been promised a safe exit from Cuba with all his family as soon as the crime was committed. He was detained and a .45-caliber pistol taken from him.

July: Damián Cruz González, Félix Alfonso Santiago and José García Gutiérrez plotted an attempt on Fidel Castro's life during the events celebrating the anniversary of July 26. They acquired a truck in which they installed a .30-caliber machine gun. They planned to intercept the leader's cars with the truck and fire on him and his bodyguards.

August: A counterrevolutionary group drew up a plot to assassinate Fidel Castro during an anniversary celebration of the CDRs. The plan was to cause a power outage in Revolution Plaza once the event had started and to then throw fragmentation grenades at the platform. Julio Sánchez Almeida, Manuel Pérez Medina, Rubén Arango González, José Antonio González Delgado, Luis Gervasio Márquez Gómez, Eduardo Rivas Pizarro, Delio Germán Sánchez Rius and Orlando de la Caridad Concepción Maura were arrested.

October: A counterrevolutionary group made up of Gregorio Nieves Rojas, Justiniano Lorenzo Espinosa García, Luis Orlando Román López, Hipólito Espinosa García and Ramiro Castillo Garcés was captured planning an assault on the Civil Defense headquarters in the town of Santiago de las Vegas, with the intention of stealing weapons to be used to assassinate Fidel Castro.

November: Members of the Democratic National Front, prompted by their handlers in the United States, planned to assassinate Fidel Castro during one of his visits to the towns of Güines and San Nicolás de Bari, Havana province. The action was to be executed via an ambush on one of the access routes to a genetics institute in the area. They planned to use various .12 mm. shotguns and two .45-caliber pistols. Gerardo Figueredo Durán, Gertrudis Cabrera Acosta, Jorge Sarmiento Lazo, Israel Ramos González, Cristóbal González Pérez and Pedro Mourdoch Benítez were detained.

December: Daniel Alberto Pérez Cruz and Samuel Nisembaun Waiider, members of the Rescate organization headed by Tony Varona in the United States, plotted the assassination of Fidel

Castro during one of his tours of Santa Clara, as instructed by their chief. During the preparations they made contact with people they knew in that city who helped them with details for the operation. They were arrested when their plot was uncovered.

1970

January: Jorge Luis Faroy Abreu and José Camejo were detained while organizing an attempt on Fidel Castro's life on the occasion of his visit to the offices of the Cuban Institute of Friendship with the Peoples. They had three AKM guns and three fragmentation grenades.

February: Counterrevolutionaries Edgardo Barrera Abreu and Bernardo Ramírez Batista plotted to assassinate Fidel Castro during one of his visits to the house of Celia Sánchez. They made a detailed study of the area, during which they were surprised and detained, and their weapons taken.

October: Common criminal Julio Guerra Guedes, influenced by radio stations broadcasting from the United States, planned to assassinate Fidel Castro with a P38 pistol at the Antillana steelworks.

December: A group composed of Emérito Cardoso Vázquez, Pedro Pablo Pérez Páez, Antonio Martínez Chávez and Santiago Felipe Martínez Chávez plotted to assassinate Fidel Castro during one of his regular visits to La Bijirita genetics institute in the vicinity of Santiago de las Vegas, Havana province. For this action they drew up a plan of the selected location and obtained khaki uniforms and two AKM rifles from a military unit.

1971

February: Nelson Pomares Fortes and José Ulpiano Torres Hernández, members of the United Army in Arms counterrevolutionary organization, conspired to assassinate Fidel Castro via an ambush on 146th Street and 5th Avenue in Miramar. The idea was to take up positions on the flat roof of the pharmacy at this intersection — where Pomares worked — and to open fire with a rifle when the leader's cars passed by.

October: Elio Hernández Alfonso, a counterrevolutionary who worked in a steel mill, tried to recruit several workers from his plant to assassinate Fidel Castro during a visit. The plot was to make the leader fall into a large vat full of melted iron when he passed by. The plot was uncovered and its instigator arrested.

November: Cuban counterrevolutionaries Antonio Veciana Blanch, Luis Posada Carriles, Orlando Bosch, Lucilo Peña, Joaquín Sanjenís, Marcos Rodríguez, Diego Medina, Secundino Álvarez and Félix Rodríguez, as well as US agents Frank Sturgis and Gerry Patrick Hemming, a Bolivian resident called Nápoles and David Phillips (by then head of the CIA's Western Hemisphere Division) planned to assassinate Fidel Castro during his visit to Chile. The plot originally had three alternatives in Chile as well as two plans in Lima and Quito. The plans were: to fire on him from the Hilton Hotel, situated beside the presidential palace; place a car full of explosives on the highway to the Chuquicamata copper mines; shoot him with a TV camera, killing the two assassins, and making them appear to be KGB agents. They also planned to throw explosives from the terrace of the Lima airport and to fire on him when his plane landed in Quito, his last stop on his way back to Cuba.

1973

September: Lázaro Hernández Valdés was detained while attempting to fire on Fidel Castro during the welcome tour of Cuba by Chilean President Salvador Allende. The plan was to ambush him in Ermita de los Catalanes, near Rancho Boyeros Avenue, where both leaders were to pass by in an open car. To commit the crime, Valdés had a .22-caliber rifle with cyanide-laced bullets. He confessed to being an avid listener of the counterrevolutionary radio stations funded by the CIA that were broadcasting from Florida during that period.

October: Juan Ortiz Ribeaux, a worker at the Antillana steel plant in Havana, planned to assassinate Fidel Castro and Raúl Castro, minister of the armed forces, during a military maneuver in which a brigade from his workplace was taking part. The idea was to fire a mortar at them when both leaders were on the stage.

December: Pablo Alfredo Álvarez Alvarado planned to ambush Fidel on 3rd Avenue and Paseo in Vedado. On being arrested, a sketch of the area was taken from him along with a pistol.

1975

February: Aureliano García Calderón was detained while checking the routes used by the Cuban leader. He had a .38-caliber revolver and a .22-caliber pistol.

March: Jorge Crespo Brunet, a worker at the Cuban Film Institute, was detained for plotting to place an explosive device in that institution during a visit by Fidel Castro. He had drawn up a plan of where to place the device and had stolen various cartridges of dynamite.

1976

September: Through one of its officers calling himself Harold Benson, CIA headquarters directed one of its agents in Cuba to compile information on Castro's imminent trip to Africa to attend the first anniversary of the Angolan revolution. The task was related to an attempt on Fidel and various terrorist attacks to be carried out by a commando unit headed by Orlando Bosch Ávila and Luis Posada Carriles. The plot against Fidel was uncovered by Cuban State Security agents. Regrettably, other acts of terrorism, including the sabotage of a Cuban passenger plane off Barbados in which 73 passengers lost their lives, were not uncovered in time.

1979

October: Antonio Veciana Blanch and Andrés Nazario Sargén, two Alpha 66 leaders in the United States, plotted to assassinate Fidel Castro during the Cuban leader's attendance at the 34th session of the United Nations. The plot consisted of throwing a contact bomb disguised as a baseball at his car during one of the Cuban leader's transits through New York. The operation was neutralized by the FBI.

1982

May: Intelligence sources reported that Luis Llanes Águila planned to infiltrate Cuba from Florida with the objective of assassinating

Fidel Castro and Commander Ramiro Valdés. He was captured attempting to enter Cuba in order to carry out the plan with Rogelio Abreu Azcuy.

1985

January: Elements linked to the Saturnino Beltrán commandos, made up of anti-Sandinista Nicaraguans and Cuban émigrés in Florida, were plotting to bring down the plane taking Fidel Castro to Daniel Ortega's inauguration in Managua. This was to be achieved by firing a ground-to-air missile when the aircraft was flying over the Nicaraguan capital. Orlando Valdés, Adolfo Calero Portocarrero, Manuel Reyes and Roberto Milián Martínez were involved in the operation.

1987

April: Intelligence sources discovered that the veteran CIA agent Mario Salabarría, who went to Miami after his release from a Cuban prison, was plotting to assassinate Fidel Castro during a tour of Spain. The operation was planned to take place when the Cuban leader traveled to his ancestors' native village. Salabarría, Marco Tulio Beruff, Cándido de la Torre and an unidentified Spanish citizen were to execute the action.

July: Terrorist Eduardo Tamargo Martín planned to assassinate Fidel Castro during a visit to Brazil. There were various meetings in the offices of the Independent and Democratic Cuba group in Caracas, attended by Ramón Méndez, Ariel Clavijo and Eduardo Tamargo himself. This group linked up with the Venezuelan police, who assumed the task of training the group selected to shoot the Cuban president.

1988

November: Cuban terrorist Gaspar Eugenio Jiménez Escobedo was organizing a plot to assassinate Fidel Castro when he made a visit to Brazil. Jiménez Escobedo was linked to the Orlando Mendoza and Luis Posada Carriles project.

December: From a Venezuelan jail, terrorist Orlando Bosch Ávila plotted an assassination attempt on Fidel Castro on the occasion of the inauguration of President Carlos Andrés Pérez. He designated an explosives expert called Eusebio for the operation, who was to prepare various devices to be activated by remote control. Pedro Corzo Eves, Pedro Martín Corzo, Gaspar Jiménez Escobedo and Eusebio himself were to take part in the action.

1990

October: A counterrevolutionary commando unit from the United States was infiltrated into Cuba to undertake diversionary actions and to assassinate Fidel Castro. Gustavo Rodríguez, Tomás Ramos, Sergio González Rosquete, Richard Heredia and Higinio Díaz Duarte were detained.

1994

November: On the occasion of the Fourth Summit of Ibero-American Heads of State and Government in Cartagena, Colombia, the Cuban American National Foundation (CANF) plotted to assassinate Fidel Castro. The plan was to fire on him with a .50-caliber Barrett rifle brought from Miami. The plot failed due to the fact that the conditions anticipated by the conspirators did not materialize. Cuban terrorists Alberto Hernández, Roberto Martín Pérez, Luis Posada Carriles, Ramón Orozco Crespo, Gaspar Jiménez Escobedo, Félix Rodríguez Mendigutía and Raúl Valverde were involved in the operation.

1995

November: On the occasion of the Fifth Summit of Ibero-American Heads of State and Government in the San Carlos de Bariloche resort in Argentina, Cuban terrorists Roberto Martín Pérez, Gaspar Jiménez Escobedo and Eugenio Llameras plotted to ambush and assassinate Fidel Castro with the support and funding of CANF.

1997

November: Luis Posada Carriles, with the complicity of Arnaldo Monzón Plasencia and the leaders of CANF, organized a conspiracy to assassinate Fidel Castro on Margarita Island, Venezuela, during the Seventh Ibero-American Summit of Heads of State and Government. In waters close to Puerto Rico, Ángel Alfonso Alemán, Francisco Córdova Torna, Juan Bautista Márquez and Ángel Hernández Rojo were detained on the boat La Esperanza. Two .50-caliber Barrett rifles were seized, one of them owned by Francisco Hernández, an executive of CANF.

1998

November: CANF, with terrorists Luis Posada Carriles, Ramón Font, Ramón Orozco Crespo, Francisco Eulalio Castro Paz and Enrique Bassas, planned to assassinate Fidel Castro during a visit to the Dominican Republic.

2000

November: Terrorist elements plotted to assassinate Fidel Castro during the 10th Ibero-American Summit of Heads of State and Government in Panama City. Luis Posada Carriles, Guillermo Novo Sampol, Pedro Crispín Remón and Gaspar Jiménez Escobedo, under instructions from CANF, planned to plant an explosive device in a university auditorium, the venue for a Cuban solidarity event at which Fidel was to speak. After being exposed by the Cuban authorities, the terrorists were caught and detained by the Panamanian authorities. Three years later, after they had been sentenced in a public court for their criminal acts, Panamanian president, Mireya Moscoso, at the end of her mandate and following the instructions of the US ambassador, granted them a pardon.

Glossary

AM/LASH: Refers to both the CIA covert operation to assassinate Fidel Castro and agent Rolando Cubela

AM/WHIP:

Brigade 2506: Bay of Pigs invasion force

BRAC: Cuban Bureau for the Repression of Communist Activities

CANF: Cuban American National Foundation

CDR: Committees for the Defense of the Revolution

CIA: Central Intelligence Agency

Contras: Nicaraguan counterrevolutionaries

CRC: Cuban Revolutionary Council 1961

DD/P: Deputy Director of Plans (CIA)

DIER: Rebel Army Investigations Department (Cuban state security or G2) 1959-1961

DRE: Revolutionary Student Directorate

DSE: Cuban State Security Department (also referred to as G-2) 1961

ELN: National Liberation Army

FBI: Federal Bureau of Investigation

FRD: Revolutionary Democratic Front 1960-61

G-2: common name for Cuban state security

JGCE: Junta of the Cuban Government in Exile 1962

JM/WAVE: CIA

MDC: Christian Democrat Movement

MID: Democratic Insurrectional Movement

MRP: Revolutionary Movement of the People

MRR: Movement for the Recovery of the Revolution

OAS: Organization of American States

Operation ZR/Rifle: CIA program to assassinate foreign leaders

OSS: Office of Strategic Services (forerunner to the CIA)

RCA: Anticommunist Civic Resistance

SAS: Special Affairs Section (CIA) responsible for covert Cuban operations, replacing Task Force W in 1963.

SIM: Military Intelligence Service

Task Force W: CIA section responsible for Cuba project (1961-1963).

TSD: Technical Services Division (CIA)